Demo

Democracy's Troubles

*Twelve Threats to the American
Ideal and How We Can
Overcome Them*

JOHN E. MILLER

McFarland & Company, Inc., Publishers
Jefferson, North Carolina

ISBN (print) 978-1-4766-8113-9
ISBN (ebook) 978-1-4766-3934-5

LIBRARY OF CONGRESS ANDBRITISH LIBRARY
CATALOGUING DATA ARE AVAILABLE

Library of Congress Control Number 2019055198

Front cover: United State Capitol Building © 2020 Lane V. Erickson
Shutterstock

Printed in the United States of America

*McFarland & Company, Inc., Publishers
Box 611, Jefferson, North Carolina 28640
www.mcfarlandpub.com*

To Lois Domsch, Mary Meier,
Dan Miller, and Tim Miller

"Democracy has always been more than a set of political practices. It is also … an ethical ideal."
—Darrin McMahon, professor of history,
Dartmouth College (2016)

"Our political crisis, if that's what it is, it not just American, but global…. All involve a dramatic weakening, if not a simple breakdown, of the authority of the established political classes and political parties. It is as if masses of people throughout the world had stopped believing in the reigning common sense that underpinned political domination for the last several decades. It is as if they had lost confidence in the bona fides of the elites and were searching for new ideologies, organizations, and leadership."
—Nancy Fraser, professor of philosophy and politics,
New School for Social Research (2017)

"To reduce conflict, there has to be basic trust, an agreement on facts and the ability to work with people who have different points of view. Those are the essential elements of a democratic system, where everyone's view gets heard and people have to work out diverging points of view."
—Darrell M. West, professor, Brown University,
and Brookings Institution (2019)

Table of Contents

Preface

We live, to quote an old expression, in "interesting times." This book was written for readers who find the current political situation to be not merely interesting but chaotic, unnerving, and difficult to interpret. Beyond the forces transforming technology, cyberspace, jobs, education, culture, religion, transportation, global affairs, and dozens of other things, the conflict and rancor surrounding our politics have few precedents in American history.

Books warning that democracy is embattled, imperiled, or even dying pour off the press almost daily, it seems. News reports bring us the latest scandal, blow-up, or outrage, often hourly. Words such as "unprecedented" and questions such as "Can you believe it?" and "Who knew?" spring from our lips. "What is going on?" we would like to know. But then again, maybe we wouldn't. "This shouldn't be happening," we think. How are we to understand our current situation?

I came of political age during the Kennedy-Nixon election of 1960 and was inspired by the soaring rhetoric of John F. Kennedy's inaugural address. As a high school and college debater, I got hooked discussing and debating public issues, became a political "junkie," and have been one ever since. As a product of the sixties, I was immersed in the issues of the day. As an undergraduate student at the University of Missouri, a graduate student at the University of Wisconsin, and an Army draftee, serving as a court reporter in Vietnam, I had front-row seats to many of the central developments of the day. My history dissertation topic was "Governor Philip F. La Follette, the Wisconsin Progressives, and the New Deal." Over the years, I wrote a book and a number of articles and book chapters on Wisconsin, South Dakota, and Midwestern political history as well as on political subjects such as Ronald Reagan and the Bryan-McKinley presidential election of 1896. Now, I've closed the circle and am working on another book on politics, a biography of Senator George McGovern, who represented my adoptive state of South Dakota. While my voting preferences trace back through to the progressive

La Follette-liberal McGovern tradition, as a historian I seek to leave my personal preferences behind and take a clear-eyed, nonpartisan, objective stance on interpreting the past.

Now, as politics seems to intrude into every nook and cranny of American life, I sometimes feel a bit jaded about the entire enterprise, but I remain no less interested in and concerned about the democratic political process and in trying to bring commitment, information, and critical intelligence to the task of understanding who we are as a people, how we got here, and where we are headed. This project began as a shorter book titled *Democracy and the Informed Citizen* dashed off in late 2017 and early 2018 as a resource to stimulate interest in and discussion about the South Dakota Humanities Council's main topic of the year during 2018. Receiving enthusiastic response to that effort, I decided to revise, expand, and update the book for a national audience. The result is in your hands.

This volume was written for citizens and students looking for a relatively brief, readable, and timely introduction to the political turmoil surrounding us today. It is intended to be used in book clubs, reading groups, civic organizations, political gatherings, and, of course, by individual readers. While ideally suited for college classrooms, it could also be used with profit by high school students. I have approached this project employing the same scholarly tools used in writing my other books, but this volume is not intended to compete with more focused and detailed studies that have been appearing in profusion of late on more specific aspects of democracy and its prospects for the future. The primary appeal of this volume is that it takes a comprehensive look at the challenges currently facing democracy, describes the situation from a dozen different angles, and attempts to demonstrate that the dilemmas we face are highly complex, long-standing, and not easily explainable by focusing on just one or a few factors.

While my approach is highly eclectic, I do bring a distinctive perspective to the analysis. It emphasizes the importance of reason, knowledge, information, and intelligence for the healthy functioning and preservation of democracy. Our Founding Fathers fully understood this. Most of them were well-versed in history, political philosophy, and what counted as the current wisdom of the day. Because of that, the new United States was blessed in a way that perhaps no other nation had been before. The inspired text for my treatment of this subject is the admonition of Thomas Jefferson: "If a nation expects to be ignorant and free, in a state of civilization, it expects what never was and never will be."[1] That advice applies both to our political leaders and to us, the citizenry, who put them into office. Unfortunately, as the following chapters illustrate, the United States is now facing problems in this area on both counts. Our citizens and our leaders need assistance in addressing the challenges we face. I hope this book will play some small role in alleviating the situation.

An initial chapter dealing with the development of governmental, educational, and journalistic institutions provides historical context for what follows. The bulk of the book describes twelve current challenges confronting democracy in the United States. It concludes with a short list of suggestions for attempting to address these problems, both individually and collectively. The emphasis is upon educating ourselves, acquiring knowledge, applying reason, and working through discussion, deliberation, and debate to resolve our differences in the spirit of democratic self-rule. An annotated list of suggestions for further reading at the end of the book provides a starting point for further investigation of the topic. That list could have been longer, just as more challenges could have been discussed. My original book dealt with ten challenges to democracy. This one upped the ante to twelve. More could have been added, but the point is made. What we're talking about is a process and a complex coming together of a plethora of problems. No easy answers present themselves, if anyone ever thought they did. It is up to us as citizens to take responsibility for our own future and for that of our children and their children.

I would like to thank Kristi Tornquist, director of the Hilton Briggs Library at South Dakota State University, and all of the dedicated staff members who work there for providing an excellent place to do my research and for all the assistance they have provided me on this project. I greatly appreciate a number of friends and colleagues who went beyond the call of duty in reading and commenting on one or more chapters or on the entire manuscript, including Donald Berg, Dave Bordewyk, Bob Burns, Becky Ekeland, Nels Granholm, Mac Harris, Cory Allen Heidelberger, Ted Muenster, and Gleaves Whitney. Special thanks to my wife, Kathy, who listened to the whole thing while it was in progress and keeps me on my toes and well-grounded.

Introduction: Democracy and the Challenges Confronting It

This book is based on the twin premises that "truth matters" and that "facts matter." Healthy democracies depend upon citizens and leaders thinking and acting upon those assumptions. Once people stop believing and acting upon the notions that honesty, transparency, the search for truth, and the willingness of people to discuss and debate questions with people who think differently from them are important, we will have entered upon the slippery slope toward tyranny. Unfortunately, some people have already moved in that direction.

Another premise of democratic society is that people naturally will disagree about many things—assumptions, goals, methods, sometimes basic principles, and, beyond that, even the nature of truth and facts. If everybody agreed about everything, there would be no necessity for politics, no need for discussion, deliberation, and decision-making. The solutions to our problems and the path to our nation's success would be laid out clearly in ways upon which everybody could agree. But experience and the lessons of history have taught us that difference, disagreement, and conflict are inherent in human nature. What is needed is some practical method of negotiating those disagreements, of channeling our different opinions, goals, hopes, and dreams through institutional means that will be able to achieve some sort of consensus or, lacking that, compromise. When compromise fails, raw power and, much too often, violence ultimately decide things for us.

"These days the question of what it means to be a 'true' American resists rational analysis," writes Stanford University professor Robert Pogue Harrison. "Whatever one can say about Americans that is true, the opposite is equally true."[1] It was not until the 1930s that the historian James Truslow Adams popularized the term "American Dream" as a way of explaining Americans' goals, ambitions, and motivations. But the concept did not have to be named to have reverberated throughout the course of our nation's collective history. Americans have followed their dreams from the very beginning; sometimes those dreams have turned into nightmares. But it has to be acknowledged that these dreams were never unitary, but rather took multiple forms and were evolving and often contradictory. The historian Michael Kammen brilliantly captured the multiplicity contained in American colonial culture in his Pulitzer Prize–winning book, *People of Paradox*, following that with other writings that described the culture that grew out of it as "The Contrapuntal Civilization."[2] American identity can plausibly be defined as both sunny and dark, imperialist and isolationist, warlike and peaceful, conservative and liberal, materialistic and idealistic, competitive and egalitarian, and democratic and authoritarian. It all depends on which individuals or groups you are talking about, what time is being described, and what the context is. Beyond that, differences exist not only among individuals and groups but also within them, for Americans—at least many of them—are notoriously ambivalent and self-contradictory on many levels and on many issues. If there is one truth that covers most of those contradictions, it might be "We want to have our cake and eat it, too," i.e., we always want more than it is possible to obtain.

Americans are rightly proud of the democratic political system their predecessors established during the late eighteenth century after declaring independence from the colonial rule of the mother country—England. They launched out onto their own to establish a new form of government that would represent the will of the people. According to an often-told story, at the end of their four-month-long Constitutional convention in Philadelphia during the warm summer of 1787, someone inquired of 81-year-old Benjamin Franklin what kind of government it was that he and his fellow delegates had just established. "A republic, if you can keep it," was his answer.[3]

Franklin's carefully chosen term—a "republic"—reflected the Founding Fathers' disinclination to think in "democratic" terms. Most of them not only did not think of themselves as democrats; they had a positive aversion to the idea of direct democracy.[4] What they had derived from their reading of ancient philosophers going back to Plato and of more recent commentators on political affairs was that democracies tend to be fragile, are susceptible to demagogues, and inevitably give way to tyranny. Ancient Athens provided one model of democratic rule—one in which every qualified citizen voted directly on governmental decisions and public policy and took his turn in filling governmental positions. Democratic Athens did not survive. Political commentators across the centuries generally agreed that direct democracy is flawed and impractical. By the 1700s, however, growing enthusiasm emerged for the idea of a republican form of government. Republican Rome was the Founders' model, not democratic Athens. Republics are regimes in which elected representatives make the ultimate decisions designed to promote the strength and stability of the state and to enhance the welfare of its citizens. In this fashion, the popular will gets taken into account and expressed, but filtered through the deliberations of elected representatives who are influenced by their knowledge, experience, and good judgment and by their interactions with their fellow legislators.

The delegates to the Philadelphia convention and the early leaders of the new republic, distrusting democracy, favored an elitist—or deferential—mode of governance. That involved having political leaders emerge from among the "best men"—the wealthiest, most prominent, most highly respected, and most powerful individuals—to whom deference was owed. (Women at the time were thought of as incompetent to participate in political matters when they were thought of at all.) In each of the thirteen colonies, political leadership tended to gravitate toward an upper cadre of planters, wealthy landowners, lawyers, ministers, large-scale merchants and businessmen, and others who commanded money, power, and prestige. Social-political hierarchy was reflected in the houses in which people lived, the carriages in which they rode, the clothes they wore, the pews they occupied in churches, and even the ways in which they addressed each other. Members of the upper "orders" (this term was generally used rather than "classes") were addressed as "Master" or "Mistress." The "middling sorts"—landowning farmers, craftsmen, small shop owners, and businessmen—were called "Goodman" or "Goodwife" (explaining why there were so many "Goodies" in colonial literature). The "meaner sorts"—landless farmers, longshoremen, sailors, day laborers, and drifters—had to settle for being referred to by their first names.

Yet, beneath this veneer of class consciousness, lay the fact, much more than had been true back in their homelands in Europe, that Americans were influenced by a vision of equal opportunity and individual liberty. The spirit of egalitarianism showed itself early, and by the early 1800s, during the decades of the early republic, people increasingly asserted their rights and freedoms and demanded equal and fair treatment from their neighbors and fellow community residents. Historians have identified a "democratic revolution" occurring in the new nation during the years after 1815 and leading up to the Civil War. The great exception, of course, was the treatment accorded to women, Native Americans, and slaves, the latter of whom accounted for around one-fifth of the population, mostly in the South but also in scattered places in the North. The Constitution counted slaves as three-fifths of a person for purposes of allocating members of the lower house of Congress among the states. This was a distinct recognition of most white Americans' refusal to accept blacks as full human beings, let alone as equal citizens. Slaves and most Native Americans were not recognized as citizens nor were they expected to contribute anything to democratic decision-making or even to enjoy the rights available to white men.

A civil war costing upwards of 700,000 lives was fought to preserve the Union and to maintain the principles first enunciated in the Declaration of Independence, incorporated in the Constitution and the Bill of Rights, and which have continued to expand and evolve in the more than two centuries since their inception. Over the decades, women, blacks, and Native Americans have received their freedom, citizenship or fuller citizenship, the right to vote, and claims on greater legal equality. Tens of millions of immigrants have become American citizens, enjoying the entire panoply of rights originally granted only to adult, white, property-owning males.

Americans fought colonial rule and the specter of even greater tyranny during the 1770s and 80s, fought a bloody civil war, and engaged in two world wars and other lesser ones in the names of freedom and democracy. Along the way, people argued about threats emanating from abroad, in the form of power politics, communism, and fascism, and from within, in the form of left- and right-wing radicalism, religious fanaticism, criminal conspiracies, and other real or imagined enemies. More than once, political groups have accused their opponents of actually being or of seeking to become dictators. Most of the time, the population never gave a thought to the possibility of democracy's demise, but complacency has never been in order. The record of other nations' travails provides ample evidence that tyranny and dictatorship can envelop a previously stable government in the proverbial twinkling of an eye.

Regardless of the reluctance of the nation's Founders to embrace a dictionary definition of democracy, the American political tradition is a democratic (or, if you prefer, a "republican") one in that it elevates the common citizenry, emphasizes popular sovereignty, and celebrates basic liberties and institutional safeguards for individual and group protection. Our particular form of democratic/republican government, as established in the Constitution of 1787 and developing ever since then, embraces the following precepts and principles[5]:

- The rule of law. Everyone, including leaders, is bound by law and deserves fair judicial proceedings, timely trials, humane punishment, right to counsel, nonpolitical enforcement of the laws, etc.
- Freedom of speech, thought, and expression.

- Freedom of religion.
- Freedom of the press.
- Freedom of assembly.
- A widely practiced right to vote in elections conducted with integrity.
- The separation of powers (legislative, executive, and judicial).
- The division of powers (national and state governments).
- Basic ethical guidelines: honesty, fairness, integrity, justice, openness, decency.
- Respect for independent institutions: the press, education, religion, the arts, business, labor, etc.
- Protection of individual autonomy against coercion from church, state, society, or any other source.
- Respect for truth. A shared sense of what is true and false. Reliance on objectivity, scientific investigation, factual knowledge, and reasoned debate.

That last criterion was famously and pithily embodied in a statement by New York Senator Daniel Patrick Moynihan when he observed, "People are entitled to their own opinions, but not to their own facts."[6] The "Moynihan Rule" has too often been ignored in recent years, as political rhetoric has heated up, partisan rivalries have prevented cooperation and compromise, and public dismay and anger have ratcheted up. People will inevitably disagree on matters large and small. But in the face of such disagreement, if both sides do not start from some agreed-upon factual basis for argument, nothing will ever be effectively resolved. Seeking closer approximations of the truth is what science is all about, including the hard sciences (biology, physics, etc.) and the social sciences (political science, sociology, psychology, etc.). The humanities (history, literature, philosophy, art criticism, religious studies, etc.) are more interpretive in general and do not usually admit of as hard and fast conclusions as do the natural and social sciences, but the goal of establishing verifiable facts and arriving at truth is of central importance to their practitioners, too.

A concern that motivates this book is the sense that in today's political and media environment large numbers of people have given up on the notion of truth itself. Many Americans feel entitled to believe their own facts regardless of what other investigators say. When disagreements arise, they are willing to accept what their group's members, leaders, and propagandists say on the matter, even if they obviously are ideologically or politically motivated or in the employ of organizations and entities that have a clear stake in the matter. This situation is problematical and bodes poorly for the future viability of democracy.

The relationships existing among politics, education, and journalism are straightforward and profound. A healthy democracy depends heavily upon an informed and involved citizenry, which in turn requires strong systems of education and fact-finding. Without adequate facts and information and the capacity to think critically and intelligently about their own situation, voters are flying blind when they enter the voting booth, or perhaps are overly influenced or even brainwashed by individuals or sources in whom they have placed their confidence to tell them "how it is." General education is important, because, if properly delivered, it confers the ability to think clearly, weigh evidence, place it in context, and make considered judgments about candidates and public policy issues. We need both our leaders and the electorate to be well-educated and well-informed in their decision making.

More specific information about political leaders, issues, and problems is likewise necessary when addressing questions about government. Our nation's Founders set an excellent example of citizens concerned about the polity as a whole and not just about their own personal welfare and advancement. Most of them were well-read, dedicated to achieving the public good, historically minded, and determined that future generations would benefit from the decisions they were making at the time. Devoted equally to personal freedom and to societal progress, they understood that they were situated at a critical juncture in history. They knew that they were acting not only for themselves but, in a sense, for their posterity and for all of humankind. Today, we benefit from their farsightedness, but in many ways our society and political system have failed to fulfill the promise they were endeavoring to achieve.

This book takes a critical look at how our democratic system is operating and how we, as a people, are or are not fulfilling our duties and responsibilities as democratic citizens. If it sounds overly critical at times, it is motivated by a sincere desire to make our democracy operate in the way it was intended to and in the way it should. True patriotism combines a love for country with a willingness to look facts squarely in the face and interpret them honestly and intelligently. These are also the purposes of the natural sciences, the social sciences, the practical sciences, the arts, and the humanities—the goal of effective thinking of any kind.

Chapter 1 begins by sketching the historical background of democracy, education, and journalism in the United States. Politics, education, and the media are integrally intertwined, the success of each depending in large part on the other two. Education and journalism provide the necessary tools for citizens and their elected representatives to make informed decisions. Factual information is required, but people also need to have effective thinking skills in order to critically analyze, interpret, and evaluate situations and make good decisions.

Chapters 2 and 3, the heart of the book, endeavor to isolate some of the most important developments occurring during the last several decades that have combined to create the current climate of discontent and political dysfunction in the United States, with particular attention being paid to the new media environment that has transformed and, to a large degree, has distorted the way in which our political system operates. Chapter 4 consists of some brief suggestions regarding how we might begin to extricate ourselves from our current dilemmas.

History, among other things, is the story of continuity and change. It is also an account of slower change and more rapid change. Some of the developments we are witnessing today have evolved over decades; others seem to have appeared overnight. Students and young people today, who have grown up in a super-charged media environment and never known anything different, may find it difficult to imagine what it was like before people had smart phones and iPads; when Facebook, Twitter, Snapchat, and cable TV were not integral parts of everyday life; and when large segments of each day were not spent on social media. They may wonder how people spent all of their time before the arrival of the Internet, television, and all of the other electronic marvels that they so assiduously take advantage of.

One thing people used to do more of than they do now was read. They read newspapers, books, and magazines, including pieces that ran longer than a page or two or three. This may be the most important take-away from this book. At least it is the message this author wants to send. Take time to read books, magazines, and newspapers. If you prefer to do it on your iPad, computer screen, smart phone, or other device, fine. But do not be enticed into continually jumping around from website to website, lingering only long enough to read a few sentences or paragraphs here and there. There is an increasing consensus among psychologists, brain scientists, teachers, and other interested observers that the attractions offered by computers and social media and the increasing time spent by people on their screens are not only making it more difficult for them to read more than a few pages of text at a time, scattering their attention, and reducing their ability to think and reason, it is actually rewiring their brains. Scary thought. Preached to for years that drug use can turn our brains to mush, we are now learning that too much screen time might have similar effects. If the only thing that suffered were the individuals affected, it would be bad enough. This book raises the possibility that democracy itself could be endangered by it. That is what we want to consider in the following pages.

1

Democracy, Education and Journalism in American History

The prosperity and success of the United States derive from many sources, not the least of which are its democratic system of government, its widely based educational system, and its far-flung array of news and information sources—from newspapers, magazines, and books to think tanks, blogs, radio, television, and social media. Despite the frequent frustrations and criticisms people express with regard to these institutions and the dysfunction they often seem to display, all three of them—government, education, and journalism—stand among the most important props of the American Way of Life, and all of us benefit greatly from them.

The three do not stand alone but are integrally related to each other. The proper functioning of government and public accountability of its leaders depend heavily upon an informed electorate. This, in turn, requires dynamic general and civic education and a vigilant press that ferrets out the information necessary to hold political leaders accountable. Qualified journalists depend on an educational system that nurtures them and on a government that protects them from zealous would-be censors and allows them to do their work. Public education, in turn, requires adequate government funding if all students are to enjoy equal access and opportunity to reach their full potential, while teachers and educators frequently turn to newspapers and other information sources to keep up to date with the work they do. This complex informational environment forms a crucial nexus within which democracy can grow and thrive.

Democracy did not emerge full-blown overnight in the United States. What we recognize today as democratic forms of governance evolved over a period of many decades in which rights, freedoms, and citizen participation expanded in response to changing conditions and the growth of political movements demanding change. The United States Constitution, ratified in 1789 and quickly supplemented by a Bill of Rights, proved to be a work of

13

genius—a supple instrument that protected basic rights and freedoms while it also provided a flexible form of governance that allowed for the expansion of those rights as time passed. The great paradox of the Constitution is that it was considered at the time by its creators, and has been judged by historical commentators since then, to have been an effort to check democracy.[1] Yet it has proven over more than two centuries of its existence to have been a generator of expanding freedom and democratic practice.

The men who met at Philadelphia during the summer of 1787 were deeply concerned about the weaknesses they detected in the Articles of Confederation, the constitution that had been adopted by the new nation in 1781 and under which the new national government finished fighting the Revolutionary War and then entered into an era of peaceful development. Political leaders such as George Washington, James Madison, and Alexander Hamilton feared that the government created by the Articles—lacking executive and judicial branches; deprived of the power to tax, regulate commerce, and do much of anything else; and facing daunting challenges from foreign powers, especially Great Britain—would not be up to the task and might easily wither and die. A general assumption among many of the fifty-five convention delegates was that democratic decision-making had been carried too far during the 1780s and that the government in place was too feeble to govern effectively. New powers to energize the national government were granted, including the powers to tax, coin money, and regulate internal and foreign commerce.

The challenge posed to governmental authority in Massachusetts in 1786 during Shays' Rebellion, in which outraged farmers and debtors forcibly closed down the courts and threatened anarchy, was a key factor leading up to the Constitutional convention. In effect, the delegates carried out an extralegal coup and initiated a new form of government for the thirteen states that had emerged from colonial status during the Revolution. Most of the Founding Fathers were determined to constrain the popular spirit that had been unleashed by the Revolution. Edmund Randolph of Virginia warned his colleagues of "the turbulence and follies of democracy." Elbridge Gerry of Massachusetts called democracy "the worst of all political evils." William Livingston of New Jersey asserted that "the people have ever been and ever will be unfit to retain the exercise of power in their own hands." Presiding over the convention, George Washington advised the delegates not to approve a document they did not favor themselves in order simply to "please the people."[2]

The Founders were, by any reckoning, elitists, relying upon the wisdom, rectitude, and good sense of other men, like themselves, who were members of the "better sort" of society. Aside from half a dozen or so exceptions, the delegates at Philadelphia were men of affairs occupying positions of considerable wealth and influence. They believed in a deferential form of politics and did not possess much faith in unadulterated mass opinion. They preferred to delegate authority to educated, cultured men like themselves, who possessed the knowledge, experience, and judgment to manage public affairs.

"And yet," as historian Richard Hofstadter noted in *The American Political Tradition*, "there was another side to the picture. The Fathers were intellectual heirs of seventeenth-century English republicanism with its opposition to arbitrary rule and faith in popular sovereignty."[3] They were determined to ward off kingly or arbitrary rule and to protect the liberties and privileges of the great mass of people, so long as ultimate decision-making power was left in "proper hands." Although they were unwilling to trust a system of direct democracy, George Mason of Virginia advised that "the genius of the people must be consulted." His Virginia colleague James Madison concurred: "It seems indispensable that the mass of citizens should not be without a voice in making the laws which they are to obey, and in choosing the magistrates who are to administer them."[4] The delegates thus were careful to refer to the form of government they were creating as a "republican" one (with a small "r"), in which the electorate delegated power to their representatives, and not a "democratic" one (with a small "d"), in which each individual had an equal say and was directly involved in determining public policy.

Limits on democratic or direct rule by the people were written into the Constitution in the form of an upper house of Congress whose members would be elected by state legislatures and whose terms would be six years; appointment rather than election of judicial officials; an electoral college for indirectly choosing the president; and the exclusion of slaves and women from voting. Generally speaking, the assumptions animating the new structure of government were that power was best placed in the hands of educated, established, and responsible men who would look out for a general citizenry that was not really capable of making important decisions and that power should be distributed widely so as to prevent an oligarchy from taking over.

Throughout most of the nineteenth century, government at all levels remained relatively small and uninvolved in regulating public and private affairs. Commentators sometimes referred to it as a "laissez faire" form of governance, from the French term meaning literally "to let to be" or, more loosely, "to leave alone." Carried to an extreme, the type of reasoning behind this kind of language would imply that there should be no government at all. But actual governing bodies were never hands-off entirely, and as time went by, they operated increasingly energetically in order to cope with the new demands and functions that were imposed upon them by a rising industrial

economy. In addition to national defense, urban police forces, and the provision of services ranging from roads, streets, and sewers to lighting, garbage
collection, and parks, state and local governments, as well as the national
government to a lesser degree, became involved in establishing and regulating
money and banking; building streets, highways, bridges, and canals; providing
poor relief; encouraging business enterprise; regulating commerce and
imposing tariff duties; regulating weights and measures; setting up time
zones; establishing grade schools, high schools, and colleges; and engaging
in a variety of other tasks and responsibilities.

Just as importantly, during the 1830s and later, the "democratic revolution" that took place in the United States eliminated most voting restrictions
for white male adults. The Civil War formally (but not actually) led to the
granting of the vote to black males, and women soon began agitating for the
vote for themselves. Democracy, in the broadest sense of the term, entailed
more than merely exercising voting privileges and engaging in political activity; it also meant breaking down class barriers, opening up social and cultural
institutions to all classes and segments of society, expanding educational
opportunities, and making information more readily available for all. The
rise of the "penny press," for example, made newspapers more easily affordable during the years before the Civil War. The astute and insightful French
observer Alexis de Tocqueville was astonished by the public's high degree of
participation in voluntary associations when he visited the United States during the early 1830s. He returned home to write one of the classic political
treatises of all time, *Democracy in America*, published in two volumes in 1835
and 1840. In it, he tended to equate democracy with equality, noting that
widespread opportunity existed for people to rise in society and making mention of the relative lack of barriers separating economic classes in America.

Americans have been reminded time and again, however, that class divisions do in fact still exist, that "power elites" continue to exert larger than
average social, economic, and political power, and that true equality always
remains more of a distant ideal than a true reality. Yet, the ideal persists. As
the political scientist Seymour Martin Lipset notably put it, the United States
was the world's "first new nation." It was an entity built not on geography,
history, blood, or conquest, but rather it emerged out of a set of ideas and
ideals that would guide and inspire it through more than two centuries of
development. America remains a relatively young nation, not finished in the
work of perfecting and fulfilling its animating principles. Those include,
among others, liberty and equality, personal freedom and personal responsibility, democracy, republicanism, individualism, and community, as well as
practical idealism, hard work, generosity, opportunity, fairness, and per-

fectibility. Some of these, especially the first several mentioned, stand out above the rest as primary. Those that were not included at the outset were added later. Some of them are or seem to be contradictory. Not all will agree on the inclusion of some items, and other observers will demand the addition of other principles. Nevertheless, few people will deny that it is ideas and ideals like these that have defined United States political culture rather than ascribed or inherited traits relating to birth, inheritance, race, ethnicity, or aristocratic privilege.[5]

Beyond these cultural characteristics, the American project was built on several foundational pillars that remain necessary today for its continued survival and success. These include adherence to the rule of law; self-government and political participation; patriotism; respect for private property; the entrepreneurial spirit, ambition, and the drive for success; educational attainment; and the scientific attitude. People harboring a realistic view of human nature understand that while perfectibility can be aimed at, in the short run people are often driven by baser or even evil motives. These must be contained, so social control is imperative, even as personal freedoms must be guaranteed. The health of the society and of the flourishing of the polity always present a delicate balancing act, something that often escapes general notice or public understanding.

Keeping this in mind, we can briefly sketch the course of governmental activity as it proceeded through the nineteenth and twentieth centuries. The Constitution established a system of mixed government which was given the name of "federalism" because it divided power between the national government and state governments. The framework established in 1787 was novel in that it was contained within a written document. While it was constructed and ratified in a pre-industrial era, it was flexible enough to remain relevant as the nation went through a tumultuous process of modernization, during which it was transformed from a primarily rural, agrarian society into a largely urban, industrial one. In the late 1700s yet, approximately 90 percent of the population continued to live on farms. During the 1810s and 20s, the first large factories were established in New England to manufacture cloth, setting the industrial revolution on its way. Railroads appeared during the 1830s, accelerating a transportation revolution that had already begun with plank roads, steamboats, and canals. With the rise of cheap newspapers, improved printing presses, the telegraph, and eventually the telephone, a communications revolution greatly speeded and facilitated messaging among individuals and businesses. Then, after the Civil War, an organizational revolution introduced bureaucracy (which was considered a good thing at the time), scientific management, new modes of business organization, and modern ideas about leadership in society, government, business, education, religion, and all aspects of social and economic life. It was inevitable that governmental institutions would modify their activities and methods of operation to accommodate those changes.

In increasing governmental size and responsibilities, the United States lagged behind Great Britain, France, and Germany. Under the direction of Chancellor Otto von Bismarck, Germany took the lead in introducing social security and welfare programs to ameliorate the dislocations caused by industrialization and urbanization. The United States was slow to imitate that model, but change did come. Governmental intrusion into economic affairs and business activities was not continuous but rather arrived in bursts of reform, which in retrospect presented the appearance of cycles of reform and consolidation. Sometimes, it was the federal government that took the lead; sometimes, it was state or local governments that assumed the task.

Federal activity along these lines had largely been limited to tariffs; subsidies for roads and other forms of transportation; banking legislation including, for a time, a national bank; a Civil War income tax; and pensions for war veterans. Major departures, responding to loud demands from farm, labor, and other groups, occurred in 1887 and 1890, when Congress passed the Interstate Commerce Act and the Sherman Anti-Trust Act, neither of which proved to be very effective at the outset. A second burst of reform occurred during the progressive period between 1900 and 1917, when presidents Theodore Roosevelt, William Howard Taft, and Woodrow Wilson took the lead in addressing the problems of monopolies, banking and finance, food and drugs, national forests, railroads, factory conditions, and so forth. The early 1900s marked the true beginnings of modern liberal democracy as we know it today.[6] During these years the United States began substantial regulation of business and industry, instituted a federal income tax, allowed women the vote, began to enforce First Amendment freedoms and to make the protection of civil liberties a priority, and made the first tentative steps toward guaranteeing civil rights.

The New Deal, launched two decades later, introduced a whole host of new regulatory bodies, agricultural subsidies, Social Security, and other federal programs. Power became concentrated in the presidency in a way that had been uncommon up until that time. By the late 1930s, Keynesian economic prescriptions, relying upon monetary and fiscal policy in an attempt to manage business cycles, had been introduced as a concept, although debate over whether and how to implement these policies continues to this day. The Roosevelt (or New Deal) coalition of pressure groups that supported the Democratic party also was instrumental in bringing new categories of people into frequent contact with politics, including women, blacks, ethnics, Native Americans, labor union members, and others.

World War II, with the huge prosperity and economic growth it generated, confirmed in the minds of many the notion that federal government action was pertinent and necessary. To conservatives, it provided a reminder of why excessive government intervention needed to be curbed. Civil liberties, to be sure, were much better protected this time than they had been during the First World War, but the internment of 120,000 Japanese-Americans in ten barbed-wire-enclosed camps in the interior of the country was a reminder that wars often place civil liberties in jeopardy. Blacks in the military remained segregated from whites during most of the war, but pressures from the National Association for the Advancement of Colored People, the Congress of Racial Equality, and other groups forced civil rights onto the national political agenda, where they would remain from then until now. President Truman's desegregation of the armed forces in 1948 and the NAACP's march down the road toward the *Brown v. Board* school desegregation decision of 1954 demonstrated how government action could force improvements in race relations even when massive resistance by whites attempted to forestall change.

By 1952, conservative Republicans had been waiting for twenty years to get back into power. They chose a military hero, Dwight D. Eisenhower, to lead them to victory, expecting that much of the New Deal could be repealed if they were able to capture control of the White House and both houses of Congress. They did briefly, but not much changed. Promises to "roll back" the New Deal proved no more realizable than were GOP promises to roll back the Iron Curtain that had descended over Europe after 1945. Instead, the 1950s were, in large measure, a period of consolidation and consensus in American politics, when the changes wrought by the New Deal were assimilated into the system, and Republicans, under the leadership of their hero, "Ike," promised to manage government programs more cheaply and effectively than the other party had been able to do. Symbolic of this was the creation of a new Cabinet-level department—Health, Education, and Welfare—which had been proposed earlier by the Truman administration but which now was actually implemented on Republican initiative. An effective bureaucracy to manage programs that were already in place was essential and inevitable, and even Republicans had come to realize that.

The 1960s, with John F. Kennedy and Lyndon B. Johnson in the White House and sizable Democratic majorities in both houses of Congress, witnessed more federal agencies and programs established under the mantles of the "New Frontier" and the "Great Society." Most significant among them were

Medicare and Medicaid, which future California governor Ronald Reagan and other conservative holdouts warned would bring socialized medicine to the United States, increase bureaucracy, and perhaps even bankrupt the nation. Once the elderly discovered the benefits of Medicare and others realized what Medicaid could do for the disadvantaged, the idea of abolishing these programs or tackling Social Security pretty much vanished.

Nevertheless, the 1950s saw the rise of a "New Right" in the United States, as conservatives discovered a crusading hero in Senator Barry Goldwater of Arizona, whose 1960 book, *The Conscience of a Conservative*, emerged as a bible for anti-government activists. The book helped jump-start a political movement that found its realization in Ronald Reagan, who captured the Republican presidential nomination in 1980. What had seemed like a lost cause when Goldwater carried only six states (including his home state of Arizona) in 1964 triumphantly emerged in the "Reagan Revolution" of 1980, when the former California governor handily defeated Jimmy Carter and launched a new era of conservative dominance in Washington. Twenty years earlier, political sociologist Daniel Bell had declared the "end of ideology" in a book of that title. Instead, what occurred during the sixties and seventies, riven as they were by anti-war demonstrations, civil rights marches, rioting in the streets, and hard-edged debates about every aspect of politics, economics, racial issues, family matters, sexual orientation, and you name it, was a massive revival of ideological conflict, the likes of which had not been witnessed since the 1930s. These ideological debates only got meaner and nastier as the years rolled by.

The American political system underwent a massive sea change in the wake of the tumultuous sixties. People at the time sensed that they were living in historic times. If they thought that things would settle down once the decade was over, they were clearly mistaken. The 1970s brought only more of the same. The country moved into a period of constant turmoil, conflict, disorientation, and sometimes chaos. Political parties seemed to be losing their functions and influence. Authority of all kinds was called into question. The young asserted their right to make their own decisions and to speak their own minds. Parents and adult figures often abdicated their responsibilities. If the Vietnam War, assassinations, marches, and rioting in the streets weren't enough to disorient everything, Watergate drove the last nail into the coffin of believing what authority figures and governing bodies said and eliminated the last vestiges of trust that many people retained in their governing institutions.

While politicians appealed to the vast "solid middle class," the "silent majority," and the "forgotten Americans," the ostensible middle ground of politics rapidly vanished. By the early 2000s, moderates on either the right or the left were losing ground. For decades, the Democrats had built a coalition around two large segments of the party—Southern conservatives (largely segregationists) and northern and western liberals, while the Republicans were split between midwestern and other stand-pat conservatives, such as Robert Taft, Bourke Hickenlooper, and Karl Mundt, on the one side, and more moderate or even liberal coastal politicians, such as William Scranton, Nelson Rockefeller, and Margaret Chase Smith, on the other. Representatives of the latter type are scarcely to be found anymore. In recent years, the most liberal Republicans have usually stood to the right of almost every Democrat, and the most conservative Democrats have stood to the left of almost every Republican. "Mavericks" in either party are in short supply. Party-line votes on divisive issues are now the rule. Congressional minorities complain when the majority party passes legislation with no help from their side, and that applies whether they are Democrats or Republicans. But when party control shifts, little changes. Compromise and cooperation have become, if not obsolete, increasingly uncommon. Politics is a mess, and prospects for improvement are not encouraging.

*   *   *

Education offers a unique subject for discussion in that it is the one area of our lives about which most of us tend to think of ourselves as "experts." All of us have spent extensive time in school, harbor our own ideas about what goes on there, and may even harbor some proposed remedies for what ails them. But education is also one of those subjects that invite unusually fervid discord and debate, because there are so many different kinds of problems identified with it and so many contradictory solutions offered for anybody willing to think seriously about them. Beyond that, there is disagreement about whether education is mainly a festering problem or whether it is truly one of the great achievements of our culture.

"Educational history," writes the educational historian Diane Ravitch, "is a particularly tempting arena for politicization because of the ready availability of the public school as a straw man, a panacea that failed." Two traditions of commentary have arisen on the subject, she suggests: "One lauds the greatness of the public school, the other laments its lowly state."[7] Many successful individuals praise the teachers who set them on the right path; most, however, are more likely to attribute their rise to their parents or to their own good character, hard work, grit, and perhaps luck. As Richard Hofstadter and many others have pointed out, a strong streak of anti-intellectualism inhabits the American mindset, one that is in constant tension with other more scholarly, scientific, book-oriented, factual leanings.[8] Writers, teachers, journalists, and other torch-bearers of knowledge always find themselves in battle with apathy, conformity, alleged common sense, and simple laziness.

The individuals who spearheaded the American Revolution and launched the democratic project in this country were unusually thoughtful, well-read seekers after wisdom, making them admirable role models for us today but also putting them in a category that sets them apart from the ordinary lot. America's Founders well understood the intimate relationship that exists between education and a healthy polity. They were, by and large, well-educated for the time. They, like the people they represented, understood that leaders in a republican system of government were necessarily people of intelligence, accomplishment, integrity, and, above all, education.

Republicanism depended heavily upon two things: good leaders or representatives, on the one hand, and education both of the leaders and of their followers, on the other. Thomas Jefferson, like his fellow statesmen of the period, understood that differences of opinion and political conflict would naturally arise, whatever the circumstances or whatever particular form of government was in place. Problems would properly be fixed by the free exchange of ideas in open forums. He believed in reading newspapers, even though they were not always reliable. Jefferson had confidence in the constructive influence of education, of which newspapers, books, and other reading material were basic elements. People, if not perfectible, were capable of great achievement with the proper education.

John Adams, his frequent political rival, adhered to a more pessimistic view of human nature, viewing humankind as inherently quarrelsome, illogical, and often perverse. The institutional solution he proposed was balance—between the rulers and the ruled, among the three branches of government, and between liberty and order. Human solutions to problems might be found in education, in stoic patience, and in wise leadership. Moral solutions lay in private and public virtue. George Washington, having presided over the launching of the new republic, left office in 1797 urging his listeners to promote, "as an object of primary importance, institutions for the general diffusion of knowledge. In proportion as the structure of a government gives force to public opinion, it is essential that public opinion should be enlightened." James Madison, recognized as the "Father of the Constitution," wrote, "A popular government without popular information, or the means of acquiring it, is but a prologue to a farce or a tragedy or perhaps both."[9]

While an unusually large proportion of the early settlers of New England, the Middle Colonies, and the South were relatively well educated for the time, the institutional props for enlightened thought in the form of schools, newspapers, books, and other reading materials remained primitive and underdeveloped throughout almost two centuries leading up to the American Revolution. Wherever they landed along the Atlantic coast, immigrants from Great Britain and other European nations carried along with them traditions from their homelands, all of which were substantially modified when confronting unfinished conditions in the New World. Puritans in Massachusetts and in the colonies that split off from it were determined to establish religious commonwealths that would serve as havens for believers of their persuasion. They sought to promote universal literacy so that their children and their children's children would be able to read the Bible and follow in God's ways. They quickly imported a printing press, set up schools, and by 1636 had already established Harvard College, primarily as a place in the beginning to educate ministers for Puritan pulpits.

Legislation passed by the Massachusetts legislature in 1642 was the first instance in the English-speaking world in which children were required to be taught how to read. Five years later, that same body ordered each town containing more than fifty households to appoint a teacher to instruct younger students in reading and writing and those with more than a hundred to set up a grammar school. Farther south, provision for schools was left primarily to families and to private and religious groups. Partly because of slavery and partly because of the scattered nature of plantation agriculture in the South, schools were slower to develop there. But many Southern slave owners were gentlemen who imported boxes of books from England, and surprising numbers of them were well-read in contemporary and classical writers. Wealthy planters could afford to hire tutors for their children and often sent their sons to England for secondary schooling.[10]

The first century established two important traditions in American schooling: first, that it would be directed beyond purely intellectual concerns toward developing the whole student in the way of moral and character training, and, second, that schools would be locally oriented and controlled. The question of where authority should remain—in the local community or in a more centralized location—was raised early on and has remained with us, in some fashion or other, ever since.

By the mid–1700s, private schools providing elementary education and academies delivering secondary education were increasing in numbers. In this, Philadelphia in the Middle Colonies took the lead. Benjamin Franklin, a man involved in many different projects during the late colonial period, sought to promote social mobility through education. One of his innovations was to help found the Academy for the Education of Youth in 1751. "Youth will come out of this school," he attested, "fitted for learning any business, calling, or profession." Instruction in practical subjects useful for jobs in trade and commerce included mathematics, electricity, mechanics, astronomy, and other scientific subjects and became increasingly common in schools during the later 1700s. Even more important in Franklin's mind, however, was the role education would play in inculcating virtue in young people. In his *Proposals Relating to the Education of Youth in Pennsylvania* he cited British political philosophers Thomas Hutcheson and John Locke, both of whom considered virtue to be the true aim of education.[11]

Most colonial schools were public, but not free, i.e., tax-supported. Progress in expanding and democratizing education proceeded slowly, but continuously. Along with the basics of reading, writing, and arithmetic, the "fourth 'r'" was religion, which in many schools, at least, was as important a part of the curriculum as the other three. Practically the only textbook to be found in New England elementary schools between its first printing around 1690 and the Revolutionary War was the famous *New England Primer*. Widely used in most schools, it leaned heavily toward religious and moral themes. In learning their letters, students would begin with "In Adam's fall, we sinned all," and end with "Zacchaeus he did climb the tree his Lord to see."[12] The book also included a page of "The Dutiful Child's Promises," beginning with "I will fear GOD and honour the King. I will honour my Father & Mother. I will obey my Superiors." Texts of the Lord's Prayer, the Apostles' Creed, and the Ten Commandments were included in the book.[13]

Colonial education remained scattered, thin, underdeveloped, and heavily religiously oriented for the most part. It tended toward rote learning, harsh discipline, private sources of funding, and ill-trained teachers. It was largely aimed at boys, excluded blacks and Indians almost entirely, and sought to replicate the social order and to maintain the status quo. Well-to-do families had much the better of it, as they usually do. Yet, great promise was there. The future was more important than the past, and the high idealism on the part of the public, students, and teachers stood out against the rather grim realities of what actually went on in the classrooms. Above all, there was a widely perceived link between education and republicanism, or democratic governance. American freedom depended upon an educated populace, it was widely believed, and the elitist social and political leadership that was in charge of things fully shared that belief.

Education goes beyond formal schooling. There is more to it than what goes on in classrooms and in institutional settings, from K-12 schools, colleges, and universities to technical schools, night schools, and on-line instruction. Relatively small numbers of school-age children attended school for any significant period of time during the 1600s and 1700s. But real learning went on continuously in a multitude of places. Harvard historian Bernard Bailyn points out in *Education in the Forming of American Society* that education is "the entire process by which a culture transmits itself across the generations."[14] In the colonies it had an elaborate, intricate involvement with other aspects of society. Colonial society's youth were tutored and socialized mainly within the family but also through apprenticeships, employment, involvement in the local community, church services and Sunday schools, evening schools, newspapers, books, magazines, libraries, and organizations like Franklin's Junto in Philadelphia. Just as is true today, factual knowledge and interpretive schemes were passed on in a variety of ways. By the time of the Revolution, adult literacy in the United States was probably the highest in the world. This was a good sign for the future of democracy.

The early decades of the republic leading up to the Civil War were a period of tremendous change, growth, openness, experimentation, learning from experience, and establishing principles and habits for later Americans to continue, discard, or modify as they saw fit. The New England model gradually spread to other parts of the country. New York and other states outside of the South set apart land and money for financing schools. Beginning around 1800, Webster's *Blue Backed Speller* became the standard textbook to teach spelling and reading. Many of the readings were straight out of the Bible, with heavy emphasis on rules of proper behavior. One lesson contained "Easy Words to Teach Children to Read and to Know Their Duty." In the question-and-answer section of the book, along with "What is a noun?" and "What is a verb?" were questions such as "What is a moral virtue?" (Answer: "It is honest, upright conduct in all our dealings with men") and "What is industry?" (Answer: "It is diligent attention to business in our several occupations"). In addition to moral virtue, the speller instructed students in the types of government and in people's civic duties with regard to it. Three types of government, as described by Aristotle, were explained: monarchy, aristocracy, and democracy. Each, in turn, was defective. Instead, the lesson to be learned was "A representative republic, in which people freely choose deputies to make laws for them, is much the best form of government hitherto invented."[15]

The three decades after the War of 1812 came to be known alternately as "The Age of Jackson," "The Era of the Common Man," and "The Democratic Revolution" in the United States, as American society and culture became increasingly democratized in a myriad of ways. Central to the story was the important role education played in expanding opportunity for those who were willing to grasp and take advantage of it. America's proliferating schools and colleges performed many vital functions, with promotion of republican political institutions being one of them. "The view that universal education was a foundation of the moral order of civil society had already become commonplace in the years before 1830," write Carl L. Bankston III and Stephen J. Caldas in *Public Education—America's Civil Religion: A Social History*. In 1825, the *Vermont Gazette* editorialized that "our common schools are the stamina for liberty and contribute to the general prosperity and moral dignity of a community, in a greater degree than any other single medium."[16]

The 1830s were a crucial decade for establishing the principle of free public schooling and creating administrative bodies and agencies for organizing education at the state and local levels. The common school movement received its biggest boost when Horace Mann, again in Massachusetts, became secretary of the state's board of education in 1837 and proceeded to set up the system and make the case for public schools. He built a solid argument for them in eleven annual reports, with a focus upon four important ideas: a reiteration of Jefferson's notion that a republic cannot remain free and ignorant at the same time; that education, while remaining moral in character, must also be free of sectarian religious influences and produce well-trained teachers; that education is primarily the responsibility of the state rather than being dependent upon the family; and that the state has the responsibility and the power to adequately fund education by raising taxes from the citizenry.

The decades before the Civil War witnessed further development and innovations in education at all levels, including the emergence of public kindergartens; the development of systematic grading in the elementary schools; slow, tentative moves in the direction of expanding secondary education; a proliferation of colleges, including the first experiments with co-educational instruction; a trend toward secularization, while Protestant morality remained a significant influence; and the introduction of the office of county superintendent of schools. There was wide agreement that the school system served as a bulwark of republican institutions. Expansion of the population into the emerging Middle West kick-started the provision in the Land Ordinance of 1785 that set aside first one and then two sections out of thirty-six in every township for the purpose of funding education. Nothing was more indicative of the Founding generation's commitment to the promotion of education than this feature.

Little controversy existed over the values expounded by the nation's early leaders. What conflict existed revolved largely around sectional issues dividing North and South, such as taxation, tariffs, internal improvements, and, of course, slavery. As educational historian R. Freeman Butts described it,

"The predominant tone of the school textbooks of the nineteenth century was a combination of Federalist, Whig, and conservative pronouncements.... To the resplendent values of liberty, equality, patriotism, and a benevolent Christian morality were now added the middle-class virtues of hard work, honesty, and integrity; the rewards of individual effort; and obedience to legitimate authority."[17]

No doubt the most famous school textbook ever published was the McGuffey Reader series, which sold more than 120 million copies between 1836 and 1920. The series editor, Professor William Holmes McGuffey, had been trained under three Presbyterian ministers, something that shone through in all of the books. In addition to teaching students how to read, the books instilled patriotic and ethical values as well as a heavy dose of Protestant religion. In this, they were simply carrying on a tradition going back to colonial times. Over the decades, the tone of the books changed somewhat (McGuffey himself died in 1873), but the books' emphasis on character and morality remained.[18]

The Civil War disrupted every major institution and activity in the United States while ushering in what some later referred to as the "Second American Revolution." Rapid economic growth, industrialization, urbanization, and bureaucratization—in a word, modernization—accelerated between 1865 and 1900. New and better modes of communication, scholarly research, scientific investigation, publication, and dissemination of information better informed and educated the public. Changes in formal education were not the least of the process.

Higher education stood out prominently in this transformation. While numbers of students and institutions remained relatively small, the foundation was laid for the huge development and expansion that would occur in colleges and universities during the twentieth century. The Morrill Land Grant College Act of 1862 provided for agricultural and technical training, along with instruction in the humanities and other subjects, a perfect marriage of the practical and the more theoretical which has characterized higher education from then until now, even though it sometimes has put each at loggerheads with the other. Research and publication became much more prevalent at the higher reaches of the system. Graduate education, heavily influenced by the German model, became a regular part of research universities, starting with Johns Hopkins in 1876 and extending to older institutions such as Harvard and Yale and newer ones such as the University of Chicago, established in 1892. As knowledge rapidly accumulated, disciplinary walls solidified; new disciplines were hatched, including psychology and sociology; scholarly organizations such as the American Historical Association, the

American Political Science Association, and the American Economic Association appeared; and research organizations, such as Thomas Edison's Menlo Park laboratory, came on line. While scholarly work remained largely an individual endeavor, teams, organizations, groups, and associations also became increasingly involved in it. With knowledge expanding at an accelerating pace, Charles W. Eliot, president of Harvard, introduced the elective system, allowing students wide discretion in choosing what courses to take, an early step on the path toward the intellectual smorgasbord that exists today. Still, colleges both public and private, especially those with a religious orientation, considered themselves developers of good character and moral values in their students. Most colleges required daily chapel attendance, some of which remained religious in nature but much of which became more secular over time. By the 1920s, "chapel" exercises in most places were better characterized as "student assemblies." Many schools featured a capstone class for seniors on moral philosophy that was taught by the institution's president. Student literary and debating societies were essential aspects of the collegiate experience on campuses all across America, and the development of oratorical skill continued to be given high priority.

High schools, whose origin went back to the 1820s, began to expand rapidly after the Civil War, although they still enrolled only a tiny proportion of the eligible student population. An 1874 court case originating in Kalamazoo, Michigan, established the principle that general tax revenues could be used for public high schools as well as for elementary and higher education. Rapid expansion of secondary education occurred after 1890, when 360,000 students were enrolled in high schools (about 7 percent of youth aged 14–17). By 1930 the number had risen to five million (50 percent of that age group). Compulsory attendance laws, which had remained largely symbolic between 1850 and 1890, began to be seriously enforced after the latter date. Teacher training improved as the period saw the rapid expansion of normal schools for the training of teachers, many of which were later elevated to the status of state colleges and universities. Vocational and technical training also increased, as larger numbers of students began enrolling in high schools.

The intellectual case for democratizing education at every level was being made by a coterie of influential thought leaders in a variety of different places. William Torrey Harris, a leading American philosopher as well as St. Louis superintendent of schools and then United States commissioner of education, was celebrated for establishing the first public kindergarten in the United States and for his promotion of educational philosophy and advocacy for the use of educational psychology in teacher training. Francis W. Parker drew upon his experiences in administering schools in Boston, Chicago, and

Quincy, Massachusetts, to promote a progressive form of education, advocating informal methods of teaching and a more relaxed social atmosphere in the classroom. G. Stanley Hall, who helped develop the new discipline of psychology at Johns Hopkins before becoming the first president of Clark University, is credited with discovering the concept of adolescence, which had huge repercussions in later years. John Dewey, a philosopher and educational theorist who was involved in dozens of political movements and organizations over the course of six decades, gained perhaps his greatest fame for his role in promoting progressive education, which began with his researches at the University of Chicago's laboratory school during the 1890s. The new philosophy emphasized cooperation and student-centered education.[19]

The twentieth century would usher in further changes and accelerate many others that were longstanding. At the beginning of the period, most children's formal education remained less than six years long. School enrollments increased rapidly as public spending rose, but debates about how to proceed and how quickly to do it were continual at all levels. During the two decades after 1910, and especially after 1920, total expenditures on education rose by a factor of four. The illiteracy rate declined from 7.7 to 4.3 percent. The decade of the twenties marked a great flowering of literature: F. Scott Fitzgerald, Willa Cather, Ernest Hemingway, Sinclair Lewis, Pearl Buck, William Faulkner, John Dos Passos, and Thomas Wolfe would be read in college and high school literature classes for decades thereafter. During the 1920s, recognized as a modernizing decade in the United States, the Book of the Month Club and the Literary Guild were inaugurated, publishing houses and bookstores did a booming business, and Americans displayed a hearty appetite for reading (or at last loading their bookshelves with) the classics. When polled, Americans included Shakespeare, Dickens, Tennyson, and Longfellow among the ten greatest men in history. During the decades after 1930, education, along with other sectors of society, faced challenges emanating from economic depression, the Second World War, the Cold War, shortages of teachers and classrooms, and continual debates about curriculum, teacher training, classroom management, and educational philosophy. The greatest, most festering problem in American society—racial segregation and discrimination—was fought out largely in its schools, ranging from K-12 to graduate and professional schools. Few of these problems and challenges were ever permanently settled.

Along the way, as pressures continually built for adding subjects to the curriculum and increasing the duties and responsibilities of the teachers and the system as a whole, the teaching of government and civics gradually was squeezed out of the curriculum and sometimes disappeared altogether. As debates over the wording of the Pledge of Allegiance and disputes regarding other patriotic ceremonies and rituals sometimes flashed in public forums, the teaching of the fundamentals of American government and American history often got substantially reduced or bypassed. Whatever was going on in the schools, polls testing Americans' knowledge and understanding of the Constitution, the Declaration, other primary documents, events in history, and basic institutions and principles of government revealed an abysmal lack of knowledge of the simplest facts on the part of people of all ages. Ability to name one or more of the three branches of government, the number of senators from each state, and the basic gist of the Declaration of Independence was beyond the capacity of large numbers of high school and even college graduates. Some Americans were more willing to sign their names to a paragraph taken out of the *Communist Manifesto* than they were to sign a paragraph from the Declaration of Independence. The culture had largely failed to educate its citizens in the fundamentals of its governing institutions, and yet it expected those institutions to deliver "the goods" that most people desired. Wake-up calls like the launching of the Soviet Sputnik in 1957, the Watergate scandal of 1972–74, the release of the report *A Nation at Risk* in 1983, and other shocks left some ripples behind, but no large waves of renewal that would transform the system emerged.

Calling up earlier episodes in the history of education is a reminder that in previous times intellectual leaders in America were strongly aware of the need for training in civics and sought to rectify deficiencies, even if the programs they proposed did not always have satisfactory results. In 1893, the report of the famous "Committee of Ten" of the National Education Association (NEA), spearheaded by presidents Nicholas Murray Butler of Columbia University and Charles W. Eliot of Harvard along with U.S. Commissioner of Education William Torrey Harris, offered up a variety of curricular proposals geared to four different courses of study and included history as a necessary core subject.[20]

As time wore on and enrollments expanded beyond all previous experience, as educational historian R. Freeman Butts wrote, "The problems of creating cohesion in civic education were especially acute at the secondary-school level, where education had to cope with a new and diverse non-college-bound majority." There was an upsurge of interest among educational leaders during the early 1900s in teaching civic education with heavy doses of political science, economics, and sociology included. A committee of the American Political Science Association in 1916 endorsed the idea of teaching "community civics," since the local level was nearest to home and was therefore most important to students.[21] Over time, however, civic education got folded into the rising influence of "social studies," as illustrated in a 1918 NEA report on the Reorganization of Secondary Education. The seven "cardinal principles" that emerged out of that document included "health, fundamental processes, worthy home membership, vocation, citizenship, worthy use of leisure, and ethical character." Along with its emphases on citizenship and character training, the result was to shift emphasis away from academic and intellectual disciplines and to broaden the social role of schools. Ever since, educators, school boards, teacher-training institutions, politicians, and the general public have argued over curriculum, teaching methods, financing of the schools, purposes and goals, and virtually every other aspect of education. Too often, understanding the need for basic teaching of civics and government has been lost. The process is never-ending. To think that our situation today is unique ignores two centuries of American educational history. But to wonder if we are in a uniquely unfortunate position with regard to student knowledge and general public knowledge of governmental institutions and issues is only natural considering the situation we are in.

Benjamin R. Barber observed a quarter of a century ago that the schools' central purpose—education for freedom—was being lost sight of. "The classroom," he said, "should not be merely a trade school. The fundamental task of education in a democracy is what Tocqueville once called the apprenticeship of liberty: learning to be free. I wonder whether Americans still believe liberty has to be learned and that its skills are worth learning. Or have they been deluded by two centuries of rhetoric into thinking that freedom is 'natural' and can be taken for granted?" The task, Barber reminded us, requires devoted effort over a considerable period of time, and the final achievement is always hard-won. "We acquire our freedom over time, if at all," he remarked. "Embedded in families, clans, communities, and nations, we must learn to be free."[22] Schools alone cannot be expected to carry the entire burden. It is the responsibility of all of us who have gone through the process to engage in the project of civic education. It is a collective effort involving families, churches, community organizations, newspapers, libraries, the media, and all the constituents of what Robert Putnam and others have labeled "social capital." The process is never complete, and democracy demands our all-out effort to push it along.

*   *   *

For most of our nation's history, journalism has been one of its most important institutions and one of the most distinctly American. From early on, the American people have been news-hungry. To feed that hunger, newspapers sprang up like weeds everywhere, peaking in numbers around the time of the First World War, when there were more than 15,000 daily and weekly editions being published.[23]

Newspapers, magazines, and other publications served a variety of roles over time, the most prominent, of course, being to bring readers news of their communities, states, the nation, and the world. Beyond that, they responded to business and commercial needs, advertised goods to be sold, boosted local businesses, promoted economic growth, provided entertainment, and were a source of literary content, humor, advice, gossip, inspiration, and communal identity. Not least of their functions was political involvement. From very early on, politics and journalism intertwined, sometimes in good ways, sometimes in bad. Informing the public about issues, problems, challenges, candidates, parties, legislation, and ordinary political affairs has always been a major service provided by the press.

Many major political figures, including scores of state governors, U.S. senators and congressmen, and lesser officials have been newspaper owners, publishers, editors, and reporters. Presidents from the days of Washington, Adams, and Jefferson have been intimately involved in trying to use, influence, and sometimes suppress the press. Newspapers have been our primary source of information about political affairs and institutions. Journalism is democracy's handmaiden, and the health of democracy depends upon the work that journalists do. That has made it, in many minds, the "Fourth Estate." Beyond the three basic branches of government—legislative, executive, and judicial—the existence of a healthy and vigorous working press has been an essential democratic institution. A dysfunctional press, on the other hand, portends democracy's decline.

For the better part of the colonial period, there were no newspapers in America, and then during the early 1700s only a handful. The thirteen colonies were fiefdoms of the British Empire, not working democracies, and government officials in London preferred things to remain that way. Colonial governments imposed stiff restraints on publishing, and colonial residents did not yet perceive a crying need for the kinds of information that newspapers might provide. Communities along the Atlantic coast remained small, isolated, and focused upon building themselves up, in addition to merely surviving. Taverns, teahouses, and casual conversations provided most of the news people thought they needed. Local trade networks and primitive levels of commercial development did not normally require much in the way of remote information, and for most people leisure to read was in short supply.

The first American newspaper was Benjamin Harris's *Publick Occurrences Both Forreign and Domestick*, published in Boston on September 25,

1690. It consisted of four small pages, the last one remaining blank for readers to write notes on, and lasted for only one issue, because Harris had not obtained the necessary license to issue it. Fourteen years passed before a second paper appeared in 1704—the *Boston News-Letter*, published by postmaster John Campbell. It lasted for 72 years, up until the American Revolution. Two new newspapers emerged in 1719, one in Boston and one in Philadelphia. More important was the launch two years later of the *New England Courant* by Bostonian James Franklin, whose younger brother Benjamin served him as an apprentice. While still in his teens, the latter started writing pieces satirizing the Boston "Establishment" and criticizing royal power. Impatient with his older brother's domineering ways, Ben escaped to Philadelphia at the age of seventeen to pursue his own career in newspaper publishing and writing, which led half a century later to his central role in the American Revolution and the writing of the Constitution. Newspapers played a huge part in fanning the flames of revolution; politics and journalism became locked in mutual embrace—sometimes in complementary fashion, sometimes antagonistically.

By 1765, nearly fifty newspapers, all weeklies, had been launched in the colonies, with about half of them still in operation at the time. The most important journalistic development of the period was the origin of the notion of press freedom, which obtained a huge boost from the jury verdict in the John Peter Zenger trial. After initiating his *New York Weekly Journal* in November 1733, Zenger, a German immigrant, became embroiled in a controversy with the royal governor and a rival paper, the *New York Gazette*, which served as a royal mouthpiece. When Zenger was put on trial for seditious libel, his lawyer, Philadelphian Andrew Hamilton, did not argue that his client had not written the offending material. Rather, he successfully argued that what Zenger had said was true and that therefore he ought to go free. The idea that truth was determinative was a novel one at the time, but truth as a defense in cases like this became a cornerstone of American liberty.

The American Revolution was a complex historical event, resulting from many different causes. Its origin and eventual success were heavily dependent upon the explosive growth of communications fostered by newspapers and the work of the new Committees of Correspondence, organized in 1772 by Samuel Adams and others. A prolific journalist, Adams emerged as the greatest propagandist of the Revolution, earning the honorary title of "Evangelist of Democracy." His agents were scattered throughout the colonies (soon to become states), attending many meetings, writing countless letters and reports, and forming, in a way, a "primitive Associated Press" three-quarters of a century before that organization arrived on the scene. Thomas Paine's

Common Sense, released in January 1776, sold 120,000 copies within three months of its first printing, placing it in the hands of most literate Americans and preparing the way for the Declaration of Independence just half a year later.

Newspaper editors used every persuasive device at their disposal to persuade public opinion, which was by no means unanimous in supporting either revolution or war. Revolutionary papers went into about 40,000 homes, but readership was much larger than that, as each copy passed through many hands. The principle of press freedom was one of the implied inalienable rights in Thomas Jefferson's eloquent statement in the Declaration. As new state governments were quickly organized, most of their constitutions included protections for press freedom, paving the way for its guarantee in the First Amendment. The war was fought, in part, in order to escape the restrictions imposed upon the press by the mother country. Freedom to publish was a pillar of democracy from the beginning and has remained so ever since, even as myriad pressures from within and without government have risen against it.

Of 35 newspapers operating when the Revolutionary War began, only twenty survived, but 35 new ones were established during the six years of conflict. Enough of them continued in business to leave about as many in operation at the end of the war as there had been at the start of it. All were weeklies and most were on the side of the patriots. The *Federalist Papers*, written by James Madison, Alexander Hamilton, and John Jay, played a crucial role in building support for ratification of the Constitution. Their publication in the *New York Independent Journal* helped spread the word to the public and established a tradition connecting politics and journalism—one that has continued in one fashion or other from then until now.

Despite the Founders' distaste for political parties, such organizations quickly emerged during George Washington's presidency. The Federalists, advocates of an active and strong central government, drafted Bostonian John Fenno into service to edit a paper that would favor their policies. Called the *Gazette of the United States*, it was launched in New York in 1789. Two years later, in order to counter it, the Jeffersonians enlisted Philip Freneau, the "Poet of the Revolution," to edit the *National Gazette*. When that newspaper expired after only two years, Benjamin Franklin's grandson started publishing the *Aurora* in Philadelphia to promote the anti–Federalist cause. Some historians referred to this period of mounting conflict and heated rhetoric as the "dark ages" of American journalism. What the Founders had not desired or expected had quickly developed. Partisan political battles, with newspapers enlisted on either side, set the terms of political debate and contestation during the early years of the republic. The two-party system established itself almost automatically and has dominated American politics ever since. Journalistic involvement in these battles was a given.

The temptation of the party in power to try to reduce—or even suppress altogether—criticism from its opponents led the Adams administration in 1798 to push through the notorious Alien and Sedition Acts. These remain today one of the most egregious assaults on press freedom and freedom of speech ever enacted. The first act was aimed against the approximately 25,000 resident aliens in the United States, while the latter was obviously intended to control the journalistic critics of the Federalists, after their voices had grown especially annoying during arguments over the United States' relationship with France and the French Revolution. In outlawing malicious and false statements published to defame public officials, the law in practice invited the government to prosecute and jail political opponents who criticized the government in any way. While the law clearly went far overboard in its violation of free speech and press, the responses of the Jeffersonians and Madisonians who made up what had become the Democratic-Republican opposition were out of bounds in their own way. Madison's Virginia Resolution and Jefferson's Kentucky Resolution both suggested that individual states had the right to repudiate, or nullify, a federal law when it was clearly opposed by public opinion. This was the same principle that later would be invoked by the South in the years leading up to the Civil War and, if allowed, would have meant the end of federal Union.

Although there were few actual prosecutions under the Alien and Sedition Acts, the opposition they stimulated was a major milestone on the way to effective enforcement of personal freedoms in the United States. In the short run, the laws provided a rallying cry for the Anti-Federalists (or Democratic-Republicans) to campaign upon in the 1800 elections and helped put Thomas Jefferson into office in what historians have called the "Jeffersonian Revolution." Ironically, once in power, Jefferson was not averse to going after his own opponents. The same man who had previously pontificated, "Were it left to me whether we should have a government without newspapers, or newspapers without a government, I should not hesitate a moment to prefer the latter," later complained that the Federalists "fill their newspapers with falsehoods, calumnies, and audacities." It should be noted that administration efforts to punish its opponents for offensive speech were much milder than had been the Federalists' actions earlier on. Nevertheless, the temptation to suppress and punish one's political opponents occurred on both sides alike. The pattern had been set: efforts by the party in power to suppress dissent have been a periodic temptation in the years since then.

The nineteenth century witnessed huge changes in the ways that journalism operated in the United States. The major impression was that of the vast proliferation and growth of the press, as the nation expanded geographically and the population grew approximately twenty-fold, from roughly four million in 1800 to 76 million by1900. While the vast majority of newspapers in the country remained weeklies or appeared less often than every day, the number of daily papers exploded along with the overall population. The first daily newspaper in America was Philadelphian Benjamin Towne's *Pennsylvania Evening Post* in 1783. By the turn of the nineteenth century, most of the large ports and commercial cities sported daily publications: Philadelphia had six; New York, five; Baltimore, three; and Charleston, two. Strangely, Boston, the mother of newspaper publishing, had none at the time. Within twenty years, two dozen of the 512 papers being published in the United States were dailies. The years 1910–1914 marked the high point in numbers of newspapers in the United States. In 1910, there were around 2,600 daily publications of all kinds, along with approximately 14,000 weekly newspapers.

A major factor in enabling such expansion was federal government policy that subsidized the newspaper industry. The Post Office Acts of 1782 and 1792 provided that educational and informational matter could be mailed at very low rates, thus making it possible for large numbers of papers to go into business in the first place and then to stay in business once they got started. Legislators believed that in so doing they were making a worthwhile educational and civic investment. Newspapers, in addition to informing the public, provided much of the kind of entertainment that would later be supplemented by magazines, movies, radio, television, and social media. During the early 1800s, while the better educated and more affluent segment of the public read books, probably half the population read nothing but newspapers.

As the population pushed west across the Alleghenies after the Revolutionary War, the press went along with it. The first newspaper west of the mountains was the *Pittsburgh Gazette*, beginning in 1786. It would be followed in succeeding decades by the *Cincinnati Enquirer, Cleveland Plain Dealer, Detroit Free Press, Chicago Tribune, St. Louis Post-Dispatch, New Orleans Times-Picayune, Milwaukee Journal, Minneapolis Tribune,* and hundreds of others. Wherever people went, newspapers were quick to follow.

There was little in the way of local news in early frontier newspapers. Much of their content consisted of letters sent in by readers, material culled from other papers, political fulminations, and editors' musings and pontifications. It took awhile until systematic efforts began to cover and report what was happening in the local environs of the paper. Staffs were tiny, and there was no provision for or even contemplation of regular correspondents or columnists furnishing their opinions. Even so, in many communities, newspapers provided the only material available to the general citizenry. They provided the major source of education for the populace until schools and other cultural institutions could be established. Before the 1830s, when prices began to go down, most people simply could not afford to pay three to six cents for an issue. In spite of this, the United States boasted the highest per capita newspaper readership in the world. As was true during the colonial period, papers often went through many hands before they fell apart or were discarded. By 1826, the United States had three million more newspaper subscribers than England had.

During the 1820s and 1830s, with the advent of Andrew Jackson and other popular leaders in politics, the extension of the vote to more and more adult males (although not to women, blacks, or other disfavored groups), the rise of industrial manufacturing, the rapid growth of organizations like lyceums and philanthropic groups, and a growing interest in reforms such as abolitionism, the United States underwent its own "democratic revolution." Notions related to "the rise of the common man" were in the air. A large part of this development was the appearance of the penny press during the early 1830s. New, faster, more efficient printing presses, new techniques for manufacturing paper more cheaply, and larger circulations and press runs all made it possible to reduce the cost of a newspaper from several cents a copy to a single penny. Thus, the term "penny press."

Benjamin H. Day's *New York Sun*, appearing in September 1833, is recognized as the first penny paper, but it was James Gordon Bennett's *New York Herald*, launched two years later, that set the pace for change and innovation with his extensive business sections, informative editorials, news from all corners of the country and the world, letters columns, society news, and critical reviews. Readership multiplied rapidly and extensive advertising revenues covered any loss in income due to the lower price of the paper. The penny press rapidly expanded readership, as most people could now afford to buy a paper.

Other innovations—the advent of the telegraph in the 1840s; the establishment of the Associated Press, bringing instant news from all over the country beginning in 1848; the development of more organized methods of collecting and reporting the news, at least in larger metropolitan areas; more careful and skillful editing; and greater specialization and introduction of separate sections of the newspaper—made for a product that by the start of the Civil War looked much different from what it had been earlier.

The "irrepressible conflict" affected all aspects of journalism, including reporting, editing, printing, advertising, and illustrating. Matthew Brady's dramatic photographs of the destruction wrought by the war, collected in books and mounted in galleries, literally changed the way in which people viewed the world around them. Detailed reports of battles and troop movements expanded readers' geographical knowledge. Politically minded newspaper editors played huge roles in party politics and even in promoting war strategy. Henry J. Raymond, who by 1861 had made the ten-year-old *New York Times* into a paper to be reckoned with, was elevated to the position of chairman of the Republican National Committee and essentially wrote the party's platform for the 1864 election, in which he also got himself elected to Congress. Newspapers had been heavily involved in political affairs from early on, but the Civil War, in part, was a result of political divisions whose every in and out had been detailed and publicized in the papers for years.

As in every war, the federal government was frustrated by its inability to control the messages and story lines that often were transmitted by newspapers, and, as president, Abraham Lincoln arrogated to himself powers that in some respects resembled those of a dictator. Especially disturbing and harmful to the prosecution of the war by the North was the presence of large numbers of war critics and anti-war advocates, referred to as "Copperheads." The role of the press in creating and maintaining morale was huge, and here again, issues of transparency, truthfulness, and control over what could be said and printed came to the fore.

Regardless of the politics and legal issues involved, the wartime situation worked results that could not have been anticipated. Besides the big boost the war gave to photography and illustration as a means of informing the public (newspapers, however, still were unable to utilize photographs, and line illustrations were mainly used by illustrated weeklies such as *Harper's Weekly* and *Frank Leslie's Illustrated Weekly*), wartime necessity actually transformed the nature of storytelling in newspapers. Pressed for space in the papers themselves and desirous of keeping tolls down on telegraph lines, writers sought to compress their stories and be more concise. Compared to today, reporting remained rambling and florid, but stylistically it was a big improvement over what it had tended to be in the past. Reporters developed the summary lead, in which they inserted the main gist of the article in the first paragraph and then followed up in subsequent paragraphs with more detailed development of the story. Most newspapers continued to use an eight-page, six-column makeup, but experimentation with headlines and the use of maps changed the look of papers. The introduction of the web perfecting press in 1863 allowed the printing of continuous rolls of paper on both sides by a rotary press, which was a distinct improvement. It took several years for most papers to adopt the innovation, but the war stimulated its introduction.

The war, which historians such as Charles A. Beard called "the Second

American Revolution," held huge implications for sectionalism, race relations, economic growth, the rise of industrialization and urbanization, politics, and any number of other social and cultural developments. The three and a half decades between the Civil War and the Spanish-American War of 1898 probably wrought more dramatic change of this sort than did any other comparable period in American history. Journalism was not unaffected. There would be a distinct move in the direction of greater objectivity and impartiality in the gathering of the news. The current notion of fairness and objectivity as a value in news reporting, which constitutes the heart and soul of modern journalism, had its inception during this period. Readers wanted to think they could form their own opinions on the basis of factual reporting they read in the paper rather than be fed a partisan line that simply reinforced what they already knew or believed. This obviously was more of an ideal than a reality, but from then to now journalism worth its salt has been motivated and driven by this concept. In addition, the notion that editorial columns should be separate from news columns reinforced the idea of fact-based reporting and objective analysis.

Beyond that, continued mechanical innovation in production drove down costs and improved the product to be sold on the newsstand or delivered to the home. Newspapers increasingly viewed themselves as crusaders for one civic cause or another (the booster mentality had never been absent from either large-city dailies or small-town weeklies). There was a continual effort to appeal to readers with a variety of types of content, such as food, sports, religion, travel, and so forth. The influence of individual editors declined (with many exceptions, such as Joseph Pulitzer, William Randolph Hearst, William Rockhill Nelson, and James E. Scripps) as newsrooms became more rationalized and bureaucratized. The introduction of efficient business methods was an essential element of what, in retrospect, can be seen as the modernization of press operations. Large newspapers increasingly came to be seen as big businesses comparable to railroads, steel companies, and mail-order distributors.

One of the most distinctive and memorable developments around the turn of the twentieth century was the development of "Yellow Journalism." Notable in triggering and accelerating this movement was the Spanish-American War in 1898. In fact, many observers considered the war to be a result of the phenomenon, since newspaper moguls saw opportunities in war to attract more readers for their product. Notoriously, the battle for circulation in New York City between Joseph Pulitzer's *New York World* and William Randolph Hearst's *New York Journal* turned public opinion and subsequently federal policy toward intervention in the civil war that had been going on in

Cuba for several years. According to the legend, Hearst sent the noted illustrator Frederic Remington down to the island to capture scenes that could be used in dispatches to his paper. When Remington wired Hearst that little was going on, that war was not in the offing, and that he was coming home, the publisher allegedly replied, "Please remain. You furnish the pictures, and I'll furnish the war. W.R. Hearst."

Whatever the truth of the story, Hearst's *Journal* worked hardest to whip up public sentiment for intervention. Exaggerated and completely fabricated stories were an essential element of Yellow Journalism. In this, Hearst was much more egregious in his practices than the more high-principled Pulitzer, but both were willing to engage in sensationalism and cutting corners with the truth in order to gain readers. Yellow Journalism, however, was more than that. It included the increased use of pictures and illustrations; screaming headlines; special attention to crime, corruption, and innuendo; expanded sports sections, cartoons ("The Yellow Kid" cartoon is what gave the name to the genre), and other feature material; and anything else that might make newspapers more attractive to potential readers. If truth was sometimes lost in the process, the cost seemed worth it to many publishers.

In a sense, what publishers and editors were doing with Yellow Journalism was what they had been doing from the very beginning: trying to attract readers. News was only one element of newspapers that made them attractive, but, of course, it was the most important magnet. Despite the willingness of reporters, editors, and publishers sometimes to bend, adulterate, or exaggerate the truth or even to make things up out of whole cloth, by 1900 the notion of truth and objectivity as an ideal—of factual reporting and acting as a gatekeeper for readers—was well in place. Without that, newspapers would have been just one other form of entertainment. In most respects, the product hawked by newsboys and sold on newsstands would be highly recognizable to modern readers. Newspaper publishers, editors, and journalists retained their partisan political affiliations and proclivities, but with a greater or lesser degree of success they attempted to separate their editorial opinions from their news stories.

Historian Matthew Pressman, in *On Press: The Liberal Values That Shaped the News* (2018), observes that for close to half a century, beginning in the 1910s and accelerating during the 1920s, major American newspapers were guided by the ideal of objectivity in reporting and writing their news stories. Interpretation of the news was reserved for editorial writers, opinion columnists, and reporters working on special sections and editions on Sundays. Foreign correspondents also were granted some extra leeway in injecting analysis and opinion into their stories. This situation began to change significantly during the 1950s and then more broadly during the turmoil of the following decade. Regular news columns began increasingly to inject analysis and interpretation into their stories, while seeking to retain a sense of objectivity in doing so. Major factors in causing this shift were the press's reflections on their failure to deal adequately with the rise of Senator Joseph R. McCarthy during the early fifties; the threat of increasing competition from television news and news magazines like *Time, Newsweek,* and *U.S. News and World Report,* requiring newspapers to go beyond simple description of events to analyzing and interpreting their implications and their meaning; and recognition that the world was becoming much more complicated, inviting reporters to help their readers navigate their way through the complexity, contradictions, and nuances of contemporary life.[24]

Formal college and journalistic education increasingly became a requirement for ambitious reporters, and journalism school values mutually interacted with the experiences of the journalists themselves. In 1900 yet, few reporters had any college experience. Later, it would be expected, and schools of journalism proliferated before mid-century to accommodate those needs. A whole new fraternity (more recently, including increasing numbers of women) of pundits and columnists would arise to offer their interpretations of the news. Opinion stars such as Walter Lippmann, Arthur Krock, Dorothy Thompson, Ernest K. Lindley, Doris Fleeson, James Reston, Drew Pearson, and David Broder would command large audiences and exert major influence on public opinion. Investigative journalism, which had always been present in one way or other, became a major function of papers that could afford to offer reporters the time and resources necessary to do the job.

During the early years of the Cold War, the external threat of communism undergirded pressures for conformity and encouraged support for institutional authorities of all kinds. Deviation from official assumptions and ways of thinking was discouraged. But a series of events and governmental failures during the late 1950s and ratcheting up during the 1960s encouraged skepticism, doubt, and resistance not only in the minds of college students, intellectuals, dissidents, civil rights activists, and anti-war protestors. Reporters and news executives joined other independent-minded thinkers and citizens in questioning the statements being made by government and military officials, business executives, and other leaders going all the way up to the White House. During the fifties, American adventurism abroad and the Russian orbiting of Sputnik called into question the leadership and wisdom of government officials. During the 1960s, the government's prosecution of the Vietnam War, especially, caused doubt, anger, and resistance among increasing numbers of Americans regarding those who were running the country.

Presidents Kennedy and Johnson let their displeasure with reporting on the war and other topics be known, but it was with Richard Nixon's ascent to the office in 1969 that discord between the White House and the press escalated to a level that had not been witnessed since the New Deal years. Conservatives, irritated by press coverage of Barry Goldwater's presidential bid, launched an assault on the press in 1964. Alabama governor George Wallace escalated the vitriol while running for president in 1968, and the following year Nixon sent Vice President Spiro Agnew on the lecture trail to lob bombs at press coverage of his administration. During the next several years, controversy over the My Lai massacre in Vietnam, the release of the Pentagon Papers, and the Watergate scandal all further intensified the conflict between politicians and the press, a split that increasingly carried over to the general population. Publisher Irving Kristol observed in 1972 that many journalists perceived themselves to be "engaged in a perpetual confrontation with the social and political order (the 'establishment,' as they say)."[25]

As newsgathering methods improved and politically-tinged reporting declined, other factors increasingly operated to call into question the factual basis, relevance, and objectivity of the news that was being delivered. Whereas political journalism and especially campaign coverage once leaned heavily toward detailed descriptions of speech content and policy proposals, now it increasingly focused on "insider politics" and behind-the-scenes maneuvering. Theodore White's hugely popular *Making of the President 1960* spawned a host of imitators that not only reported on the brand of cigarettes that candidates were smoking and the color of socks that they were wearing but also let their readers in on the conversations, interactions, and maneuvers that they and their minions were involved in. Reporters' focus on personalities and celebrities tended to downplay other, more systemic and institutional factors that were operating to influence developments. They also shaped their stories within a variety of different framing devices that may or may not have had a political bias attached to them.

Newspapers are peculiarly geared to making money at the same time that they seek to promote the public good. In either case, they depend on attracting attention, which in our modern, fast-paced, media-saturated world becomes an increasingly scarce resource. Just as the Yellow Journalists at the turn of the twentieth century resorted to sensationalism, exaggeration, fact-bending, and personality-focused stories to appeal to readers, recent practitioners have relied on similar techniques, up-dated for current times. Unfortunately for them, while shifting focus to more "soft news" and becoming involved in "infotainment" sometimes work well in the short run, experience has shown that in the long run they seldom have staying power. The problem is not only an issue of supply, however; ultimately demand determines what will be consumed and what will be bought. If people are too complacent, preoccupied with other things, distracted by easy alternatives, disinterested in politics and other important subjects, or simply too lazy to bother, the consumption of news will continue to decline. Democracy cannot long thrive in that instance.

2

Social/Cultural Challenges to Democracy

Democracies are not guaranteed to last forever. Many have come and gone over time, sometimes to recover and reappear in somewhat changed form. Democracies are always fragile, something most Americans are reluctant to acknowledge. As Abraham Lincoln indicated at Gettysburg, the Civil War exposed the United States to the test of whether a nation so conceived and so dedicated could long endure. Gilded Age economic developments suggested that democracy might be replaced by some form of plutocracy. The Great Depression witnessed the rise of autocratic and dictatorial governments around the globe, and some observers in this country wondered how long democracy would last here. The Cold War raised the question of whether democratic institutions were capable of standing up to communism. Now, once again, alarm bells have been rung about democracy's long-term survival.

Identifying and classifying the challenges confronting democracy is a rather arbitrary exercise, for they are all interconnected in a variety of ways, with causal lines flowing in various directions and influences interlaced with each other. One could consider other factors operating within the family, popular culture, industry and finance, ethics, and so forth. Governmental institutions and the political figures running them do not operate within a vacuum. The culture surrounding them establishes the basic climate of opinion, attitudes, values, beliefs, habits, desires, expectations, and motivations that influence and drive people to feel, think, and act the way that they do. Institutions such as agriculture, labor, industry, education, journalism, health, transportation, religion, and publishing provide the context within which they operate. Developing intelligent, ethical, visionary, and practical leaders is an important function of culture. Effective leadership requires good followers, and they, too, need developing and nurturing. Democratic flourishing requires a virtuous citizenry, one that fulfills its duties and responsibilities as well as defends its rights and privileges. Good character is a quality of individuals, but it always operates within the wider context of community. Good characters work to create good community, and good communities foster good character. The reverse, unfortunately, is also true. This book places special emphasis on the importance of knowledge, education, and intelligence in the decision-making process. These, in turn, flow out of regard for facts, respect for knowledge, and a willingness to listen to experts while also maintaining an attitude of independence and self-reliance. The fusion of individualism and community-mindedness, vision and practicality, generosity and frugality, and far-sightedness and respect for tradition feeds into the health and vitality of democracy and makes for a livable society and a vibrant culture. This chapter describes a social/cultural system that is currently in disarray, a situation that poses serious risks for the future of democracy.

Challenge 1—Education in Need of Renewal

Few areas of American life engender more disagreement and debate than education. Writings on the subject, Richard Hofstadter once observed, constitute "to a remarkable degree a literature of acrid criticism and bitter complaint."[1] Blue ribbon reports going back to and before the widely publicized *A Nation at Risk*, issued by the National Commission on Excellence in Education in 1983, as well as scores of books and articles since then have driven home the point that our students, teachers, administrators, and therefore our schools in general are failing, endangering economic growth, job placement, cultural flourishing, and democracy itself. A short list would include E.D. Hirsch, Jr.'s *The Schools We Need and Why We Don't Have Them*, Steven Brill's *Class Warfare: Inside the Fight to Fix America's Schools*, Jane M. Healy's *Endangered Minds: Why Children Don't Think and What We Can Do about It*, and Charles E. Silberman's *Crisis in the Classroom: The Remaking of American Education*. Against these kinds of critiques are studies purporting to show that while some schools are doing poorly, the educational system as a whole is working fine or, at least, as well as could be expected. Most of these positive findings tend to be contained in articles and reports rather than in books, and the newspaper press often fails to publicize them. Books taking a more optimistic viewpoint than usual about American schools include Diane Ravitch's *The Revisionists Revised: A Critique of the Radical Attack on the Schools*, David C. Berliner and Bruce J. Biddle's *The Manufactured Crisis: Myths, Fraud, and the Attack on America's Public Schools*, and Warwick B. Elley's *How in the World Do Students Read?*

Ultimately, as they are on so many other subjects, Americans are ambivalent about the education being served up to their children and young adults from kindergarten through the various levels of higher education. People perhaps remember their own school days and their own lack of effort and that of others around them, they question just how rigorous classrooms are, and by and large they don't respect teachers enough to pay them what they're worth or to entice a larger number of college students to want to go into the profession. Some don't agree with what they think goes on in the classroom. Others don't like the content of the courses. Many worry and complain about education's cost. A considerable number think education is getting too politicized or listen to critics who say that it is. Most look at their own children and realize that they could and should be working harder to learn and have more respect for learning. Always, of course, there are exceptions; there are always a certain percentage of students—fluctuating from time to time and place to place—who really enjoy learning and are highly motivated. They may be the ones who appreciate education the most or, on the other hand, who criticize it most for being so slack.

Ultimately, according to *New York Times* columnist David Leonhardt, "whatever complaints people may have about their local school or college costs, most have no doubt that their children need a good education. People see it as the most reliable path to a good life, and they are right." He goes on to suggest that the journalists and academics who publicly question the value of education may be two-faced. "Many are desperately trying to get their own children into strong school systems and colleges. Their skepticism apparently applies only to other people's kids."[2]

Anecdotal evidence about what is happening in the schools is not encouraging. In 2012, the Texas Republican party's platform actually opposed thinking. "We oppose teaching of higher order thinking skills, critical-thinking skills, and similar programs," it stated.[3] A Pew Research Center poll taken in June 2017 revealed that a majority of Republican respondents think colleges and universities have a "negative effect on the way things are going in the country." Democrats, on the other hand, overwhelmingly believe that they have a positive effect.[4]

Facts, information, and knowledge at every level are all critical for the effective functioning of democracy. The electorate needs to be able to make well-informed decisions at the polls and to operate productively in their daily activities, lest they become subject to demagogues and susceptible to all sorts of misinformation and falsehood. Legislators require evidence-based information to fashion laws that are rational, fair, and effective. Administrators, bureaucrats, and judges need it to carry out their mandates and render just decisions. Unfortunately, all too often these days, reality veers greatly away from the ideal.

Rising educational levels, in the form of attendance and graduation rates, are misleading indicators of effective learning. Today, about 40 percent of the 18–24 age group is enrolled in college, up from 26 percent in 1980. Recent high school graduation rates are approximately 84 percent for young women and 81 percent for young men, compared to 79 percent and 75 percent, respectively, in 1980. The more important question, however, relates to how much students are actually learning in school. Here, uncomfortable truths emerge. A 2015 *New York Times* article reported that Berea High School, with a student body of a thousand, saw its graduation rate rise in four years' time from 65 percent to over 80 percent. On their college entrance exams, however, only 10 percent of the students were deemed college-ready in reading and 7 percent in math. Across all schools, only 40 percent of the twelfth graders were ready for college-level work in reading and math.[5] The National Assessment of Educational Progress, considered to be the most reliable indicator of student learning, describes 46 percent of high school seniors as being below the "basic" level of proficiency in science, with only 2 percent being "advanced." Only 24 percent of students are "capable of composing organized, coherent prose in clear language with correct spelling and grammar."[6]

The deficiencies evident in elementary and secondary education carry over into post-secondary education. Richard Arum and Josipa Roksa's much-cited investigation of the impact of college and university study on student learning finds that while perhaps as many as 10 percent of students make notable gains, there are few or no gains for large numbers of students in critical thinking, complex reasoning, or writing skills. Emphasis on social life tends to exceed that placed on academics. More than one-third of students give evidence of no significant learning at all. There is a huge gap in potential that is being wasted or not being fully taken advantage of.[7]

Rapidly escalating college costs have caused rising numbers of individuals—especially among young adults, men, and rural residents—to conclude that going to college isn't worth the cost. Much of this shift in attitude is job related, as people calculate whether investing large sums of money in a college degree will pay off in landing a desirable position. Many rightfully conclude that learning a trade or a skill through technical education makes greater sense. In a 2017 *Wall Street Journal*/NBC News poll, 49 percent of respondents believed that a four-year college degree would result in a good job with higher lifetime earnings, while 47 percent concluded the opposite. College graduates split two-to-one on the positive side of the issue; those with none or only some college, who had previously divided evenly on the question, now registered their skepticism by double digits. Democrats, people living in urban areas, and middle- or upper-class individuals generally believed college was worth the cost; Republicans, rural residents, and lower- or working-class Americans tended not to.[8] Clearly, those who have benefited most from the educational system retain greater faith in it, while those who have not participated in it as much or at all are more skeptical about it. It should be observed, however, that there is considerable overlap among different groups in these trends, and that increasing doubts about the value of education beset the system.

Here, we focus upon on how well American students are doing with civic education—how well they have absorbed fundamental facts and truths about their governmental system and the politics that surround it. The report card on that count is not reassuring. Poll after poll suggests that for decades public knowledge has been deficient regarding governmental processes, goals, and results. Political scientist Philip Converse's pioneering studies during the 1950s revealed just how little average voters understood about government and politics and just how illogical and incoherent their political choices often were. Lack of knowledge does not necessarily correlate with lack of intelligence. Many researchers have confirmed the reality of "the Flynn effect," which indicates that general IQ scores have risen steadily during past decades as educational levels have gone up. What is at issue here is knowledge levels—the possession of factual information and the ability to interpret and derive meaning from those data. In *Against Democracy*, political philosopher Jason Brennan cites evidence indicating that rising educational levels have not made people more knowledgeable about politics.[9]

In 2011, *Newsweek* magazine invited 1,000 people to take the test immigrants are required to complete during the naturalization process. Thirty-eight percent of the test-takers flunked the exercise; 29 percent could not name the vice-president, only 27 percent could say why we fought the Cold War, and only 34 percent knew how long U.S. senators serve.[10] A recent poll by the Annenberg Policy Center indicated that 37 percent of Americans interviewed could not name any of the five rights mentioned in the First Amendment, and 33 percent were unable to name any of the three branches of government. Only 26 percent could name all three.[11] Other polls have shown that the general public thinks that foreign aid eats up around 10 percent of the federal budget (the figure is closer to 1 percent) and that public broadcasting consumes 5 percent (in reality it is about1/50th that much).[12] Columnist George Will succinctly sums up the situation: "Despite dramatic expansions of education and information sources, abundant evidence shows the scope of political ignorance is remarkably persistent over time."[13]

Poll after poll and study after study have documented the low levels of information and high levels of misinformation characterizing large segments of the American electorate. If this were just a matter of curiosity, it would be bad enough. But a healthily functioning democracy depends upon a certain basic level of public information about its institutions, leaders, issues, and public problems. Without that, political debate devolves into gibberish and leaders are left to see who can out-demagogue each other. "It is nearly impossible to have sensible public deliberation when large numbers of people are out of touch with reality," writes Harvard professor of government and the press Thomas E. Patterson in his 2013 book, *Informing the News: The Need for Knowledge-Based Journalism.* "Without agreement on the facts, arguments have no foundation from which to build. Recent debates on everything from foreign policy to the federal budget have fractured or sputtered because of a factual deficit."[14] The knowledge deficit of the American electorate has led a growing minority of scholars to seriously question whether democracy should be replaced by some other kind of system that depends more upon informed decision-making and expert advice.[15]

Explanations for the current situation are many. They start with the educational system. "In every society there is an integral, reciprocal relationship between education and politics," writes Diane Ravitch, and "the kind of education available (however broadly it is defined) influences the nature of politics and society, just as the nature of politics and society has a determinative effect on educational policy."[16] Unfortunately, in recent decades, time spent on the study of history and government has steadily been squeezed out of the curriculum as other demands have expanded. Equally problematic, if not even more distressing, is the impression that many, if not most, of today's students express little concern about or interest in politics and history. In this fast-paced, frenetic, screen-oriented era, stopping to wonder about what makes society tick, how the economy works, how democratic decision-making proceeds, and what happened in history seems to be beside the point for many of the young.

Psychological researcher Jean M. Twenge has labeled the current crop of students the "iGeneration"—"iGen," for short. This group of super-connected kids, she concludes, is growing up "less rebellious, more tolerant, less happy— and completely unprepared for adulthood" (the subtitle of her book). IGen'ers obtain all or most of their news online. Few read newspapers. They are considerably more poorly informed on government and politics than were previous generations.[17] A high school teacher told a *Dallas Morning News* columnist that her students didn't know how to read. "Oh, they've cracked the alphabetic code," she indicated. "What I'm saying is they don't have the ability to sit still with a text and read it for comprehension. Even worse, when they come across something they disagree with, they think it isn't true. I'm not talking about opinions; I'm talking about facts." The problem isn't so much that her students were wrong but that they didn't realize that they needed to employ reason to come up with the answers. The teacher was concerned that ordinary people were now accepting the notion that truth is relative and that they could rely on emotion to discover it. "For many of us, what's true is whatever is pleasing and useful," concluded the interviewer.[18]

Emory University English professor Mark Bauerlein calls the current crop of students "The Dumbest Generation," placing the blame heavily on the impact of cultural and technological forces—especially social media—which distract them from better use of their time and denies them the opportunity to read widely and consider seriously their civic duties and responsibilities. "Most young Americans possess little of the knowledge that makes for an informed citizen, and too few of them master the skills needed to negotiate the information-heavy, communication-based society and economy," he worries. "Furthermore, they avoid the resources and media that might enlighten them and boost their talents. An anti-intellectual outlook prevails in their leisure lives, squashing the lessons of school, and instead of producing a knowledgeable and querulous young mind, the youth culture of American society yields an adolescent consumer enmeshed in juvenile matters and secluded from adult realities."[19] NAEP (National Assessment of Educational Progress) data show that 46 percent of high-school seniors think it's "very important" for them to be active and informed citizens at the same time that only 26 percent of them are rated "proficient" in civics.[20]

Paradoxically, however, while fewer students are interested in becoming informed or actually participating in politics, more of them have developed strong views on the subject. Political apathy and political polarization appear to go hand in hand. Many iGen'ers are deeply cynical about whether they can have any impact on politics, and lack of trust in governmental institutions and leaders is rife. For them, according to Twenge, change will come from individuals rather than from government, if it comes at all. Yet, to put a more positive spin on the situation, it should be noted that all of these observations are based on trends disclosed by interviews and polling data and that there continue to be sizable numbers of students who are interested in civic affairs and what government can and should do. Student volunteering to do good in their own communities has increased noticeably in recent years, spurred on partly by classroom assignments, partly by students' own initiative.

Recent poll data reveals that more 18- to 24-year-olds hold favorable views of socialism (58 percent approval) than of capitalism (56 percent approval), which is less surprising when we consider the strong attraction Bernie Sanders, a self-declared democratic socialist, presented for young voters in the 2016 presidential race. More disconcerting are polls showing many young people losing faith in democracy itself. One survey indicated that during the decade and a half after 1995, the percentage of young Americans thinking that democracy was a "bad system" increased by half (16 percent to 24 percent).[21] Speaking of the Western world in general, British author Edward Luce observes that "elite disenchantment with democracy has been rising for years." He cites a World Values Survey indicating that "support for democracy has plummeted across the Western world since the fall of the Berlin Wall." The phenomenon appears to manifest itself most strongly with upper-income groups, but also has made surprising inroads among younger voters. When asked how essential it was for them to live in a democracy on a scale of one to ten, Americans born before World War II gave it a ten. Fewer than one-third of American and European millennials gave it a ten. Twenty years earlier, young people had made living in a democracy a high priority.[22]

Beginning in the 1960s, the teaching of civic education in the schools began to lose out to other subjects deemed more important. The launching of the Soviet Sputnik in 1957 elevated the priorities of math and science education. A new emphasis on accountability during the 1980s and later shifted attention to tests of things that could be measured, notably math and reading. Commenting on the situation, Christopher Dale of the Tribune News Service notes the anomaly: "A functioning democracy depends on an informed citizenry, including baseline knowledge of societal laws and institutions. Bafflingly, many schools no longer teach children how our government works and what basic rights Americans are guaranteed."[23] Perhaps as important as schools' failure to teach civics effectively are the huge distractions posed by television, teen culture, and social media, all of which appear to be much more exciting to most students than learning about civics.

Low levels of information about and participation in politics among millennials (born 1980–2004) are worrisome indicators to many observers. The group seems less involved in civic affairs than earlier generations. Voting rates of those under the age of 25 dropped from 51 percent in 1964 to 38 percent in 2012. In 2016, only 16 percent of millennials said they trusted government and political institutions such as Congress, while 18 percent said they trusted the major news media.

This sort of information has contributed to a growing movement to beef up instruction in civics and government in the schools. A recent federal assessment indicates that just a little over 20 percent of students rated "proficient" on a test dealing with the principles and operations of American government.[24] During the last several years, a number of states have joined in promoting civics education in the classroom, working through programs such as "Generation Citizen," a nationwide civic education group. As a result, 15 states require high school students to take the U.S. Citizenship Test and 17 more are considering making the move. One review of several studies concluded that such kinds of civic education actually have little or no effect on whether people will vote later in life, but it does make some difference in whether they will register their opinion in ways such as signing petitions.[25]

Thomas Jefferson's warning bears repeating: "Those who expect to remain ignorant and free, in a situation of civilization, expect what never was and what never will be." Our nation's Founders put their faith in popular sovereignty, but they also expected voters to be possessed of what they referred to as "virtue," a quality that included attention to facts, a willingness to discuss, openness to persuasion, and devotion to reasoned deliberation. Exercise of democratic rights needs to be accompanied by fulfillment of one's responsibilities and duties to the community. Only improved education and a concerted effort by government leaders, civic officials, and opinion influencers to rectify the deficit can foster such an active, duty-driven populace.

Challenge 2—Journalism in Free Fall

The presence of a free and vigorous press is an essential requirement for democracy to operate effectively, or at all. This necessity was recognized in 1791, when the Bill of Rights was added to the Constitution, aimed at guaranteeing press freedom, and it is all the more important today. In addressing the question of what large-scale democracy requires, political scientist Robert A. Dahl listed six prerequisites of modern representative democracy, including elected officials; free, fair, and frequent elections; freedom of expression; freedom of association; and inclusive citizenship. Requirement number four was access to alternative and independent sources of information, including other citizens, experts, newspapers, magazines, books, Internet sources, and similar entities.[26] Throughout the course of our nation's history, a free press has been an essential presence. Our confidence in the future of democratic institutions is bound up with the continuation of the free flow of information, but the condition of the newspaper press in America today is anything but secure.

Journalism's woes derive from two directions: from the newsrooms, where the news is made, and from the living room, day room, classroom, and coffee room, where it gets consumed. Fewer and fewer readers are subscribing to or reading the product that the newspapers publish. Evidence of declining readership is abundant. The percentage of adults who read a newspaper every day declined from over 70 percent in the late 1960s to a little over 50 percent in the 1980s and slightly more than 30 percent by 2010. On average, readership was declining by about 1.4 percent per year over these four decades, and the trend has continued downward. Combined with declining revenue from advertising, as the Internet began to gobble up ad revenues, profit margins declined drastically, producing dangerous incentives for investors to scavenge resources.[27]

Disturbing statistics document young people's consumption—or, rather, non-consumption—of the news. In this, as in so many other things, the 1960s constituted a watershed. A little more than half a century ago, young people were still nearly as informed about the news and governmental affairs as were older adults. Now, however, according to journalism historian David Mindich, "the decline in news consumption, which has taken place over the past four decades, has produced two generations of young adults who, for the most part, have barely an outline of what they need to make an informed decision in the voting booth." Compared to the 70 percent or more of older Americans who continue to read newspapers, fewer than 20 percent of young Americans do so now. Nor do most of them watch TV news or get onto news websites. Most young people access the Internet for everything but the news. Their political awareness, according to Mindich, is "remarkably shallow."[28]

If fewer and fewer people are reading or following the news as time goes by, it might seem that it really doesn't make that much difference what goes on in the newsrooms. But even if a smaller and smaller portion of the population are news consumers, the sorts of things published in the *New York Times, Washington Post,* and *Wall Street Journal,* as well as in the *Omaha World-Herald* and the *Monett Times,* do have indirect effects in important ways. Their stories are consumed by policy elites, educators, intellectuals, business leaders, and other socio-economic influentials; they have a big part in setting the agendas of important institutions; and they establish the groundwork for the climate of opinion that reigns at any given time. The working press is our most important definer of reality in an era when the whole notion of reality has come into question.

The prospects for American newspapers are dismal, and the implications for democracy are frightening. Words like "debacle," "disaster," and "catastrophe" to describe the situation are not uncommon. Presidents have long battled the press for better coverage as a matter of course, but honest ones recognize the essential work that newspapers do. Barack Obama's response to a question in 2009 about their decline described a situation already looming: "I am con-

cerned that if the direction of the news is all blogosphere, all opinions, with
no serious fact-checking, no serious attempts to put stories in context, that
what you will end up getting is people shouting at each other across the void
but not a lot of mutual understanding." Media historians Robert W. McChesney and John Nichols paint a developing picture in which there is minimal
reporting and distributing of information and informed analysis, both of
which are required for effective democratic governance: "A world without
journalism is not a world without political information. Instead it is a world
where what passes for news is largely spin and self-interested propaganda—
some astonishingly sophisticated and some bellicose, but the lion's share of
dubious value. It is an environment that spawns cynicism, ignorance, demor-
alization, and apathy. The only 'winners' are those that benefit from a quiescent
and malleable people who will 'be governed,' rather than govern themselves."[29]

Unfortunately, newspapers also suffer from a significant credibility problem. In polls, only 32 percent of the public say they trust the media, the lowest
level recorded since Gallup began asking the question in 1972. When asked
to rate the honesty and professional standards of 22 different professions, 41
percent of respondents ranked those of journalists "low" or "very low," which
placed them below every other category except members of Congress and
car dealers. Furthermore, 62 percent thought the media favor one political
party over the other, which is more than the usual 50 percent that had been
recorded in previous years. Reasons put forward for this lack of trust included
inaccurate news stories, dislike of the news that is printed, the use of anony-
mous sources, blurred lines between hard news and editorial commentary,
and the entrenched political divide that exists in the country. The political
preferences of news consumers obviously color the way in which they interpret what they take in. Only 45 percent of Democrats and 76 percent of
Republicans find Fox News to be credible, while 76 percent of Democrats
and 52 percent of Republicans find the *New York Times* to be credible.[30]

News organizations are in dire straits these days. Between 2004 and
2018, nearly 1,800 newspapers in the United States disappeared, including
more than 60 daily papers and approximately 1,700 weeklies. The total number of papers went down from 8,891 to 7,112, a 20 percent drop. Print readership disappeared even more rapidly during that decade and a half. Total
weekday circulation of dailies and weeklies combined fell 40 percent, from
122 million to 73 million. Numbers provided by the Bureau of Labor Statistics
show newspapers staffs declining by 45 percent during the same period of
time (from 71,640 to 39,210), compared to a decline of 26 percent in coal
mining. Other surveys report the number of journalistic jobs at even lower
levels.[31]

The damage being done to the business emanates from both sides of the equation, resulting in an ever-accelerating feedback mechanism that has led to devastating results in a very short period of time. As newspapers become thinner and thinner, with less and less hard news, especially of the local variety, even as subscriptions and the cost of daily or weekly papers keep going on up, readers who are attracted by an increasing variety of other news sources calculate that it is no longer worth it to buy print editions of the news. As ad revenues continue to tank, reporters get laid off, print editions shrink, and papers become a shell of their former selves (getting referred to as "ghost newspapers"), leading even more readers drop away as the death spiral accelerates.

Efforts to replace declining subscription revenue with digital sources of income have been disappointing in a situation where Google and Facebook between them control about four-fifths of the digital market. According to a report by University of North Carolina journalism professor Penelope Abernathy, the result is "news deserts," where people living in hundreds or even thousands of communities have only limited access to the kinds of news and information that have historically been the lifeblood of democracy. People living in these areas tend to be poorer, older, and less well educated than their counterparts elsewhere. Many subjects, from organizational and political news to sports, health, and economics often get short shrift or do not get covered at all.[32] Areas affected extend all over the map, but rural and suburban areas are especially vulnerable to the process. Metropolitan regions are not exempt. For them, the problem usually consists of losing alternatives to choose from, as papers disappear or merge with others. The papers that are left become hollowed out by reduced numbers of reporters and other personnel, and thinner editions, lack of coverage, and plain neglect are the result.

Especially troubling in recent years has been the upsurge of hedge and private equity firms swooping in to purchase newspapers and chains of them for purely pecuniary motives, exhibiting no concern for the resulting decline in the quality of the product. Companies such as Digital First Media, Citadel, New Media/GateHouse, and Alden Capital have purchased more than 1,500 small-city dailies and weeklies in recent years, enabling them to extract exorbitant profits by way of management fees, dividends, and tax breaks, while simultaneously slashing staff, reducing quality, and losing readers. Their game plan involves aggressive cost cutting, newsroom layoffs, a focus on quick-hit stories, and the neglect of more expensive investigative pieces. Financial restructuring and bankruptcy proceedings, leading to further staff reductions and salary cuts are often part of the process. After Tronc, which owned 77 other papers, purchased the *New York Daily News* in 2017, it laid off half the newsroom staff, leaving 50 reporters to cover all five boroughs of the city. In 2014, when GateHouse acquired the *Providence Journal*, winner of four Pulitzer Prizes over the course of its history, layoffs began immediately. In four years time, newsroom staff was cut by 75 percent. Staffing at the *Denver Post*, owned by Digital First, fell during the past six years from 180 to fewer than 70.[33] The result of these kinds of activities is often to drive papers into the ground. "This corporate stuff is killing local newspapers," says the editor of a GateHouse-owned paper. According to the authors of an article in *American Prospect*, Robert Kuttner and Hildy Zenger, "Whether private equity is contained and driven from ownership of newspapers could well determine whether local newspapers as priceless civic resources survive to make it across the digital divide."[34]

Recently, the most aggressive chain along these lines has been Digital First. Its unsuccessful hostile bid to purchase the Gannett group of papers, including *USA Today*, was called "terrible news in an industry that's almost become numb to grim new developments" by *Washington Post* media critic Margaret Sullivan. "Controlled by a hedge fund, Digital First strip-mines its newspapers, drastically cutting newsroom staffs and squeezing profit from these operations with no apparent regard for journalism or their future viability."[35] The inevitable result of these kinds of activity is that quality goes down while prices go up. It becomes a never-ending cycle of self-devouring wasting away.

The newspaper business has become increasingly oligopolistic in recent years, driven by an unrelenting wave of mergers. One-third of all the newspapers in the country in 2018 were owned by the largest 25 companies. One-fourth of all the weeklies and two-thirds of all the dailies were in this category. New Media/GateHouse alone controlled 451 of them, while the largest 50 companies together owned 45 percent of them. Just 10 companies owned almost half of the country's daily newspapers.[36]

Print newspapers currently are rapidly giving way to digital platforms. The 62 percent of the population who obtain their news on social media (18 percent doing it often) like to get their content for free. In 2014, only 11 percent of U.S. readers expressed a willingness to pay for online news. The rest said they'd never pay or would be willing to pay only a small amount (around $8 a year on average) for it. Thus far, print journalism has not figured out how to stem the tide, leading some informed observers to predict its imminent demise. "Journalism is collapsing, and with it comes the most serious threat in our lifetimes to self-government and the rule of law as it has been understood here in the United States," write John Nichols and Robert W. McChesney.[37]

These developments are hampering journalists from doing the kinds of investigative work they used to do. The best, most intensive coverage is devoted to the White House and Congress, but reporting what is going in in statehouses and in city halls around the country necessarily suffers. Making the situation dangerous and ultimately threatening to democracy is the fact that the institutional press alone possesses the knowledge, expertise, and access to the people who make the news that allows for the kind of independent, objective coverage that is necessary to hold powerful individuals and institutions accountable. There is huge value in having that kind of access, even though critics will complain—in some cases rightly—that such proximity has the potential to compromise journalistic principles.

It is easy to understand why presidential adviser Steve Bannon decried President Trump's willingness to talk to the press and his allowing other administration officials to do likewise. Shutting the press out of informational channels has always been a secret or not-so-secret stratagem of people in power. But power also flows out of ability to get information out, and while new social media channels have provided multiple opportunities for making end-runs around the mainstream media, the latter still matter. The president has engaged in the contradictory practice of benefiting from publicity provided by the press while at the same time excoriating it as "fake news."

The ongoing relationship between the press and presidential politics was succinctly summed up by *Time* magazine in a December 1968 article, and not much has happened to change things in this regard since then: "Every recent administration—not only [Lyndon] Johnson's but also Dwight Eisenhower's and John Kennedy's—has been accused of manipulating the news, or at least of an occasional lack of candor. The press wants to know everything, preferably before it happens and preferably handed to it on a silver platter. Presidents and their Administrations naturally want to feed out information as they see fit, preferably in such a way as to make them look good."[38]

Historically, the power of the newspaper press to determine what news is and even to reshape governmental priorities as a result has been immense, which is why the rise of cable television, talk radio, and a variety of social media outlets has brought such vigorous efforts to exploit them as ways of bypassing traditional channels. "News," Douglas Cater wrote in 1964 in *Power in Washington*, "is a fundamental force in the struggle to govern. Each day hundreds of thousands of words are spoken, tens of dozens of events occur. The press and other media perform the arduous task of sorting out and assigning priorities to these words and events."[39] The gatekeeper role of reporters, editors, and publishers has been central to the way in which Americans view and understand the world around them in all of its aspects—social, economic, political, cultural, artistic, religious, educational, and so forth.

News reporters most often determine what is watched on television and what is heard on radio and other media outlets. Their power is primarily threefold: first, to determine what gets attention and what does not; second, to establish the facts of the matter, seeking the truest version they can muster; and third, putting the facts into context in such as way as to interpret their meaning, or at least to set the reader on track to discovering that meaning.

All of this undergirds our sense that press freedom is absolutely essential, that press competence is hugely important, and that press integrity, fairness, and objectivity are all crucial to the welfare of the citizenry and to the health of democracy. In politics, economic decision-making, family relationships, community affairs, education, philosophical reflection, scientific investigation, organizational leadership, and virtually every important aspect of life, truth matters. This is doubly true of journalism. Yet it is perfectly obvious that reporters and the press in general, just like every one of us in our everyday lives, come to the table with particular knowledge, assumptions, preferences, and biases. *Washington Post* reporter and columnist David Broder underscored this point in a talk given to journalism students at the University of Maryland in 1970, when he referred to "All the News That's Fit to Print," the *New York Times* slogan at the top of its masthead, as "a splendid slogan" but nevertheless "a total fraud." Despite the paper's massive resources and large amount of space available, it can not begin to cover all of the important news in New York City, let alone in Washington, D.C., and the rest of the world, Broder noted. Like all other papers, its first important decision is what to cover, and that choice is colored by what it deems important, which, in turn, is influenced by the knowledge, opinions, and biases of the people on its staff and the people who run the operation.[40]

President Trump did not invent criticism of the press. What he has done is carry the assault on the press to an unprecedentedly high level, and leading people to wonder where it all will end. The rhetoric of the president is shocking but, in some ways, understandable; he honed his craft as a reality television star, world wrestling promoter, and beauty pageant impresario, venues that seem to be especially made for breaking the rules. He is essentially a showman. What is less understandable has been the willingness of political figures both within and without his camp to tolerate and even applaud his behavior.

The press itself is implicated in its own current travails, for right up until election night in 2016, the smart money was on Donald Trump's losing. Even the candidate himself, by all accounts, was totally surprised by his victory. During the presidential primary season and even into the general election campaign, many newspapers continued for too long to believe that they could benefit from their unusually extensive coverage of the candidate, since it would boost their own revenues by attracting readers who wanted to find out what Trump had said or done during the previous twenty-four hours. For all their handwringing about Trump once he entered the White House, the press had benefited hugely from their attention to him during the primary season and continued to sell papers with stories about him after he became president.

The perpetual dance or gladiatorial battle occurring between the White House and the press goes all the way back to our nation's founding. John Adams got things off to a tumultuous start when his Federalist party enacted the Alien and Sedition Acts in 1798. Thomas Jefferson, when he wasn't calling the press an essential component of republican government, hurled sharp barbs at opposition reporters and started his own alternative press. Most presidents have grown annoyed to one degree or other with press commentary, some more than others. Woodrow Wilson vigorously enforced the Espionage and Sedition Acts during and after World War I. Modern no-holds-barred conflict between the press and Washington administrations started during the 1960s, triggered mainly by the Vietnam War. After running as a "peace" candidate in 1964, during which he engineered the Gulf of Tonkin Resolution, granting him basically unlimited power to wage war in Southeast Asia, Lyndon Johnson quickly began sending Marines and other military personnel into Vietnam, increasing troop numbers there in 1965 from 23,000 to 184,000. All the while, he and State Department and Pentagon spokesmen insisted that nothing had changed in official policy. That was the year the press began using the term "credibility gap" to describe what was going on in Washington, and the public—slowly at first but in a rush later on—began buying into the notion. Presidents had lied before, and they would continue the practice, but after Vietnam the public became somewhat inured to the practice, and some came to view it as the new normal. People had been shocked in 1960 when they learned that President Dwight Eisenhower had lied to them after U-2 spy plane pilot Francis Gary Powers got shot down while flying over Soviet air space. But as Watergate unfolded, as President Reagan later got caught up in the Iran-Contra scandal, as President Clinton asserted he had not had sex with "that woman," and as Bush 43 and his minions insisted that weapons of mass destruction endangered American security in 2003, more and more people came to expect that their President would lie to them as standard operating procedure.

A major problem for the press was that when reporters uncovered and exposed these prevarications, they were not universally applauded. What once might have been perceived as a public service now increasingly began to divide the electorate between two highly politicized and opposing sides. Opinion polls revealed a public split along partisan lines not just on questions of policy and other issues. Now they actually viewed the world and adjudicated facts and lies along political lines. Your fact had become my lie, my fact had become your lie, and it seemed that never the twain would meet.

As the press attempted to carry out its duties of ferreting out facts, contextualizing them, and offering plausible interpretations, reporters increasingly found themselves involved in the middle of this polarization. People in the press thought they had already heard themselves called everything in the book, but 2016 found them in new, uncharted territory. As Alex Shephard pointed out in the *New Republic*, they heard a major-party presidential candidate refer to them as "bad," "dishonest," "crooked," "lying," "scum," "disgusting," and "crazy." Donald Trump blacklisted news organizations and had political reporters thrown out of his campaign rallies. He said he would get the libel laws changed to make it easier to sue media companies, tweeted a video showing him body-slamming a CNN reporter, and called the media (or at least the parts he didn't like) "the enemy of the American people." He whipped up a crowd at a rally by promising, "Believe me, if I become president, oh, do they have problems." His chief strategist, Steve Bannon, told the *New York Times*, "The media here is the opposition party." Skeptics might say that all of this was just Trump being Trump, but in the past people learned to be sorry for not taking demagogic politicians at their word.[41]

Attacks on the press by politicians from the president on down are nothing new, but they seem to be increasing in frequency and virulence in recent years. Some of the press's problems are self-inflicted wounds and require some soul-searching and changes in its own behavior. With so many different forms of information delivery—from newspapers, magazines, journals, and reports of various kinds to news radio, talk radio, network television, public television, cable television, Facebook, Twitter, blogs, and on down the line—it is impossible to generalize broadly about the news media. But in observing the press in the process of trying to compete and even to survive in a rapidly expanding, super-heated media environment, several things might be mentioned. Too much reporting is entirely event-driven and fails to put the facts presented within a larger context. In the effort to compete with direct rivals as well as with different forms of journalism, too many newspapers and other outlets resort to emphasis on personalities, fluff, diversion, and various kinds of "soft" news. Not enough journalists are deeply informed about the subjects they cover, something that could be alleviated by more emphasis on "knowledge-based journalism." Pack journalism, in which most reporters and media outlets routinely "follow the leader," is all too prevalent. Too little provision is made for deep research and longer forms of presentation. Much room exists for improvement. Still, the journalism profession in the United States can take deep pride in how far is has evolved over time, and the product it provides is certainly an improvement over what prevailed decades ago. Quality journalism is available for readers who possess the desire and tenacity to search it out. They just need to take the time to do it.

It is a two-way street: we need improvement on the part of the press as well as on the part of consumers of its output. Politicians need to be called to account when they attack or abuse the press and violate long-standing norms, succumb to political expediency, and express comfort with assaults on fundamental tenets of American democracy—freedom of the press, freedom of expression, and freedom of assembly. Democratic institutions cannot long survive when a vital, effective press does not deliver news that enables citizens to arrive at an accurate understanding of the world they live in. Citizens, for their part, need to make a conscientious effort to seek out responsible, fact-oriented journalism that is geared to uncover the truth and avoids excessive partisanship.

Media fragmentation has accelerated in recent years, abetted by the decline of the major television networks as news sources proliferated with the rise and expansion of talk radio, cable TV, blogs, iPods, and the Web. Farhad Manjoo, in his book *True Enough: Learning to Live in a Post-Fact Society* (2008), argues that "the limitless choice we now enjoy over the information we get about our world has loosened its grip on what is—and isn't—true."[42] Just as inflated currency tends to lose value over time, the explosion of news sources in the information hothouse in which we live make us more susceptible to receiving information from sources that may be ignorant, uninformed, incapable, or—more seriously—malignant or intentionally deceptive. Former mayor of New Orleans Mitch Landrieu describes the situation well: "We live in an age of disinformation, with so many overloaded circuits that journalism and news gathering is part of a strange digital stratosphere with few restraints and with easily doctored images that distort reality, and where the old role of spin doctors—those who seek to turn public opinion—is fast subsumed by con artists on social media, or even Russian manipulation. This is an atmosphere in which demagogues thrive."[43]

The gatekeepers we used to depend upon to certify the credibility of the news we consume have largely faded away or disappeared entirely, either by circumstance or by our disregard of them. There still are plenty of reliable sources of believable news, if we only choose to use them. The trouble is, too many people either do not know of their existence or fail to use them. Author and columnist Max Boot raises the alarm in observing that "there are no gatekeepers anymore. The democratization of politics via the internet has empowered the cranks and conspiracy-mongers, while making it impossible for more erudite eminences, to the extent that they still exist, to shape the conversation."[44]

When gatekeepers are unavailable or when people fail to rely on those that do exist, we get propaganda feedback loops that simply reinforce the assumptions, preconceptions, and prejudices of those who rely upon them. Scholars at the Berkman Klein Center for Internet and Society at Harvard University conclude that there is no left-right division in the presentation of network news. Rather the split that exists lies "between the right and the rest of the media ecosystem. The right wing of the media ecosystem behaves precisely as the echo chamber models predict—exhibiting high insularity, susceptibility to information cascades, rumor and conspiracy theory, and drift toward more extreme versions of itself."[45] Democrats and liberals also gravitate to their own preferred news sources, such as MSNBC, the *New York Times*, the *Washington Post*, and Public Radio and Television, but they are much more likely than conservatives to access a wide variety of sources, including ones that don't necessarily hew to lines similar to their own.

When we contemplate the current situation and wonder what we might do to extricate ourselves from it, the challenges facing us appear to be overwhelming. Our efforts to retrieve the ideal of objectivity, to recreate conditions in which opposing political ideologies are able to find some common ground, to restore economic viability to journalistic business models in any way similar to the ones we have been familiar with, or to restore confidence in and credibility to journalism, broadly conceived, might appear destined to fail. Yet there are some encouraging signs around us. The insistent hunger many people harbor for the truth, for knowledge about the world around them remains strong. The widespread and growing intelligence of the culture accumulated over time provides it with tools and resources that can be tapped, given the determination and will to succeed. In times of trouble and challenge, Americans in the past have risen to the occasion. Now is no time for despair.

One encouraging indicator is a growing demand for journalism degrees as applications increase and enrollments rebound in journalism schools and departments. Reports indicate that that investigative journalism classes are filling up. "The Trump era, overflowing with news, and the emergence of new ways to tell stories appear to be giving a jolt to journalism schools that in recent years struggled to cope with industry contractions," according to the *Washington Post*. New students occupy all points on the political spectrum—conservative, liberal, independent, and places in between. "The president might be having a positive impact on us," suggests Lorraine Branham, dean of the Newhouse School of Public Communications at Syracuse University. "In some ways, it's almost like a Watergate moment."[46] With traditional sources of funding for journalism in decline, new ones may be coming on board along with new modes of investigating and reporting the news. In New York City, a new nonprofit website called "The City" is joining forces with *New York* magazine to fill gaps in investigative journalism. Private philanthropic efforts have been increasing in various guises in other places. Beneficiaries include outlets such as ProPublica, the *Texas Tribune*, and Chalkbeat, a nonprofit website covering educational issues in seven cities. The Knight Foundation and the Democracy Fund are supporting the American Journalism Project, which makes grants and supplies consultants to local news outlets around the country. Implausible and scattered as such initiatives may appear to be, they bespeak a widespread recognition that effective reporting of the world around us matters a lot to many people.[47]

Thomas Patterson in his book *Informing the News* proposes a beefed-up curriculum for journalism students that will equip them to more effectively dig out stories and make better sense of the issues they investigate. Better journalism can occur only in an improved public culture that makes education a higher priority. It will emerge with a new, more mature attitude that people take toward their national identity and destiny. Over the course of more than two centuries, the United States has evolved as a unique beacon for freedom and engine for progress in the world. Experiencing ups and downs, it has proven that practical idealism works, that seemingly insoluble problems and challenges can be successfully engaged, and that optimism is always a better choice than resignation.

Challenge 3—The Shifting World of Ideas

Ordinary people in their everyday lives are shaped and channeled by a variety of influences—the people around them, their economic circumstances, psychological instincts and drives, family background, education, place of residence, employment, social relationships, and so forth. Nothing is more important in affecting their thoughts and behavior than their preconceptions, attitudes, the ideas that jangle around in their heads, and the intellectual climate within which they operate. As the renowned British economist John Maynard Keynes famously said, "The ideas of economists and political philosophers, both when they are right and when they are wrong, are more powerful than is commonly understood. Indeed, the world is ruled by little else."[48]

While continuing controversy swirls around the question of just how exceptional a country the United States is and has been, few would deny that, as a people, we have been exceptionally fertile in our ability to develop theories, spin yarns, imagine fantasies, and pursue dreams. The first Europeans to reach these shores brought along with them—in addition to their Bibles, books, guns, treasure chests, and tools—an abundance of plans, schemes, and blueprints for wresting wealth out of the ground and accruing happiness within their communities. They moved to escape poverty, oppression, and stasis. They came to find land, freedom, opportunity, and progress. In America, their plans changed, their expectations escalated, and their practices altered as they confronted new environments and new challenges. While it certainly cannot be said of everyone, an unusually large number of them exhibited enormous powers of imagination, creativity, and innovation. Much of this was tethered to reality, to facts on the ground, to empirical test; much of it was not, rather displaying impulsiveness, fatuousness, and lack of restraint. Deceit, deception, fakery, fraud, hoaxes, shams cheating, and pretending were always part of the American story. Americans, in truth, were practical dreamers, usually stable but frequently susceptible to being caught up in the grip of unreality.[49]

By the early 1900s, the primary story Americans were telling themselves about their own history, as recounted by the majority of academic writers of history themselves, was that of the expansion of the frontier. As explicated by Wisconsin and later Harvard historian Frederick Jackson Turner, the central theme of American development had been the continuous westward march of people across the continent, occupying the land, even as Native Americans, who had been here first, were driven back and quarantined on reservations. The latter unpleasantness was largely disregarded, as triumphal Europeans celebrated their own putative qualities of individualism, freedom, democracy, practicality, inventiveness, energy, idealism, courage, and industry.[50]

In the broader realm of popular culture, school children and adults alike thrilled to tales of adventure on the frontier. They read of the exploits of Daniel Boone, Davy Crockett, Andrew Jackson, Leatherstocking, Mike Fink, Paul Bunyan, Annie Oakley, Tom Sawyer, and Huck Finn. In the process, fact and fiction got all mixed up, and, after all, did it make any difference? As I was growing up in the 1950s, television programming still revolved largely around western shoot-em-ups. We boys could dream of adventures on the gridiron and baseball diamond alongside Frank Merriwell, "the Gipper," and Mickey Mantle, even as girls took turns playing Laura Ingalls Wilder, Nancy Drew, and Little Women. By then, Superman, the Green Hornet, and Dick Tracy were paving the way for Batman, Spiderman, and Wonder Woman.

With the rise of Hollywood, teen culture, and rock and roll, everyone could dream of becoming Elvis, James Dean, Elizabeth Taylor, Cher, or Madonna. The boundary between "reality" and "fantasyland" became ever more blurred and indistinct. If you were an intellectual, you even started putting quotation marks around the words.

Folklorists and intellectual historians will tell you that this sort of behavior has been prevalent since the beginning of time. Think Homer, Achilles, and Odysseus. But there is something unusual in Americans' proclivity for dreaming dreams, reaching for the stars, entertaining fantasies, and, in a surprisingly large number of cases, actually realizing some of them. That keeps the cycle going. Kurt Andersen, in his book *Fantasyland: How America Went Haywire, a 500-Year History* (2017), suggests that the California Gold Rush was an inflection point in American history, "permanently changing the way we thought about impossible dreams and luck and the shape of reality." It was a time when people's lives "could become a fabulous romance, reality as marvelous as any tall tale. Personal reinvention was not just theoretically possible but suddenly happening wholesale."[51]

Southerners entertained their own peculiar sets of dreams, and nightmares. The Nat Turner–led slave rebellion of 1831, resulting in scores of lives lost, sent shudders down the spines of magnolia-land residents. It led them to heighten their precautions, tighten up their controls, and suppress dissent in last-ditch efforts to preserve "the Southern way of life," which all revolved around slavery. The decade leading up to the Civil War unloosed verbal invective, physical violence, and the kind of political polarization that we measure ourselves against today. Fantastic tales and speculations abounded. None of this declined after the war ended, for white Southerners took heart in and gained courage from their fanciful version of the "Lost Cause," while northerners pursued their own dreams of wealth and progress as told and retold in the stories of Horatio Alger.

The tales, yarns, fantasies, lies, myths, and exaggerations that gained adherents in the United States over the decades are countless. People were less skeptical in the past than they are now, but the proclivity to accept wholesale falsehoods and matters directly contrary to empirical fact is hardly less prevalent today than it was in the past. The appearance, rise, and fall over the years of mesmerism, phrenology, confidence men, Lost Cause promoters, racism, anti–Semitism, the Ku Klux Klan, McCarthyism, UFO sightings, Holocaust deniers, and Scientology remind us of the impulse to delusion that is recurrent and impossible to eradicate. Knowledge of human nature, psychology, sociology, and history would predict it.

To arrive at the situation we are in today, when widespread skepticism exists regarding the possibility of agreement on facts and truth, required a coming together of a number of social, cultural, and political forces that in concert have created a new, hyper-charged atmosphere of misstatements, dissimulation, and posturing that call into question the truthfulness of all kinds of assertions and judgments. Literary critic Michiko Kakutani notes that the Rand Corporation's use of the term "truth decay" to describe the "diminishing role of facts and analysis" in American public life has joined other familiar "post-truth" terms such as "alternative facts" and "fake news." Not to mention fake history, fake science, fake Facebook participants, and fake followers on social media. Forces operating to undermine belief and confidence in truth have been churning for a long time, she reminds us. "For decades now, objectivity—or even the idea that people can aspire toward ascertaining the best available truth—has been falling out of favor."[52]

The current climate of opinion in the United States, with all of its shape-shifting implications, derives from a number of historical forces and trends, only a few of which can be noted here. In the first place, there was the American Revolution, which itself was promoted by a confluence of powerful ideas that had emerged out of the European Enlightenment. Our Revolution made its impact felt subsequently both here and abroad through its promotion of freedom and liberty, equality, individual rights, responsible citizenship, civic duty, individualism, and community. The French Revolution, much inspired by ours, added to liberty and equality a third prominent ideal—"fraternity." Marxists, later on in their revolutionary zeal prized equality over liberty to the degree that they ever actually implemented what they purported to favor. All three revolutionary movements had the intellectual impact of undercutting old certainties, such as the divine right of kings, introducing greater fluidity and uncertainty into people's ways of thinking, and promoting the notion of continual progress, which, in turn, fostered rising expectations, with both good and bad consequences.[53]

Democracy was never a fixed goal but rather one that evolved over time, as political participation, power, and influence extended their reach to more and more groups. The nineteenth century was the century of Darwin, among other thinkers, and his evolutionary mode of thought, with its emphasis on fluidity, constant change, and development, was pervasive in its impact. Marxist revolutionary ideas and those emanating from the American and French Revolutions also rejected fixedness in favor of change, promoted fluidity over stability, and advocated openness rather than closure. Marx and Engels' phrase "All that is solid melts into air" captured the spirit of the time, although their utopian plans for societal transformation were hugely flawed, ultimately resulting in tragic consequences when implemented in specific countries.

American democratic (or republican) institutions and practices projected no final utopian dream, positing a time when history would essentially end and a new and perfect society would begin. They opted rather for incremental change, with adjustments being made to accommodate new conditions and to correct previously flawed assumptions. This was entirely in keeping with the emergence of pragmatism, a major shift in thinking that gained adherents in the United States during the decades after the Civil War. Its advocates proposed that the meaning of conceptions flows from their practical effects. The function of thought is to guide people's actions, and the best way to ascertain the truth of propositions is to ask what the consequences of believing them would be. Pragmatism goes down as the most characteristic philosophical movement to emerge in American history.

In his classic study *Social Thought in America*, Harvard intellectual historian Morton White called the multifaceted movement a "revolt against formalism"; it was opposed to fixed notions of all kinds. Pragmatism influenced virtually every domain of American life. In sociology, it begat social Darwinism and reform Darwinism; in economics, institutional economics and economic determinism; in law, legal realism and sociological jurisprudence; in psychology, behaviorism; in history, the so-called "new history"; and in education, progressive education. Some of the results were salutary, others not so much, but none of these developments constituted an end point, and further evolution in the disciplines occurred as the twentieth century wore on. The point to make here is that change, openness to new ideas, empiricism, and a rejection of fixedness and finality were essential in all of these ways of thinking. Considered here, pragmatism had the effect of destabilizing firm principles, established formulas, and fixed notions of truth.[54]

The philosophy also flowed naturally into the most important political development of the early twentieth century in the United States—the rise of progressivism at the local, state, and national levels. Mayors such as Joseph Folk of St. Louis, Hazen Pingree of Detroit, and Tom L. Johnson of Cleveland; governors including Robert M. La Follette of Wisconsin, Hiram Johnson of California, and Albert B. Cummins of Iowa; and presidents Theodore Roosevelt and Woodrow Wilson led the charge toward more active governmental intervention in various areas of American life. It is at this point in history, especially during Wilson's presidency, that many conservative critics of government today locate the point at which American political institutions went off track. The consensus at the time, however, was quite favorable to the progressive movement as a whole, and for many decades thereafter widespread agreement existed among government officials and ordinary citizens that reforms such as wages and hours legislation; regulation of food and drugs, railroads and other forms of transportation, commerce, and monopolies; federal income taxes; protections for organized labor; and equal rights for women were sensible responses to the economic and social changes unleashed by the industrial revolution. In recent years, that consensus has begun to break down, as reform Darwinian ideas undergirding these types of government activities began receiving serious competition from, among others, older social Darwinian ideas that denied the legitimacy of most kinds of government intervention in the economy aside from national defense, the maintenance of social order, public schooling, and the establishment of minimal rules for business operations.

Undergirding progressive reform activity during the early 1900s was a transformation that took place on American university campuses and in thought centers such as New York, Chicago, and Washington that provided intellectual ballast for enhanced governmental intervention. The writings of social scientists such as Thorstein Veblen, Edward A. Ross, and Algie M. Simons; political scientists such as J. Allen Smith, Charles E. Merriam, and Frank J. Goodnow; educational theorists such as John Dewey; historians such a Frederick Jackson Turner, Charles A. Beard, and Vernon L. Parrington; advanced social thinkers such as Jane Addams, Alice Paul, and Horace Kallen; and journalists such as Lincoln Steffens, Ida Tarbell, and Ray Stannard Baker exerted a huge intellectual impact in paving the way for new ways of thinking and modes of action.[55]

Gaining currency as the bible of progressive reform was 1909's *The Promise of American Life* by journalist Herbert Croly, who five years later became the first editor of the *New Republic*. The magazine emerged in the late teens as the most influential journalistic organ of the progressive movement. Croly's 452-page book made the case for a larger, more active federal government in order to grapple with the challenges posed by huge new business combinations emerging out of the industrial revolution of the late 1800s. Croly argued that these big businesses, along with the new unions, smaller business, and agriculture, would all have to be regulated in the national interest. Horace Kallen, an intellectual disciple of John Dewey, viewed pragmatism as a philosophy dissolving "dogmas into beliefs, eternities and necessities into change and chance, conclusions and finalities into processes."[56] In abandoning security, certainty, and permanence, this new way of thinking opened up novel possibilities, but along with them came profound doubts, anxieties, and unfinished business.

Theological speculation and religious practice also were caught up in the spirit of the times. *The Origin of Species* (1859) hit the world of intellect in Great Britain and the United States like a meteor, and its reverberations echoed through succeeding decades. It is not surprising, writes intellectual historian Jon H. Roberts in *Darwinism and the Divine in America: Protestant Intellectuals and Organic Evolution, 1859–1900*, "that defenders of the faith within the American Protestant community tended to view any challenge to the idea that each species had been independently created by means of a 'special' divine creative act as a threat to the faith." For fifteen years, most Protestant thinkers castigated Darwin's "theory and all its possibilities" as "the dream of an inebriate or the visions of a madman." Gradually, however, many of them began to come around, and by the turn of the twentieth century many of them felt fully comfortable in their ability to reconcile the findings of Darwin and his scientific cohorts with their continued belief in a transcendent, benevolent God. Others, like Thomas Huxley, became unbelievers, unable to reconcile the claims of religion with the discoveries of science.[57] The emergence of Social Gospel Christianity during the early 1900s not only elevated social and economic concerns in the thinking of theologians and laypeople; it also made historical-critical methods of investigating Scriptures essential practice for its followers, rejected literal interpretations of the Bible for a looser, more figurative approach, and placed its confidence in reason, evidence-based argumentation, and willingness to change over against tradition, authority, and sticking to the past. In that context, religion emerged as a major participant in a fundamental shift in the American climate of opinion, one that welcomed fluidity, skepticism, empiricism, argumentation, multiple perspectives, contingency, and—ultimately—relativism. Fixedness was out; change was in.

Much of this emanated from the confidence instilled by American inventors, builders, entrepreneurs, businessmen, artists, academics, and intellectuals of all kinds. They celebrated economic growth, military success, industrial might, technological marvels, and intellectual progress. Notions of relativism found support in evidence of progress that could be witnessed all around, confidence that tomorrow would bring even greater change, willingness to discard old ideas and practices for new ones, and a general feeling that fluidity, improvement, and constant novelty were to be welcomed and accepted as facts of life.

The sense of change abroad in the land before the First World War is contained in the title of a classic book on American social and cultural history by the historian Henry F. May: *The End of American Innocence: A Study of the First Years of Our Own Time, 1912–1917* (1959). At the beginning of the time period, he writes, "religion, history, and current politics all seemed to bear out both the eternal verities and their relevance to the problems of today." World War I brought an end to American "innocence," May argues. "The most obvious aspect of change was the complete disintegration of the old order, the set of ideas which had dominated the American mind so effectively from the mid-nineteenth century until 1912." These included, first and foremost, "the certainty and universality of moral values," and along with them, the inevitability of progress and the importance of literary culture.[58]

Matters of this scope usually do not change overnight, and intimations of the cultural/intellectual transformation described so well by May were present long before the war, but historians largely agree that World War I was a crucial turning point in the history of Western thought on many counts. For our purposes here, it is enough to observe that the post-war period saw the rapid rise of relativism in many areas and that these intellectual trends all fed into out present moment of doubt and wonder regarding the rise of lies, fudging the facts, post-truth, and "fake news."

Beyond its impact on theology, Darwinian evolution, of course, had huge implications for biology, which, after all, is what the British biologist's theory was all about. It also reinforced similar trends in the other natural sciences, as well as in the social sciences, the humanities, including history, and many other elements of American life. History is the story of change and continuity. Many things undergo slow, gradual change, ideas among them. But the 1920s were an especially fertile period for changes reinforcing the notion of relativism in the United States.

Peter Novick's book *That Noble Dream: The "Objectivity Question" and the American Historical Profession* (1988) does a masterful job of pulling together various strands in this historical moment. "Science had offered pre-war historians not just a method," he writes, "but above all a vision of a comprehensible world: a model of certitude, of unambiguous truth; knowledge that was definite and independent of the values or intentions of the investigator. None of these characteristics were to survive the first third of the century. The very mathematical and logical foundations of empirical science seemed to be at risk in the interwar years." Novick describes how Albert Einstein, in constructing his general theory of relativity, demonstrated the inadequacy of Euclidian geometry for describing the physical universe. Beyond that, C.I. Lewis and others developed non–Aristotelian, multivalued logics. Notions of "truth" and "falsity" could not be relied upon to ground our interpretations, he and other thinkers argued, because the very terms are context-dependent.[59]

Physics provided the most dramatic example of the new relativity that was sweeping the intellectual world during the decade. Niels Bohr's principle of "complementarity," Werner Heisenberg's "indeterminacy" theory, and the rise of quantum mechanics all worked to reinforce notions that nothing was fixed or absolute and that everything was fluid, changeable, indeterminate, and subject to debate. When it came to ethical analysis, the journalist and all-around intellectual Walter Lippmann's *A Preface to Morals* (1929) did a masterful job of illustrating how "the acids of modernity" were working to undermine old certainties, truths, dictums, and rules, leaving "whirl as king." Speaking of modern man, Lippmann pronounced, "There is no theory of the meaning and value of events which he is compelled to accept." Beyond that, "there is no moral authority to which he must turn now, but there is coercion in opinions, fashions and fads. There is for him no inevitable purpose in the universe, but there are elaborate necessities, physical, political, economic."[60] Joseph Wood Krutch echoed those sentiments in *The Modern Temper*, published that same year, a book that some credited as being the best analysis of intellectual conditions as they existed in America at the end of the twenties. Once there had been a world of certainty, widely agreed-upon by most people, Krutch observed, but that world no longer existed. Whereas Newtonian physics proposed a universe that could be understood like the table we sit at, modern science suggested that people could not even know the table: "So remote is this 'real' table—and most of the other 'realities' with which science deals—that it cannot be discussed in terms which have any human value," Krutch concluded.[61]

No less affected by this relativistic turn were social scientists, who found themselves abandoning long-held ideas and traditions. Cultural anthropology, which had attracted little interest before the war, found itself with new readers and adherents. Cultural relativism became a watchword for major figures such as Franz Boas, Ruth Benedict, and Margaret Mead. Not only were alien folkways tolerated by researchers who did field research in foreign countries; increasingly, detached skepticism toward the norms of one's own society became commonplace. Peter Novick suggests that "the main thrust of cultural relativism in the interwar years furthered that disintegration of certainty and absolutes in every realm."[62]

Ethical relativism flowed naturally out of cultural relativism. Operating along a parallel track, legal realism flourished, advancing an approach to the law that went back at least as far as Oliver Wendell Holmes's influential treatise on *The Common Law* (1881). Orthodox legal theory held that the law was based upon unchanging principles of right and justice. Legal realists and proponents of "sociological jurisprudence" adopted a more inductive approach, contending that the law essentially is "what judges do." The process might well be colored by judges' fallibility, biases, misunderstandings, and prejudices. During the 1930s, Dean Roscoe Pound of Harvard Law School lent his prestige to the movement.

Historians, as much as other intellectuals, became enthusiasts for relativism during the interwar period. Two presidential addresses at annual meetings of the American Historical Association—Carl Becker's "Everyman His
Own Historian" (1931) and Charles Beard's "Written History as an Act of
Faith" (1933)—were classic statements of the idea that interpretations of history vary widely from person to person; that context, bias, personal interest,
and many factors go into how the past gets construed; and that no fixed and
final version of the past will ever gain universal assent. Both scholars boldly
reflected the kind of relativistic thinking that prevailed at the time. Facts did
not speak for themselves, in their opinion. One's own values entered into the
process as soon as one decided on a topic that was worthy of historical investigation, and their influence expanded from there.[63]

Franklin D. Roosevelt's New Dealers, to a significant degree, inherited
the pragmatic/progressive legacy of the early 1900s. No one exemplified this
better than Thurman Arnold, appointed by the president in 1938 to head the
Justice Department's anti-trust division. Ironically, the new man in charge of
prosecuting anti-trust cases had earlier, as a law professor at Yale, lampooned
anti-trust prosecutions for being obsolete and meaningless in a world in
which large size in business was inevitable and government efforts to slow
down further consolidation could be only symbolic and ineffective. In a
broader sense, *The Symbols of Government* and *The Folklore of Capitalism*,
which Arnold published in 1935 and 1937, consigned efforts to challenge large
scale in business to the "folklore of capitalism." Such folklore, along with
mythology and social rituals of various kinds, paraded as basic principles in
the public imagination, Arnold contended. Human action, he believed, was
fundamentally symbolic in nature. Words, theories, principles, ceremonies,
and other symbolic activities were basically aimed at prompting the typical
voter to "believe in the reality of his dreams and thus give purpose to his
life." Thus, a paradoxical situation arose: "Social institutions require faith and
dreams to give them morale. They need to escape from these faiths and
dreams in order to progress. The hierarchy of governing institutions must
pretend to symmetry, moral beauty, and logic in order to maintain prestige
and power. To actually govern, they must constantly violate those principles
in hidden and covert ways." When people confronted contradictions between
myth and reality, they typically reacted in one of two ways, Arnold suggested:
"The first is ceremony, drums, and oratory. The second is reason and dialectic.
The conflict must be made to disappear under a thick blanket of incense of
some sort or other."[64]

No one had previously described the dilemma of democracy more clearly
or persuasively. Democracy (or a republican form of government) depends

upon popular support. But to achieve the popular support necessary to govern, public office seekers can either be honest and appeal to facts and reason or they can bang the drum and seek to connect with emotion and irrational modes of thought. Unfortunately, the latter method often, if not usually, seems to work more effectively than the former. Ironic rather than cynical, Arnold understood that successful politicians often feel compelled to resort to folklore, myths, and dreams, because they have proven to be effective tools of persuasion. He anticipated by more than three-quarters of a century the situation we find ourselves in today.

In the meantime, other intellectual currents coalesced to promote anti-foundationalist notions that serve to bracket as unprovable and even fictional concepts such as "truth," "reality," "facts," "evidence," "proof," and "objectivity," while they favor terms such as "unknowable," "undecidable," "paradoxical," "ironical," "conventional," and "problematical." For the past several decades, theories of postmodernism, deconstruction, and other anti-rational approaches have been blowing through the intellectual arena. Postmodernism admits of numerous interpretations and misinterpretations.

Picking up where post-structuralism leaves off, postmodernism, traces its roots back to European philosophers such as Friedrich Nietzsche and Martin Heidegger. Nietzsche, whose views on truth, like so much else in his philosophy, were shot through with ambiguity and contradictions, did much to undermine conventional thinking on the subject and inspired legions of followers to question the possibility of discerning objective truth. Observing that human life "is sunk deep in falsehood," he contended that what people take to be truth is basically spurious and that the schemes people use in attempting to impose meaning on the world, while useful in a practical sense, are fundamentally deceptive. Proffered truths, in effect, are illusions, less likely to illuminate things than to mislead. In his inquiries into the essence of being and truth, Heidegger did not follow many of his colleagues in analyzing the correspondence between people's judgment and the world they lived in. For him, truth was always perspectival, and every "truth" that was advanced simultaneously concealed other potential truths. Postmodernism also draws upon twentieth century trends in the arts and in literature, such as Surrealism, Dadaism, and abstract expressionism, all of which were associated with rupture, discontinuity, irrationality, and the subconscious. The counterculture of the 1960s and the writings of French thinkers ranging from Jacques Derrida and Michel Foucault to Jean Baudrillard and Jacques Lacan invigorated the movement in the United States just as it was beginning to become passé in Europe.[65]

Taking the American pragmatic tradition to its logical conclusion in his

1979 book, *Philosophy and the Mirror of Nature*, Richard Rorty recommended that philosophers abandon epistemology altogether. Suggesting that early Western philosophers had developed a metaphor of the mind as a mirror that reflected accurate representations of reality, Rorty contended that the time had come to move on to other, more fruitful lines of inquiry. In place of a vocabulary anchored by "objectivity" and "representation," he proposed substituting one of "justification" and "solidarity," indicating that "we understand knowledge best when we understand the social justification of belief, and thus have no need to view it as accuracy of representations." In the process, he said, "justification becomes a 'social phenomenon' rather than a transaction between a 'knowing subject' and 'reality.'" His fellow philosopher Hilary Putnam laid things out more colloquially, suggesting that "truth is what your contemporaries let you get away with."[66]

Contrasting attitudes toward truth and its apprehension divide thinkers and groups into absolutists and relativists, objectivists and subjectivists, rationalists and social constructivists, traditionalists and postmodernists.[67] While postmodernism remains a fuzzy concept, open to many approaches and different meanings, it joins with post-structuralist theories in moving beyond modernism, once radical in its implications but which also assumes integrated social formations and coherent human subjects that live within them. Fragmentation, incoherence, and instability are key attributes of postmodernism and deconstruction. Among their characteristics are "human interiority split apart," the "death of the author," a "decentered, fluid subject," and the absence of "essential being." In them, representation gives way to "constructivism." "Natural" or "essential" categories such as race, gender, and sexuality give way to "transgressive" modes of being. "Disruption," "difference," and "fluidity" become the new norms. A prominent theme of postmodernism is its aversion to "master narratives" (examples of which would be "the rise of American democracy," "the superiority of American devotion to civil rights and civil liberties," and "the inevitability of progress"). While largely associated with left-wing thinkers in the academy, these strands of thought worked their way into literature, film, theater, music, and every aspect of American popular culture and many parts of standard culture. While certainly not dominant and countered by more traditional and predictable ways of thinking, these ideas and inclinations had a major impact on Americans—direct and indirect—and facilitated new kinds of thinking and behavior in a variety of areas of American life, including politics. Without necessarily meaning to do so, they helped prepare the way for what is now being referred to as the "post-truth era," leaving many people deeply disturbed and worried for the health and perhaps even the survival of democracy.[68]

Challenge 4—Fake News, Alternative Facts and the Assault on Truth

Taking off from Thomas Jefferson's famous statement in the Declaration of Independence, "We hold these truths to be self-evident...," Harvard professor Jill Lepore's recent textbook, *These Truths: A History of the United States*, observes that the Virginian's original draft of the document had used the words "sacred & undeniable." Upon reading them, Benjamin Franklin scratched them out with his quill, replacing them with the term "self-evident." Either way, the phrase suggested that the fundamental principles of political equality, natural rights, and sovereignty of the people were not to be questioned or disputed; they were fixed, certain, and based upon empirical fact.[69]

"Americans, it is said, hunger for facts," *Time* magazine informed its readers in 1967.[70] If the statement was true then, it seems much less applicable today, at least among a large segment of the population. One of the greatest threats to American democracy at the present time is proliferating accusations of "fake news," an actual increase in the practice of it, and, ultimately, the assault on truth that these phenomena portend. One of the larger ironies of the situation is that the people most likely to accuse others of purveying fake news are the very ones who are actually most likely to engage in the practice themselves. President Trump has called fake news "our country's biggest enemy," just as he has labeled the mainstream press "the enemy of the people."[71] Neither accusation is convincing.

"Our information environment is sick," observes author David Patrikarakos in *War in 140 Characters* (2017). "We live in a world where facts are less important than narratives, where people emote rather than debate, and where algorithms shape our view of the world."[72] He is not alone in his concern. "Lies are coming at the American public in torrents—raining down on them everywhere they turn," writes journalist Margaret Sullivan. "The intentional spreading of disinformation on every platform—from Facebook all the way to PayPal—should frighten everyone who cares about democracy."[73] During 2015, the term "post-truth" became wildly popular, its usage by one measure exploding by 2,000 percent over a year's time. Understood variously by different people, "post-truth" generally referred to circumstances in which emotional appeals and personal beliefs trumped objective facts in the shaping of public opinion. Oxford Dictionaries named it 2016's word of the year.[74]

The term "fake news" originated as a way to characterize a specific act— that of manufacturing fictional stories that could be spread on the Internet in return for a fee, providing a source of income for an individual or a group. Fake news can be defined as "false, misleading, and often sensational information that is disseminated as if it were actual news." In the infotainment atmosphere in which we live, people can be lured into reading almost any sort of frivolous story that is circulated. Ironically, studies have shown that false news progresses through Twitter "farther, faster, deeper and more broadly" than the truth.[75] In the process of liking, sharing, and searching for information, social bots (automated accounts that impersonate humans) are capable of accelerating misinformation exponentially. It has been estimated that 9 to 15 percent of all Twitter accounts are bots, many originating in Russia. At one time, as many as 60 million bots may have been active on Facebook. They played a huge role in muddling the information environment during the 2016 presidential campaign. Only a tiny fraction of Twitter users— less than one-tenth of 1 percent—disseminated nearly four-fifths of all the misinformation or "fake news" that year. The vast majority of users never look at these stories; fewer than 5 percent of left-leaning voters and centrists shared any fake information, 11 percent of right-leaning ones, and 21 percent on the extreme right, according to the study.[76]

Political operatives grasped that this kind of misinformation could easily be manipulated to promote their own objectives. Jan-Werner Muller, author of *What Is Populism?*, reminds us that "ignorance and misinformation are not just facts of life; they are often also the result of fully conscious decisions by political elites who would like to protect and extend their interests."[77] Once installed in the mainstream, the term "fake news" was transformed by politicians and their supporters who were confronted with valid information and critical comments that they disagreed with or simply didn't like. They turned the notion of falsehood around 180 degrees and flung it back at their critics, accusing *them* of purveying "fake news." The practice morphed into an all-purpose smear technique used to deride journalists, politicians, and others they disagreed with. The epithet became a common one in 2016, but the person reverting to it most often and vehemently was Donald Trump, first in his quest for the presidency, and then after he entered the Oval Office. Having enjoyed listeners' enthusiastic reactions to it during the campaign, he began resorting to it over and over again. It was named *Collins Dictionary's* word of the year for 2017.[78]

The day after the inauguration, on the president's orders, his press secretary, Sean Spicer, called reporters in to dress them down for misreporting the number of spectators on the Washington Mall the previous day. Despite clear photographic evidence that the crowds for both of President Obama's inaugurations had been significantly larger than Trump's, the president insisted that his had been "the biggest audience in the history of inaugural speeches." Compounding the disbelief of onlookers in the press room and news consumers who read, watched, or heard about it, Kellyanne Conway, Trump's senior counselor, defended Spicer's statements by saying that he had given reporters "alternative facts." Wherever that idea originated, it struck an immediate nerve within the media and the public, indicating the mentality that seemed to be operating in the White House. The phrase immediately entered the American lexicon.[79] The week after the inauguration, George Orwell's dystopian book about the disorienting lies and propaganda of a tyrannical fictional government in what in 1949, the year of its publication, was the distant future, shot up to number one on Amazon's best-seller list. Readers noticed disconcerting parallels between the Trump administration's attempts to manage the news and the fictional Ministry of Truth's efforts in *1984* at "reality control."[80] "The degree to which they are creating their own reality, the degree to which they simply make up their own scripts, is striking," remarked Peter Wehner, who had been a top political strategist in George W. Bush's White House. "It's a huge deal, because in the end you really can't govern, and you can't persuade people, if you do not have a common basis of fact."[81]

It is clear that the Trump White House and people outside if it were operating in different epistemological universes. One could also say that the president and the people who identified with him were at one spot on the truth spectrum and those on the other side were at another. The list of "alternative facts" grew in the days and weeks thereafter. Trump claimed, without any evidence, that between three and five million illegal voters had caused him to lose the popular vote, that President Obama had wiretapped his phones in Trump Tower, that Cuban-Americans had given him 84 percent of their vote, that he had saved the Defense Department over $700 million in negotiations for the purchase of F-35 fighter jets, that nobody cared about his tax returns except the reporters, that he would not personally benefit from his proposed tax cuts, and that the United States was the most highly taxed nation in the world. None of these assertions was true.

Donald Trump's whole political career was jump-started by the "birther" myth that he repeated continually—the assertion that Barack Obama had not been born in the United States. The *Washington Post*'s fact-checking project, begun during President Trump's first hundred days in office, revealed an average of 4.9 false or misleading presidential claims a day (he repeated some of them, such as the high rate of U.S. taxes, many times). By the end of his second year in office, the *Post* counted 7,600 untruths. The president's average of more than 15 erroneous claims a day in 2018—almost triple the first year's rate—resulted in part from the discontinuance of regular press briefings in the White House, which he made up for with impromptu give-and-takes with reporters, staged rallies for supporters, and continuous tweeting.[82] In the parlance of their critics, what Trump and the people around him were practicing was "gaslighting," a term defined by Tony Schwartz, the repentant ghostwriter of Trump's *Art of the Deal* book, as "a blend of lying, denial, insistence and intimidation designed to fuel uncertainty and doubt in others about what's actually true." This kind of behavior led Margaret Sullivan to observe, "There can be no doubt: We're in a whole new phase of the Orwellian nightmare in which black is called white, and you'd better not dare object to that."[83] Beyond the direct harm that fake news inflicts on the news environment, the way in which it often leads legitimate media sources to investigate or report on the allegations has the effect of helping shape the journalistic agenda. This wastes time and resources and for a certain segment of the population will incline them to accept fake news as real.[84]

The president obviously disagreed with criticisms being leveled at him as a purveyor of falsehoods. In a meeting in the White House with *New York Times* reporters Peter Baker and Maggie Haberman and the paper's publisher, A.G. Sulzberger, in early February 2019, he denied that he was responsible for the noxious political atmosphere in the country or that he was guilty of misrepresenting the truth. He tried to refocus the conversation toward his own personal grievances. "I do think it's very bad for a country when the news is not accurately portrayed," he said. "I really do. And I do believe I'm a victim of that, honestly." Observing that Fox News treats him "very well," he called NBC News and *Washington Post* coverage of him and his administration "terrible" and asserted that the *Times* "treats me unbelievably terribly."[85]

The president obviously dislikes the negative coverage he often receives and wishes it were better, but his motivation in constantly attacking the news media is obvious. The tactic works, and in moments of candor he has admitted it. Polls show that among strong Trump supporters, 91 percent trust him to supply accurate information, while only 11 percent expect to get it from the news media. In a 2016 conversation with CBS News reporter Leslie Stahl, he revealed, "I do it to discredit you all and demean you all, so when you write negative stories about me, no one will believe you."[86]

The president is an outlier in the sheer quantity of his unprovable or downright false statements, but he is not alone in his penchant for playing fast and loose with the truth. Over the course of American history, many American presidents have had a spotty relationship with the truth. Woodrow Wilson, Franklin Roosevelt, and Lyndon Johnson ran for the presidency as "peace" candidates in 1916, 1940, and 1964, months before each of them led the United States into war. Harry Truman's "Truman Doctrine" speech in

March 1947 started a tradition of American presidents painting the United States' Cold War allies as undisputed lovers of freedom and democracy, when many of them actually were authoritarians or out-and-out dictators. Americans were shocked in 1960 to learn about Dwight Eisenhower's bald-faced lying during the U-2 spy plane episode, but by 1965, when Lyndon Johnson's prevarications about the Dominican Republic incursion and the Vietnam War introduced the term "credibility gap" into the vocabulary, onlookers had become used to lies emanating from the White House.

No one expects politicians and bureaucrats to be 100 percent transparent in all of their dealings and statements, especially when it comes to foreign policy. But a minimal standard of truth is essential if trust and credibility are to be maintained and if democracy is to function effectively. The signature symbolic moment in the evolution of lies in Washington may have occurred during the frequently cited interview between journalist Ron Suskind and an unnamed George W. Bush assistant, rumored to have been political adviser Karl Rove, in which the latter referred sarcastically to journalists and others who inhabit what he referred to as the "reality-based community." Making judicious studies of "discernable reality" is not the way the world works anymore, that aide asserted. "We're an empire now, and when we act, we create our own reality.... We're history's actors ... and you, all of you, will be left to just study what we do."[87]

Numerous precedents existed for the developments of 2016. Many streams of mendaciousness fed into the swirling waters of truths, half-truths, lies, and outright BS. Hypocrisy can be thought of as the grease that keeps society rolling smoothly along, and politicians, of all people, recognize this. But historically, with certain exceptions, there had been limits regarding what politicians say, and most people understood that that was the way things operated. Nixon's unleashing of Vice President Spiro Agnew on the press in 1969 with his alliterative accusations of press bias had been quite disturbing. Conservative discontent with what many of them labeled the "mainstream liberal press" had been growing for years. The repeal of the Fairness Doctrine in 1987 meshed with AM radio's search for new program content, as music migrated to FM channels, providing an opening for new talk-radio shows. Within two years after entering national syndication in 1988, Rush Limbaugh was attracting five million listeners. He spawned a battalion of imitators, most prominently Sean Hannity and Ann Coulter, and in 1996 Roger Ailes launched Fox News, reaching ten million households at launch. Four years later, spurred on by the Clinton impeachment spectacle, Fox network programs were being aired in 56 million homes. Liberals, endeavoring to compete with conservative talk radio and cable television programming, never came close to catching up, but they did enjoy greater success with major media outlets such as the *New York Times*, the *Washington Post*, the three major television networks, and Public Broadcasting. The difference was that while conservative-leaning media generally were much more outspoken and open in reflecting their biases, liberal-leaning papers and television and radio stations tended to be more wedded to objectivity and were less overtly propagandistic. Selective consumption of information was more common on the right than on the left. Polarization was "asymmetric," concluded a 2015 study conducted by researchers from MIT's Center for Civic Media and the Berkman Klein Center for Internet and Society at Harvard University. The loss of common points of reference and the willingness to engage in open, give-and-take conversation was not a natural result of new technologies, they concluded, but rather emanated from conservatives' "habit of rejecting information that was not congenial to their side and denying the legitimacy of the sources of inconvenient facts."[88]

Some people exhibit an almost unlimited capacity for accepting assertions and made-up stories that conform to their preconceptions and biases, something psychologists refer to as confirmation bias. For example, rumors circulated that Obama at the end of his time in office was plotting to secure another term by helping Hillary Clinton win the election and then indicting her. Or that Clinton was a Satan worshipper involved in "an international child enslavement and sex ring." Or that Chelsea Clinton wasn't actually the Clintons' daughter but rather Hillary's love child by another man. All of these slurs were manufactured by alt-right or fake news websites.[89] The zaniness of the things some people accept as truth knows no end: that vaccinations cause autism, that climate change is a hoax, that Supreme Court Justice Antonin Scalia might have been murdered, that Texas Senator Ted Cruz's father was involved in John F. Kennedy's assassination, and the list goes on.[90]

Too many people are willing to buy into such falsehoods. The idea that the U.S. government was involved in planning the 9/11 terrorist attacks was believed by 26 percent of Democrats and 21 percent of Republicans in one poll. The notion that millions of illegal votes were cast in the 2016 election was accepted by 52 percent of Republicans and 36 percent of Democrats. Sixty-four percent of Republicans and 26 percent of Democrats believed that unemployment had increased between 2009 and 2016, when in fact it had declined dramatically. The Dow Jones industrial average had more than doubled under Obama, but 39 percent of Republicans and 9 percent of Democrats thought it had gone down.[91] Simple ignorance or misinformation explains some of these departures from factuality, while political bias and polarization are also major factors.

There is also the simple, but profound, problem of "information glut" affecting people's ability to take in and comprehend the reality of the world around them. In one post-election story in 2016, *Time* magazine, observing that political debate had become unhinged from reality, suggested that it was "a problem of quantity as much as quality: there is simply too much information for the public to accurately internalize, which means that distortions—and outright falsehoods—are almost inevitable." And since mainstream journalists are no longer trusted to fulfill their familiar gatekeeping role to verify facts and kill falsehoods, phony conspiracy theories often become part of the information mix along with accurate journalism.[92]

Beyond cold political calculations made by candidates, consultants, speechwriters, and outside observers that lead them to believe that utilizing falsehoods and distortions works to one's advantage, the current popularity of lies, exaggerations, misinformation, and pure BS derives from several other factors, first of all, the degradation and manipulation of political language. George Orwell warned almost three-quarters of a century ago that political speech and language had become, in a large sense, "the defense of the indefensible." He said it was designed to "make lies sound truthful and murder respectable, and to give the appearance of solidity to pure wind."[93] While descriptive of some political discourse, this statement, taken literally and out of context, would relegate all political argument and debate to the trash bin. But the contention serves to put us on our guard. When Nancy Pelosi and some of her fellow Democrats referred to the Republican tax cuts of 2017 as "Armageddon," it made sense to discount what they said as wild exaggeration. When Donald Trump employs the simplistic language of "terrific," "phenomenal," and "incredible" to describe people and things that he likes and words like "loser," "lightweight," and "sad" for people and things that he dislikes, chalk it up to a failure to think and to pay attention as well as to a darker tendency to belittle and degrade anyone who opposes him or stands in his way.[94]

Secondly, we need to place the current political environment within the broader context of "infotainment." "Being part of the entertainment-industrial complex is part of being president," says Robert Thompson of Syracuse University. Donald Trump understands that the president has become the nation's entertainer-in-chief.[95] Within certain bounds, recognizing it as such can be productive. Carried to extremes, as is currently the case, it becomes dysfunctional.

Thirdly, as a real estate mogul, reality television personality, and promoter of the Trump brand, the president developed a penchant for "truthful hyperbole"—the term he used to describe one of his techniques to promote his businesses in his autobiographical *The Art of the Deal*. Often, the technique seemed to work well for him. While other politicians have not used this particular term, it seems to be an accurate description of a good deal of what many of them do. There may be some merit in mixing one's hopes and highest expectations with a forceful determination to follow through to make one's wishes come true. In many ways, America became great because of people's effectiveness at promoting the booster spirit and then possessing the grit, determination, and work ethic to make things happen. Hope, however, always needs to be tethered to reality. Problems arise when truth is heavily outweighed by hyperbole. Words have to be connected to fact, or eventually they will have no effect at all.

Fourthly, for some voters and politicians, the use of words progresses beyond the usual variations of truths, half-truths, exaggerations, and lies and into the realm of what professor of philosophy Harry G. Frankfurt examines in his best-selling book, *On Bullshit* (2005), published by Princeton University Press. At some point, a penchant to exaggerate, misrepresent, or simply lie descends to an entirely different level. Something Frankfurt talks about in his brief but insightful book is the point at which any concern that people might have for truth is set aside. The truth values of BSers' statements are of no real interest to the speaker, Frankfurt asserts. The bullshitter ignores the demands of truth, fact, and reality altogether and just throws words out there: "He does not reject the authority of truth, as the liar does, and oppose himself to it. He pays no attention to it at all."[96]

But attempting to explain the prevalence of "fake news" and misinformation of all types by concentrating exclusively on its purveyors is to miss half of the story. As the saying goes, "it takes two to tango." Or, as an economist might observe, "there is supply, and then there is demand." Without receptive audiences and willing consumers, false information and clouds of unreality would have no purchase. Americans—or, we should say, large segments of the American public—have long shown themselves to be gullible and easy to fool. "We've been spun to for generations, and it has hardened us into a nation of cynics who live in a time when 'truthiness' has actually become a plausible notion," Ted Anthony and Ron Fournier observed in February 2008, long before Donald Trump arrived on the scene. If anything, the notion rings even truer today. "Our faith has flagged—in our schools, our churches, our media, our corporations, and, of course, our president. Lies and manipulations, the kinds of calculated untruth that are different from myths, have come close to owning the day. But they don't," the writers hopefully concluded.[97]

New York Times reporter Timothy Egan, probing the kind of reasoning that such conditions prompted, recorded a Wyoming Trump supporter's circumlocution: "I can't really say that anything he says is true, but I trust him."[98] For large numbers of voters, facts are less important than the narratives that organize them. "Trump's supporters," David Brooks surmises, "follow him because he gets his facts wrong, but he gets his myths right. He tells the morality tale that works for them."[99] Journalist and author of several books on the American military Max Boot grew so concerned with the antics in the White House that he disaffiliated from the Republican party. He viewed President Trump as not so much trying to sneak lies by people as trying to shove them down their throats. "From now on the truth will be whatever he says, and he expects every loyal follower to faithfully parrot the official party line, no matter how nonsensical," he chides. Beyond that, it all seems to be working for him. "The frightening thing is that Trump's insistence on redefining reality is working, at least with his base."[100]

During the 2016 election campaign, Trump supporters and apologists justified his tenuous connection with the truth by suggesting that people should not take his statements literally but rather should take them seriously. These kinds of rationalizations may be convincing for devoted followers, but they are not for skeptics who ally with newspaper columnist Richard Cohen in observing, "Trump and his people have collapsed the space between lies and truth. The president uses one and then the other—whatever works at the time."[101] Press outlets from the *Washington Post* and *New York Times* to individual websites and cable-TV networks have enumerated and attempted to correct Trump's mistakes, misstatements, and prevarications during the last several years, but experience and scientific experiments reveal that in the face of such corrections, people actually tend to cling even more strongly to their original views.[102]

Any explanation for the effectiveness of lies, hoaxes, fake news, and other violations of the truth has to grapple with the fact that most people most of the time do not actually decide things or arrive at their notions of reality individually through private research, investigation, and reasoning. Rather, they rely on friends, neighbors, associates, and the groups they belong to. People usually obtain their information and work out their viewpoints second-hand. They identify with people, groups, and organizations they trust and come to rely upon, and they take their word for things. As cognitive scientists Philip Fernbach and Steven Sloman indicate in *The Knowledge Illusion: Why We Never Think Alone*, individuals are not well fitted to distinguish between truth and falsehood. Ignorance is our natural state. What we know, how we learn, and how we view the world is a result of group activity; it depends on whom we know, trust, and work with. Almost all of the ideas in our head get there second-, third-, or fourth-hand, and on down the line.

There is no sharp boundary between people's ideas and those of others around them.[103]

Books such as *The Unreality Industry: The Deliberate Manufacturing of Falsehood and What It Is Doing to Our Lives* (by Ian I. Mitroff and Warren Bennis), *Dumbing Down: Essays on the Strip-Mining of American Culture* (edited by Katharine Washburn and John Thornton), and *The Age of Manipulation: The Con in Confidence, the Sin in Sincere* (by Wilson Bryan Key) suggest that we have a problem on our hands.[104] Social media distract and mislead us, advertisers bombard us with bogus appeals aimed at the gut rather than the brain, and public relations techniques seem to rule in every kind of situation, 24/7/365. Hyper-politicized radio talk shows, cable TV stations, and politicians of all types have learned the techniques of "spinning" and "framing" stories while seeking to capture our attention and win our assent. The biggest problem that all of this entails is the threat it poses to democratic institutions. Law professor and former Obama advisor Cass Sunstein, in his book *#republic: Divided Democracy in the Age of Social Media*, suggests that because people possess "a growing power to filter what they see," our modern technologies stand in the way of what the Founding Fathers envisioned for a democratic republic: exposing people to different perspectives. He calls for an "architecture of serendipity" that exposes voters, whatever their assumptions and biases, to different people, groups, organizations, and ideas.[105] If Americans congregate primarily with their own tribal members, absorb "fake news" and manufactured "facts," and follow leaders who themselves are caught up in the whirl of self-referential discourse and thought patterns, democracy will have little chance to operate as it was intended to. We are in a pickle, and it will take some rigorous thought, bold creativity, and hard work to get us out of it.

No one will take any comfort in the knowledge that for all of our present discomfiture with regard to the fragility of truth in our daily comings and goings, the time is coming soon when rapidly developing technology, including the development of virtual reality and artificial intelligence, will make possible the creation of totally fake photographs and videos that will be basically indistinguishable from the "real thing." In fact, that time is already here. Technology producing such "deepfakes" is progressing rapidly. We are just waiting for it to become widely available and put into practice. Once that happens, not only will people be lured into believing totally phony fabrications, many of them will be inclined to reject legitimate videos, a phenomenon referred to as "the liar's dividend."[106] "Fabricated videos will create new and understandable suspicions about everything we watch," writes former *New Republic* editor Franklin Foer. "Perhaps society will find ways to cope with these changes. Maybe we'll learn the skepticism required to navigate them. Thus far, however, human beings have displayed a near-infinite susceptibility to getting duped and conned—falling easily into worlds congenial to their own beliefs or self-image, regardless of how eccentric or flat-out wrong those beliefs may be."[107]

Historians like to situate events in historical context. It is reassuring to realize that current problems and perplexities have their counterparts in history and that people somehow moved beyond them and learned something from them. Reading Walter Lippmann's acerbic analysis of public opinion in the 1920s in the United States, Thurman Arnold's more ironic interpretation of the "symbols of government" and the "folklore of capitalism" written during the 1930s, Richard Hofstadter's books on the long run of American anti-intellectualism and political paranoia, and Daniel Boorstin's discussion of the huge importance of images and the growing prevalence of "pseudo-events" along with more recent discussions of bunk, buncombe, and other varieties of weirdness can, perhaps, help us feel a little better about where we are today. But then again, we continue to be surprised and even shocked by continuing developments that we observe around us every day. We wake up in the morning asking, "What will *he* do or say today?" and "What shall *we* expect will happen?" The *New York Times* recently editorialized, "Without a Walter Cronkite to guide them, how can Americans find the path back to a culture of commonly accepted facts, the building blocks of democracy? A president and other politicians who care about the truth could certainly help them along. In the absence of leaders like that, media organizations that report fact without regard for partisanship, and citizens who think for themselves, will need to light the way."[108] We can only hope they are right.

Challenge 5—Declining Faith in Institutions and Leaders

Democracy and republican institutions depend upon trust to operate effectively and thereby undergird a free and flourishing society: trust in people to perform their civic duties and to carry out their lives in responsible ways; trust in leaders to fulfill their obligations and meet the challenges presented to them; trust among leaders to transcend differences of opinion and purpose and to work together to pursue the common good; and trust in institutions to operate efficiently, fairly, and in accordance with the purposes for which they were established. Sadly, levels of trust in the United States and confidence of people in their leaders and institutions to function fairly and effectively have drastically declined in recent years. A 2015 Pew poll indicated that only 19 percent of Americans trusted the government most of the time, down from 77 percent in 1964.[109]

This is a relatively new phenomenon in American history. While partisan criticisms of the other party and its leaders are standard fare and cyclical waves of frustration and resentment have arisen over wars, foreign policy issues, economic downturns, and government scandals, large generalized and persistent dissatisfaction and discontent with government and its institutions have arisen only during the past several decades. During the nineteenth and early twentieth centuries, large influxes of immigrants were happy to have escaped poverty and oppression and willingly assimilated into their new, freer society. Children pledged allegiance every day in their schools, read stories about American patriots, and were taught in civic classes about how to become good citizens. The entire culture coalesced to induce respect, appreciation, and admiration for democratic institutions and leaders.

The social scientist Francis Fukuyama addresses the broad issue of trust in his 1995 book, *Trust: The Social Virtues and the Creation of Prosperity*. In it, he notes the necessity of having a healthy and dynamic civil society for generating lasting economic prosperity and for preserving liberal, i.e., free and independent, political and economic institutions. Civil society consists of a complex array of intermediate institutions, including businesses, schools, churches, charities, unions, clubs, voluntary associations, and the media. Behind them, the family is the foundational institution in which young people are socialized into the culture, acquiring knowledge, obtaining social skills, imbibing values, and acquiring the habits that contribute to their own advancement and to the welfare of society as a whole. "A thriving civil society," Fukuyama writes, "depends on a people's habits, customs, and ethics—attributes that can be shaped only indirectly through conscious political action and must otherwise be nourished through an increased awareness and respect for culture."[110]

Statistics documenting Americans' declining trust in institutions of all kinds are staggering. During the past four decades, the number of people expressing confidence in organized religion declined from 65 to 41 percent. Confidence in banks dropped from 60 percent in 1979 to 27 percent in 2016 (after dropping as low as 22 percent in 2009). Comparable numbers for public schools were 53 percent to 30 percent; for newspapers, 51 percent to 20 percent; for labor, 36 percent to 23 percent; and for big business, 32 percent to 18 percent. The police, the military, and small business were the only categories that by these measures retained over 50 percent of public confidence. Most disturbing, perhaps, is that people have increasingly lost trust in one another. The General Social Survey of the University of Chicago revealed that 46 percent of those polled in 1972 agreed that "most people can be trusted." By 2012, that figure had fallen to only 32 percent.[111] The trend is unmistakable, as younger people display less trust in their neighbors than do their elders. While 40 percent of the baby boom generation express trust in other people, only 19 percent of millennials do. "This is a thoroughly globalized and linked generation with unprecedentedly low levels of social trust," David Brooks observes.[112]

"No one denies that in its current form, the U.S. government is failing," writes Harvard political scientist Graham Allison. "Long before Trump, the political class that brought unending, unsuccessful wars in Afghanistan, Iraq, and Libya, as well as the financial crisis and Great Recession, had discredited itself. These disasters have done more to diminish confidence in liberal self-government than Trump could do in his critics' wildest imaginings, short of a mistake that leads to a catastrophic war."[113] Nothing did more to diminish the public's intrinsic trust in its leaders and institutions than Vietnam, an event that, in the words of columnist George Will, "continues to haunt some elderly men who live among us. And the war's legacy lives in Americans' diminished trust in government. Since 1968, trust has not risen to pre–Vietnam levels."[114] Following upon the massive anti-war demonstrations, political assassinations, and urban riots of the 1960s, in a series of cascading shocks starting in the early 1970s, the American public lost trust in in the leaders and institutions it had traditionally depended upon: Watergate, diminishing economic expansion, poor job growth, increasing income and wealth gaps, Iran-Contra, threatened and actual presidential impeachments, 9/11, misbegotten and seemingly unending wars—the list of causal factors goes on.

Declining levels of trust coincide with reduced levels of participation in civic institutions. Harvard political scientist Robert Putnam documented the phenomenon is his much-discussed 2000 volume, *Bowling Alone: The Collapse and Revival of American Community*. The book's title derives from the observation that whereas once people bowled together in leagues, now they are more likely to "bowl alone." Putnam expands his purview to the scores of groups, clubs, and organizations that have seen their membership rolls drop, sometimes precipitously, in recent decades: PTAs, service organizations, Scout troops, religious congregations, veterans' organizations, professional associations, recreation clubs, political parties, and so forth. Putnam estimated that people's involvement in public and civic affairs declined by 40 percent over the course of almost four decades.[115] Some analysts remain unconvinced, arguing that people have found outlets in other venues, connecting with friends and total strangers on the Internet, for example. But the evidence is fairly convincing, and people's personal experiences seem to confirm that the kinds of personal, face-to-face social interactions that used to occupy so many of their off-work hours have indeed declined significantly in many places, at least, in recent years.

All of this goes counter to the kinds of activities that Alexis de Tocqueville observed and was so impressed by as he traveled around the country during the 1830s. If anything stood out most prominently on that journey, it was the universal penchant of the Americans that he encountered to join voluntary associations and to express their social and political opinions in those venues. The virtues of community and social capital have long been praised by social observers and critics as a counterforce to the opposite impulses driving Americans' behavior—expressive individualism and competition in the marketplace. There is no doubt that both forces have operated powerfully to drive American development and progress and have contributed to the prosperity and benefit of the population. While sometimes standing in opposition to each other, individualism and communalism have co-existed over the decades in fruitful tension with each other, reflecting complementary tendencies and needs. The tension exists not only between individuals and groups, but also within them, for most of us wish and need to work and play alone at times, while at other times we prefer to coalesce and cooperate with others. In the context of our discussion here, it is important to note that when we do come together to work and interact with each other, we should be able to do it cooperatively and be bound together by high measures of trust and truthfulness in our activities.

Declining trust in institutions has gone along with similar drops in confidence in leaders, authorities, and experts. A glance around the social landscape readily confirms that authority of all kinds has lost respect and influence in recent decades. Whether we think of teachers, ministers, and parents, on the one hand, or television news anchors, law enforcement officers, and government officials, on the other, the general tendency has been to hold them in lower esteem and to question their word and their authority to speak for us or to dictate our actions. Children talk back to their parents, students disrespect their teachers, ministers get addressed by their first names, and we all seem ready to push back at individuals whom we generally used to defer to and follow. Where are the Walter Cronkites, the Norman Vincent Peales, and the Miss Bradfords who taught us tenth-grade history? And where are the Dwight Eisenhowers and Franklin Roosevelts we used to respect and admire? The fact is, many of us still do; that is, we admire, respect, and even love our favorite presidents, authors, talk-show hosts, and musical groups. Increasingly, though, the leaders and experts we listen to and admire are ones we identify with along party lines, ideological alliances, or organizational boundaries. The generalized respect we used to readily offer to people that we listened and deferred to more generally has trended downward for decades.

The growing distrust of and declining respect offered to leaders and authorities finds its most extreme expression in pushback directed against experts. Expertise isn't dead, writes Tom Nichols, a professor of national security affairs, in *The Death of Expertise: The Campaign against Established Knowledge and Why It Matters* (2017), "but it's in trouble. Something is going terribly wrong. The United States is now a country obsessed with the worship of its own ignorance." Examples abound, whether it is the anti-vaccine crusade, the raw milk movement, the multiplication of conspiracy theories being purveyed, or a host of other unsupported notions. In many cases, it is highly educated people with the purest of motives who get caught up in the web of irrational thinking. Nichols again: "Indeed, ignorance has become hip, with some Americans now wearing the rejection of expert advice as a badge of cultural sophistication." In part a reflection of people's overconfidence in their own ability to ferret out the truth of things without the help of outside experts, the phenomenon also results from growing cynicism about and distrust of the media, education, and government. "Americans increasingly don't trust anyone anymore," Nichols concludes. "They view all institutions, including the media, with disdain."[116]

Journalist Charles P. Pierce, referring to "the breakdown of the consensus that the pursuit of knowledge is a good," asserts that there is essentially a war on expertise going on in the United States. "In the new media age, everybody is a historian, or a scientist, or a preacher, or a sage," he writes. "And if everyone is an expert, then nobody is, and the worst thing you can be in a society where everybody is an expert is, well, an actual expert." To contend otherwise is to identify oneself as an "elitist," and elitism is bad.[117] It is hard to convince people about something when they think they already know the truth. When people who identify as or are labeled by others as "populists" express their antipathy to journalists, scientists, college professors, experts, and "elitists" of every type, they are not reacting simply against those particular individuals or groups. Rather, they are registering their opposition to entire systems of representation or ways of thinking. They are likely to call into question the whole of education or journalism or government.[118]

The problem is a two-way one, because experts themselves sometimes behave badly, expressing disdain for the public, wading into areas beyond their expertise, failing to understand why people distrust them, and not making clear enough distinctions among conclusions that may have varying probabilities of proof. The citizenry needs to utilize reason and judgment in their affairs, while authorities and experts need to exhibit sensible humility and respect for the opinions of those who disagree with them while also upholding standards of truth and evidence that, in the end, can be the only practicable means whereby we can arrive at the truth. "Here, then, is the crux of the West's crisis," author Edward Luce tells us, "our societies are split between the will of the people and the rule of the experts—the tyranny of the majority versus the club of self-serving insiders."[119] Ways need to be found to bridge the gap between the public and the experts. "Elites, who define the issues, have lost touch with the people," historian and social critic Christopher Lasch wrote in *The Revolt of the Elites and the Betrayal of Democracy* (1995). "The unreal, artificial character of our politics reflects their insulation from the common life, together with a secret conviction that the real problems are insoluble."[120]

The dilemma posed by complicated problems that demand expert attention within a democratic political system was first analyzed in depth nearly a century ago by a young Walter Lippmann in *Public Opinion* (1922) and *The Phantom Public* (1925). By then, in Lippmann's view, society had become so complex and problems so complicated that average voters had been rendered incompetent to decide on solutions. It was time to turn decision-making over to knowledgeable administrators with access to reliable information, which would immunize them against the effects of the kinds of emotion-laden symbols and stereotypes that contaminated public debate. The brilliant Lippmann, whose career lasted long enough for him to change his views several times, later softened his disdain for public opinion, but the question of how to arrive at fact-based, rational, and doable solutions that can achieve some sort of consensual support in a democracy has remained with us ever since.

To an extent, the debunking of elites and criticisms aimed at leaders and institutions were a healthy development, for far too often in the past people had fallen into the thrall of poseurs, know-it-alls, and mountebanks, whose positions of leadership and authority was obtained through questionable or illegitimate means. Who needs a Senator Joseph McCarthy to tell them how government agencies have been infiltrated? Who needs tobacco officials to tell them that cigarettes are healthy for them? Who needs L. Ron Hubbard to tell them how to live their lives? Declining deference to authority can indicate a healthy egalitarianism, a justifiable skepticism regarding the truth of things, or an admirable desire to elevate justice and progress over tradition and inertia. Nevertheless, resistance to and denigration of authority and expert knowledge also eats away at the sinews of a society that promote progress, self-correction, and achievement.

Various proposals to cut the Gordian knot have been offered over time. "Although the struggle between experts and the public has become adversarial, there can be no such thing as the 'victory' of one side over the other," public opinion analyst Daniel Yankelovich wrote in 1991. "If the experts overreach themselves and further usurp the public's legitimate role, we will have the formal trappings of democracy without the substance, and everyone will suffer. If the public dominates and pushes the experts out of the picture altogether, we will have demagoguery or disaster or both. A better balance of power and influence is needed, with each side performing its function in sympathy and support of the other."[121]

These recommendations apply to many issues that have increasingly polarized public debate in recent years: abortion, drugs, climate change, stem-cell therapy, law enforcement, penal practices, sexuality, religion, gender issues, family life, and patriotism. As early as the late 1970s, researchers such as Kevin Phillips, Ben Wattenberg, and Richard Scammon were telling us that social issues were overtaking economic ones in dividing the electorate along oppositional lines. Their books—Phillips's *The Emerging Republican Majority* (1970) and Scammon and Wattenberg's *The Real Majority: An Extraordinary Examination of the American Electorate* (1970)—ushered in several decades of increasing attention being paid by all parties—researchers, political operatives, and voters alike—to geographic, ethnic, religious, and personal identities that ranged across all dimensions. Momentum building in this direction perhaps was inevitable, but its consequences for democracy were in many ways pernicious. Increasingly, the public has divided into tribes, and tribal identities too often trump concern for the general welfare—exactly the danger that James Madison predicted and sought to remedy in *Federalist #10*, which he, John Jay, and Alexander Hamilton wrote to promote ratification of the Constitution.

Growing disrespect for authority, loss of trust in institutions, and general discontent with conditions as they are coincide with an increasing lack of faith in our leaders. The relationship between the public and its leaders has posed a core concern for thinking about democracy from the very beginning. The American Revolution, like the French Revolution which followed it and was inspired by it, was a rebellion against kingly rule and the whole notion of the "divine right of kings." The Constitution's Framers spent much of their time on Article II, attempting to rein in the power and possible tyrannical ambitions of the executive that they were in the process of creating. The first president, George Washington, took care to minimize the regal trappings of his office, and he returned to Mount Vernon, like the Roman Cincinnatus before him, to retire alone and unattended. Throughout the nineteenth century, the office of the presidency remained, with two major exceptions (Jackson and Lincoln), a largely ceremonial office with little power attached to it. That all changed with the arrival of William McKinley, the first Roosevelt, and Woodrow Wilson. By the time of Franklin Roosevelt during the 1930s, the Cold War presidencies from Truman through Reagan, and more recent occupants of the White House, what Arthur M. Schlesinger, Jr., labeled "the Imperial Presidency" led to the accretion of vast new powers and influence in the office. Americans remain somewhat ambivalent in their thinking about "the most powerful person on earth." Do they want someone who commands enough power to keep the peace and solve society's problems or do they want to limit presidential power in order to prevent the kinds of unsanctioned actions that drove Richard Nixon out of office and threatened more than one of his successors with impeachment?

Americans' thoughts about leadership and the leaders who are in power at any particular time are clothed in ambivalence. On the one hand, they long for leaders they can admire, trust, depend upon, and be willing to follow. On the other hand, they remain skeptical, demand results, question performance, and are quick to criticize. The burdens of leadership in an increasingly massive, complex, contradictory, and difficult to understand society are seldom fully appreciated. We expect our leaders to be all things to all people, but especially to be responsive to our own needs and personal demands. A seldom recognized requirement for good leadership is that they have good followers, and in many respects Americans are not good followers. The demands on leadership are immense, and the resources for fulfilling those demands are seldom sufficient. Sometimes individuals who have been highly successful as leaders in business, the military, education, entertainment, and other fields think, and others think along with them, that their management and leadership skills should be transferable to governmental positions. Sometimes they are; sometimes they aren't. It turns out that running governmental institutions usually is much different from running other kinds of institutions.

There is no lack of advice available on how to become a good leader; large sections of bookstores and libraries are filled with volumes on the topic. The advice offered in them tends to be relevant and helpful but not sufficient to explain everything or to guarantee success. Authors differ on whether leaders are born or made. They often offer contradictory advice. Once stated, much of that advice differs little from common sense. One highly successful advice book titled *The Leadership Challenge* approaches the subject from a positive, hopeful, optimistic point of view, focusing upon five practices that should prove useful in many situations: model the way; inspire a shared vision; challenge the process; enable others to act; and encourage the heart. Lists of essential qualities and skills are abundant. Fred I. Greenstein, presidential historian and political scientist, advances six leadership characteristics by which to judge presidential success: effectiveness as a communicator, organizational capacity, political skill, vision, cognitive skill (or intelligence), and "emotional intelligence." Former auto magnate Lee Iacocca proposes "Nine C's of Leadership": curiosity, creativity, communication, character, courage, conviction, charisma, competence, and common sense. A college professor of English upped the number of qualities recommended for an academic setting to fourteen: listening, inclusiveness, delegation, sincerity, decisiveness, accountability, optimism, realism, frankness, self-effacement, collegiality, honesty, trustworthiness, and morality.[122] Who would argue against any of these propositions?

Other advice-givers have also weighed in, opting for a more aggressive, take-charge sort of approach. Context matters. Legislators, judges, bureaucrats at various levels, advisers, executives from some deputy assistant this-or-that on up to the president all face different challenges at particular times in unique circumstances. Each task or responsibility may call for a different kind of action. That said, author Robert D. Kaplan, for example, recommends that foreign policy makers adopt a "warrior" mentality, while Harvard government professor Archie Brown finds the "exercised leadership" of Mikhail Gorbachev to have been successful for what he had to accomplish. Citing the example of Yankees owner George Steinbrenner, Benedict Carey refers to research on status and power suggesting that "brashness, entitlement and ego are essential components for any competent leader, the precursor to ascent and its spoils; they are the traits that provide the seedbed for risk-taking and a soft place to land when some of those risks go wrong." In the right circumstances, being impatient and "over-the-top" can bring rewards.[123]

The winning strategy of New England Patriots football coach Bill Belichick, who has now triumphed in six Super Bowls has been attributed less to his strategic vision, good as it is, than to his management style, which emphasizes team-building and connecting his players to higher purpose. "Players talk about 'buying into' the 'Patriot Way,' which means the Belichick way," writes Christopher Caldwell. Possessing a larger vision and executing it on a day-to-day basis are also the two major challenges facing any president. Too often, the press and the public focus on visible accomplishments, legislation enacted, foreign deals and agreements worked out, rhetorical flourishes, and symbolic gestures. Too seldom do the day-to-day operations of government in the departments, bureaus, and offices come under close and meaningful scrutiny. Yet, that is where the actual function of the government most closely touches most people most of the time. Michael Lewis's *The Fifth Risk* provides some startling descriptions of how this is all working in the Trump administration. The fact is, both skills are necessary for any successful government leader. Douglas A. Ready observes, "Ground-level execution and networking are essential leadership skills, but so are framing and communicating broad, sweeping issues of national importance."[124]

Our nation's Founders, operating in exceptional circumstances, put trust, integrity, virtue, and constraints on power at the center of their thinking about how a republic should function. They recognized the crucial importance of mechanisms, structures, rules, and prohibitions in making government work and heading off tyrannical usurpers. They also realized that norms, virtue, and integrity were required in both the electorate and in their elected and appointed officials. These requirements are age-old, and their necessity is no more obvious than at the present moment.

Public scrutiny of and skepticism about their public officials is always in order, but widespread lack of faith in them and the institutions they administer is not healthy for democratic functioning. Officials need to earn public respect, but at the same time the electorate needs to appreciate the difficulties and dilemmas they constantly encounter. People want the benefits of government without having their taxes in creased. They generally expect from government more than it is able to give. Realism is always called for. Evidence and truthful reporting are necessary to make informed decisions.

Challenge 6—The Need to Revitalize Character and Community

During the past several years, the news has been full of reports about sexual harassment and assault; serial shooting episodes; CEOs walking off with salaries in the double-digit millions of dollars and windfall bonuses of hundreds of millions while thousands of employees are thrown out of work or pensions are slashed or eliminated altogether; the degradation of the language we use; politicians promising one thing and delivering another or simply bald-faced lying to the public; clothing "mal-functions" at Super Bowl half-time shows; video games that portray every form of violence and depravity imaginable. Our capacity for surprise, shock, and indignation seems to be disappearing, until the next assault on our senses occurs.

Along many dimensions, the values, constraints, customs, behaviors, and manners of many Americans seem to have backslidden in recent years. These developments are not inconsequential for American democracy. Alexis de Tocqueville observed that democracy's survival and success depend more upon the habits, customs, and opinions of people than upon formal government structures, written laws, and institutional processes. Picking up on that theme, journalist and author Colin Woodard writes that the "habits of the heart" Tocqueville understood as undergirding liberal democracy "include a degree of restraint and civic-mindedness, an ethic of internalized altruism and trust in others that limits the need for public authority and state intrusion, and a personal commitment to liberal values." As Peter Wehner, a senior fellow at the Ethics and Public Policy Center, has indicated, politics is about character and ethics as well as about practical affairs. In the words of Aristotle, it is about "shaping souls." In the *Nicomachean Ethics*, the seminal Greek philosopher said that politics' major concern is "to engender a certain character in the citizens and to make them good and disposed to perform noble actions."[125]

To a considerable degree, we have become a nation of consumers more than one of citizens engaged in fulfilling our civic duties. It is, in many ways, a worldwide phenomenon, not just an American one. The British journalist and author David Selbourne captures the shift that is so visible both here and abroad: "Today's 'liberty' is … not the freedom fought for in the French and American Revolutions. Rather, it is the liberty of 'customers' promised 'more of their own money,' of the moral free-chooser for whom self-realization is the highest good, and of those for whom the slogan 'live and let live' is the sum of their ethics. The awareness that liberty is a civic and social construct has been displaced by the belief that it is a birthright for which nothing is owed."[126]

*   *   *

Binges of nostalgia frequently arise among us. You will often hear people say, "When I was a kid…," with a wistful look on their face, or "Back in the good old days…." A couple of years ago, in the process of interviewing members of the Baby Boom generation who had grown up in Sioux Falls, South Dakota, I heard many similar stories that tended to go like this: "When we were kids, our mothers would feed us breakfast, and then we would hop on our bikes and ride all over town all day long until dark, except to come back home for lunch and dinner. We had no thought of danger. Our parents had no concern about our welfare. If we got into any kind of trouble, they probably would have heard about it before we got home. Some neighbor or friend would be on the phone to them reporting the incident in detail for their information. The forthcoming punishment would be sure and swift." It takes only a little reflection about what life was like back then to remind us that those "good old days" were also marred by economic privation, technologies that seem quaint to us today, segregated schools, closed access in many areas of life to all sorts of minorities, patriarchal social institutions, misogyny, and widespread ignorance (which, of course, is prevalent during all periods of human history).

People behaving badly casts human character in a bad light, while the quality of the surrounding community also appears to be on the decline and in disarray. The two are not unrelated. People are embedded in the communities and societies in which they live, and few are able or inclined to venture far outside of the channels and limits that they present. "We live through institutions," write sociologist Robert N. Bellah and his associates in *The Good Society*.[127] It is difficult to be a good person when you are not living in a good society. A culture, observes Princeton professor Jeffrey Stout, is "an enduring collection of social practices, embedded in institutions of a characteristic kind, reflected in specific habits and intuitions, and capable of giving rise to recognizable forms of human character."[128] The task of a democratic society is to create a culture that will cultivate the kinds of institutions and social practices within which democratic habits and practices can exist and flourish, giving rise to democratic forms of character.

"Man's action is interpersonal," the sociologists Hans Gerth and C. Wright Mills note in their book *Character and Social Structure: The Psychology of Social Institutions*. (We would want to update their gendered terminology six decades after this book was written.) "It is often informed by awareness of other actors and directly oriented to their expectations and to anticipations of their behavior.... Man as a person is an historical creation, and can most readily be understood in terms of the roles which he enacts and incorporates. These roles are limited by the kinds of social institutions in which he happens to be born and in which he matures into an adult."[129] These observations do not negate the freedom that is available to people and the choices they are bound to make, but they do remind us of the vital importance of the surrounding communities within which people live. When one of these thrives, the other is likely to do so also; when one is in disarray, the other inevitably suffers.

As much as they value equality, equal rights, and equal opportunity, Americans are probably even more devoted to liberty, freedom, and independence. As David Brooks reminds us, individual liberty emerges out of shared community. The Constitution begins with "We the People," not "We individuals." "Most of us require communal patterns and shared cultural norms and certain enforced guardrails to help us restrain our desires and keep us free," Brooks writes. "Any society has to perform at least two big related tasks—raising the young and pursuing the good. It takes a village to do both those things."[130]

To Alexis de Tocqueville, the seemingly contradictory nature of the American character—highly individualistic and independent-minded, on the one hand; drawn to associational activities and robust community, on the other—was central to defining the uniquely democratic society that was emerging in the United States during the early 1800s. After the nation almost self-destructed during the Civil War, a new, more excessive form of individualism emerged during the latter decades of the century, leading the period to be called "the Gilded Age." The progressive movement of the early 1900s promoted a new cultural synthesis that supported a more resilient and complex form of individualism within a civil society even as it encouraged a stronger sense of community. Following the excesses of the 1920s, the Great Depression and participation in the Second World War reinforced Americans' sense of a "common good" that benefited all even while it imposed duties and requirements on citizens that would make it possible. Christopher Lasch, Tom Wolfe, and others popularized the notion of the 1970s as the "Me Decade" and a time of narcissism, but the individualistic strands they perceived in the culture go far back in time. In recent years, public intellectuals such as Robert Putnam, Robert Wuthnow, Michael Sandel, Barbara Ehrenreich, and Robert Reich have been emphasizing the need to restore and reinvigorate a vital notion of the common good, making it a notion that everyone can rally around.[131]

Signs of community breakdown and slippage have multiplied in recent years. J.D. Vance's best-selling *Hillbilly Elegy: A Memoir of a Family and Culture in Crisis* (2016), about growing up on the edge of the Appalachian Mountains in eastern Kentucky and southwestern Ohio, describes how individuals, families, and entire regions are affected when traditional community bonds begin to break down, leading to increased poverty, violence, abuse, drug use, alcoholism, and family dysfunction. Not unsurprisingly, in regions like this, and especially in rural areas, large numbers of people welcomed Donald Trump's expressions of concern for their plight and expressed their backlash against a perceived failure of government when they went to the polls.

Sociologist Robert Wuthnow warns that "individual identities now become so important that common purposes are difficult to pursue." He is concerned that "we now find ourselves worrying that individual freedom has advanced to the point that community loyalties have been lost." Attempting to promote cultural renewal and revive a stronger sense of community poses a difficult task. Wuthnow envisions culture as a kind of "deep meaning" that "is concerned with the tacit knowledge that guides human behavior without our needing to think very much about it. It is composed less of beliefs and values and more of orientations and understandings." In a similar vein, Harvard political theorist Michael Sandel refers to the "unreflective background" that undergirds public discourse and policy as "assumptions about citizenship and freedom that inform our public life."[132]

These kinds of moral tenets and behavioral guidelines get implanted in people's minds and behavioral patterns in the form of habits, gradually formed and nurtured, as Aristotle taught long ago. They are powerful and effective only insofar as they are firmly rooted in a strong sense of community and in civil society. It is within families, religious groups, schools, community organizations, and neighborhoods, where people interact, converse with each other, reinforce their neighbors' morale, and keep a watchful eye on their behavior, that people's actions and personal relationships are channeled in healthful and productive directions and deviant behavior is headed off.

The exaggerated individualism that has become so prevalent in American society of late has had the effect of undoing the kinds of social relationship, the sense of duty, and the feeling of responsibility that bound people together in community in the past. These developments, in turn, have had profound effects on the way in which politics operates, since social life, the culture, and the political system are all bound intimately together. "I think we all realize that the hatred, fragmentation and disconnection in our society is not just a political problem. It stems from some moral and spiritual crisis," writes David Brooks. "We don't treat one another well. And the truth is that 60 years of a hyper-individualistic ... culture have weakened the bonds between people. They've dissolved the shared moral cultures that used to restrain capitalism and the meritocracy."[133]

Citizens of a free society, in order to function effectively as individuals, in the terminology of Harvard sociologist Robert Putnam, need generous amounts of "social capital." Community building, as well as the nurturance of individual thriving, requires trust, shared values, and civic virtue. As individuals, we are called upon to find meaning in life, to cultivate reason, to seek what is moral and true, to assume responsibility, and to do our duty. As members of the community, we are obliged to act with civility, engage others with empathy, make connections, and act cooperatively. As social creatures, we seek friendship, contact with others, and reinforcement for the values we hold dear.[134]

Evidence abounds that American behavioral patterns today are out of synch, reflecting the types of human character that currently prevail. What once was taboo has become commonplace. What once aroused disapproval has become acceptable. Life continues to go on in many of the same ways, but the boundaries have shifted and many of the old standards have disappeared. This is not to deny that in some ways, people's attitudes and behavior have considerably improved, e.g., within the family, between the races, and among various groups. What is harder and harder to do, however, is to provide coherent rationales for saying "no" to what once was discredited or absolutely forbidden, e.g., premarital sex, abortion, certain kinds of drug use, pornography, vulgar language, and resort to violence. In his seminal book *After Virtue*, the philosopher Alasdair MacIntyre observes that the language of morality is in a state of "grave disorder" and that we have very largely "lost our comprehension, both theoretical and practical, of morality."[135]

To be sure, the path followed by moral principles and prohibitions over time has resembled that of a roller coaster rather than one of a straight highway taking the traveler in one direction or another. In *A Farewell to Arms*, written in the wake of the First World War, novelist Ernest Hemingway famously had his protagonist say, "I was always embarrassed by the words sacred, glorious, and sacrifice, and the expression in vain.... Abstract words such as glory, honor, courage, or hallow were obscene beside the concrete names of villages, the numbers of roads, the names of rivers, the numbers of regiments and the dates."[136] For many people, language lost the capacity to accurately convey the horror of war as well as ordinary happenings. The old moorings seemed to have been cut loose. Now, almost a century after the events Hemingway wrote about, the foundations of morality are shakier. In the words of psychologist Jonathan Haidt, "Where the ancients saw virtue and character at work in everything a person does, our modern conception confines morality to a set of situations that arise for each person only a few times in any given week: trade-offs between self-interest and the interests of others."[137]

The importance of personal character for societal flourishing should be obvious. Biblical sources emphasize the connection between the two. "The association between individual character and collective well-being was equally clear to the ancient Greek philosophers," writes James Davison Hunter, the current dean of character studies in the United States. "In the *Republic*, Plato held up character as the defining qualification of the ruling class." The French political philosopher Montesquieu, whose work was well-known by the Founding Fathers, made a similar case, observing that "the corruption of each government almost always begins with that of its principles." This was especially true, he said, in a democratic regime. "The steady character of our countrymen," Thomas Jefferson wrote in 1801, "is a rock to which we may safely moor." James Madison agreed. "Is there no virtue among us?" he asked. "If there be not, we are in a wretched situation. No theoretical checks—no form of government, can render us secure. To suppose that any form of government will secure liberty or happiness without any form of virtue in the people is a chimerical idea." These ideas constituted core principles of the democratic faith for these two leaders. Thirty years later, Tocqueville, in his travels around the country to gather material for *Democracy in America*, concluded that virtue was indeed a central condition for the vitality of democracy in the United States. Sound "habits of the heart" were essential to the prosperity and progress of a nation and to the health of its political institutions. "How could society escape destruction if, when political ties are relaxed, moral ties were not tightened?" he wondered.[138]

None of the thinkers just mentioned would have been reassured by what is happening in the United States today. Our media-dominated, sex-drenched, violence-oriented, and often crude, rude, and vacuous popular culture is guilty of trashing the taste of Americans, according to Professor James B. Twitchell, if they really need any help in the project. "In a world now consuming images as never before, what will be shown is what most paying customers want to see," he writes. "What most customers want to see is, almost by definition, what a generation ago would have been labeled common, unwashed, scumular, barbaric, or *vulgar*."[139] Meanwhile, a new, highly-educated, and well-credentialed elite has taken over control of society from the old WASP Establishment. "Yet, as this meritocratic elite has taken over institutions, trust in them has plummeted," writes David Brooks, whose position as a writer, radio-TV personality, and columnist with the *New York Times* certainly qualifies him for inclusion in the elite. "The meritocracy has not fulfilled its promise," he contends. This is not to say that many of their number are not doing excellent jobs and do not present a distinct improvement over the older "racist, sexist, and anti–Semitic old boys' network" that used to run the country. What the latter did possess, however, was belief in "restraint, reticence, and service," qualities often sorely lacking, at least among a segment of the new regime. "Wall Street firms, for example, now hire on the basis of youth and brains, not experience and character. Most of their problems can be traced to this," Brooks believes.[140]

The machinations of the Bernie Madoffs of the world, the top executives at Enron, and other sleazy operators remind us of the continuing greed, malignancy, and shameful behavior that remain commonplace in business and society, ranging from top to bottom. Memories of the Holocaust and numerous wars that occurred in the twentieth and twenty-first centuries underline the fact that "civilization is immeasurably fragile, and is easily turned to brutality and barbarism," writes Adam Gopnik. "The human capacity for hatred is terrifying in its volatility."[141] By those measures, some of the political shenanigans going on in recent years might seem tame in comparison. Nevertheless, a "red line" of acceptability was breached in 2016 when candidates hurled insults at each other regarding their physical looks, the size of their hands, their dissimulation, and their relative lack of intelligence. We have come a good distance from 1960, when the distinguished historian Henry Steele Commager could complain that the formula that had been agreed upon for conducting the televised debates between Nixon and Kennedy was "designed to corrupt the public judgment and, eventually, the whole political process."[142]

One wonders what he would have thought of the 2016 debates or, say, the toxic content of many of the movies, television programs, songs, and other products being turned out by the cultural industry these days. Just as political candidates seek to gain the attention of the public by ramping up their rhetoric, television producers feel the need to crank up violence on the screen in order to attract audiences. In 2016, fans of *The Walking Dead* cried foul when two of their favorite characters met their ends in the fall premiere by having their heads bashed in by a villain with a barbed wire-covered baseball bat. One of them had half his skull gone and an eye dangling from its socket. A program later in the season featured a close-up of a disembowelment. There seemed to be few limits beyond which the show's creators were unwilling to go.[143] During the election campaign that fall, Donald Trump sometimes seemed intent on seeing how far he could go to violate previously adhered-to taboos. As Adam Haslett in the *Nation* described it, his "endless acts of public verbal violence that have broken one unwritten rule of political discourse after the next … have had the effect that all violence does: to shock those who experience it into a kind of stunned passivity."[144] The Republican candidate was picking up where some of his predecessors had left off.

Four years earlier on the campaign trail, an Associated Press writer had asked what was going on with some politicians, in this particular case the New York City and Philadelphia mayors and the governor of New Jersey. They had all uttered some choice vulgarities in G-rated public settings where such language was not usually indulged in by such officials. "While foul language has been uttered in politics before," the reporter wrote, "the blue streak is making some wonder whether it reflects the coarsening effects of pop culture in this reality-TV era of 'Jersey Shore' and 'The Real Housewives,' a decline in public discourse, a desire by politicians to come across as average Joes, or just a really hot summer."[145] *New York Times* columnist Paul Krugman observes that "republican institutions don't protect against tyranny when powerful people start defying political norms. And tyranny, when it comes, can flourish even while maintaining a republican facade…. The erosion of democratic foundations has been under way for decades, and there's no guarantee that we will ever be able to recover. But if there is any hope of redemption, it will have to begin with a clear recognition of how bad things are. American democracy is very much on the edge."[146] Members of Congress and appointive officials tend to talk more frankly about the situation after they depart office. "There is such a loss of faith in the institution of Washington, in the government itself," Virginia representative Eric Cantor, who had been on track to be Speaker of the House, said after losing a re-election bid to an upstart candidate, that voters "can't listen to any politician at this point and believe them."[147]

The entrance of Donald Trump into electoral politics in 2015 reshaped the parameters of American politics, and not for the better. Untutored in the history of American politics and unfamiliar with commonly understood norms and practices, he brought his business, reality TV, and sports-influenced behaviors into the political realm, and the clashing of gears, so to speak, was heard around the planet. Republican candidates for the presidential nomination and other party functionaries were reluctant to take him on during the primary season, hoping to win his favor in case he prevailed, and after he won they became even less likely to call him out on his unusual and unprecedented behaviors. One who did was newly elected United States senator from Utah and former presidential nominee Mitt Romney. After the election, he wrote an op-ed piece for the *Washington Post* in which he stated, "To a great degree, a presidency shapes the public character of the nation. A president should unite us and inspire us to follow 'our better angels.' A president should demonstrate the essential qualities of honesty and integrity, and elevate the national discourse with comity and mutual respect." By stating what the goal should be, Romney was implicitly criticizing the way President Trump actually was playing out his role.[148]

An explanation for the tolerance many people afforded President Trump's wild rhetoric and intemperate actions before and after he won the election of 2016 is the influence that expressive individualism has come to assume in a culture where a sense of community has been in significant decline. Andrew Root in the *Christian Century* observes that consumerism, heavy drinking, and unbounded sexual activity have seduced many young people into violating established norms and taboos. The article cites Christian Smith, a professor of sociology at Notre Dame, who worries that many young adults suffer from lack of a moral compass: "They seem unable to enter into any kind of serious moral reasoning at all. Instead, they default to hyper-individualism, believing that whatever seems right to each person is moral." About the only thing that many of the individuals Smith interviewed were willing to judge others on was … judging others![149]

"Without ethics, politics has no limits," Earl Shorris, founder of the Clemente Course in the Humanities, tells us.[150] Our nation's Founders implicitly understood this. A republican form of government depends upon the virtue of the people and of their representatives even more than it relies upon institutional safeguards. Yelling "Lock her up!" or traducing the rule of law to promote one's own prospects or the welfare of one's party violates the first principles of democratic governance. It also obviously provides an egregious expression of infantile behavior, the kind of thing an arrested-development adolescent might engage in. This is not politics; it is emotional wallowing.

The infantilization of politics constitutes not just a moral failure of individuals; it is also a failure of community. We depend upon communities for companionship, friendship, sustenance, recreation, and, ultimately, survival. "No man is an island" is not just a slogan to hang on the wall, even if people who should know better have been quoted as saying that "there is no such thing as society." In a real sense, society comes before the individual, but it would be more accurate to say that the individual and the society are equally important—co-dependent and collaborative. Without one, the other could not exist.

This is why indications that community is imperiled attract our attention. Most famously, Harvard political scientist Robert Putnam's book *Bowling Alone* caused such a stir when it appeared that many people took note of it. Declining participation in the traditional kinds of civic organizations, such as Boy Scouts and Rotary clubs, which have played such a big role in community formation, signaled a serious challenge to our democratic society. While many immigrants came to America during the colonial period as individuals or families, many of them arrived along with corporate groups. Most famously, the Pilgrims at Plymouth and the Puritans at Boston provided seeds for the Puritan culture that swept west from New England and across the northern tier of states into the Midwest, Great Plains, and on to the West Coast during the nineteenth century. The diaspora from New England brought along with it a communal culture that was economic, social, religious, educational, and intellectual in nature. Lying at the heart of it was a devotion both to the welfare of the community and to individual choice, opportunity, and advancement. This involved a strong sense of duty and responsibility to others as well as a commitment to democratic deliberation and decision-making. The town-meeting tradition and the development of self-government, as practiced in colonial assemblies and town-hall meetings, provided a paradigm that inspired the writers of the Constitution in 1787.

The communal nature of the American experiment was dramatically illustrated in the sermon delivered by Massachusetts governor John Winthrop on shipboard the *Arbella* in Boston harbor in the spring of 1630 before he and his fellow immigrants disembarked. In some of the most famous words ever uttered by an American, he told his assembled listeners, "We shall be as a city upon a hill; the eyes of all people are upon us." In recent years, these words have come to be interpreted as self-congratulatory, attesting to the greatness of the Puritan endeavor and entailing a prediction that the rest of the world would look upon America as a shining example of what they, too, could become if only they modeled themselves after their excellent, high-minded, freedom-loving, success-bound predecessors. But Winthrop never used the word "shining" in describing the Puritans' "city upon a hill." Instead, he was warning his little flock of Puritan believers that not only the eyes of the world but also the eyes of God would be upon them, and that if they failed to honor him and follow faithfully in his pathways they would be made "a story and a byword" of unfaithfulness and thus suffer shame and be cursed for their failure. Regardless of how we interpret the meaning of Winthrop's entreaties, however, we can all agree that the Puritan experiment was a communal venture.[151] The historian Perry Miller characterized its purpose accurately when he entitled one of his books *Errand into the Wilderness*. The Puritan polity was not a democracy. It constituted a religious errand and was more of a patriarchy or theocracy than a democracy, but it bore the seeds of democracy. One of the major reasons for its ultimate success was that it emphasized individuality and communalism in equal measure.

Without going into further detail about the communal hiving out from New England during succeeding years and decades, it is enough to emphasize that American democracy has always depended heavily upon a strong sense of community. Community and individual are not at odds with each other. As democratic philosopher John Dewey and many others have stated so well, the thriving of the individual and the flourishing of society are co-dependent. Democracy's success and survival depend upon the health of both. A corollary of this is that character and community are inextricably intertwined. When both are imperiled, democracy is at risk.

3

Political Challenges
to Democracy

Since politics is driven by conflict and since conflict is ubiquitous in society, political divisiveness is something we will always have with us. The question is not *whether* we shall engage in it but rather in what *manner* we shall get involved. So far, the United States has managed to play the political game in a generally peaceful and practical manner, allowing that often the competition gets quite heated, many problems are left unresolved, and some people and groups get treated quite badly while others enjoy considerable rewards from the process. The most grievous exception, of course, was the Civil War, and many examples of exploitation, unfairness, failed initiatives, oppression, and dysfunction could be cited.

The United States has gone through cycles of extreme polarization in the past. Charges of executive tyranny or even dictatorship, congressional malfeasance and ineptitude, judicial activism and misconduct, and bureaucratic incompetence and overreach have often arisen. Party competition guarantees that it will happen again and again. In recent years, especially after the Great Recession of 2008, the American electorate has seemed to be more out of sorts than usual. When voters are "in a funk," they can behave in unpredictable ways. Congress often seems to have "thrown out the textbook." Presidents increasingly seem set upon defying long-established norms. The judiciary is not exempt from political involvement. Outside of Washington, in the states, cities, towns, and rural areas of America, willingness to abandon long-established norms, traditions, and guidelines is visible almost every day. The fragility of democracy is on display.

Challenge 7—Voters in a Funk

As the 2016 election approached, American voters had been in similar situations before—upset, testy, sour about the status quo, and in the mood for change. Conditions in 1920, 1932, 1946, 1974, and 1980, for instance, come to mind. Confronted by post–World War I and World War II let-downs, the Great Depression, Watergate, or double-digit inflation, the public displayed varying degrees of restlessness and frustration. In those elections, a widespread desire to "throw the bums out" was operating. That is the ultimate sanction voters possess in a democracy to express their objections to the way things are going. It is a blunt instrument, to be sure, but effective nonetheless as an expression of criticism and disgust. Whether it brings positive results is another matter, but politicians have learned to live in fear of voters' wrath.

In 2016, voters were in a funk not so much because of President Obama. Although he generated considerable distrust and dismay among some individuals and groups, his overall popularity ratings remained strong. Rather, it was because of widespread unease, frustration, and anger caused by a variety of factors—sluggish wages; waning job opportunities; actual or perceived high rates of crime, drug use, and other social problems, especially in specific regions; crumbling moral and ethical norms; ongoing foreign wars; and, not least of all, immigration. In addition, there was the matter of the president's race. Polls indicated that 62 percent of the population thought the country was headed in the wrong direction.[1] The two presidential candidates offered up to them by the major parties were less than attractive. Hillary Clinton and Donald Trump both possessed coteries of enthusiastic fans, but 55 to 60 percent of the public did not trust either one of them, many viewing them with distaste, if not contempt.[2]

It is always useful when considering the mood of the times to remember that the American public is never all on the same page. It consists of a continually churning array of groups and individuals whose thoughts and feelings are often hazy, ambivalent, contradictory, and liable to reversal, depending upon the circumstances. The "40 percent rule" generally operates, that is, whichever political party is in the majority at any particular moment, the opposing party usually commands at least 40 percent of the vote when election time rolls around. The formula does not always operate, but it does manifest itself much or most of the time. Many factors operate to maintain this equilibrium. While people's thoughts, beliefs, and emotions are often strongly held, they are always contested by other people, and what may hold true at one point in time will not always carry over to the next. Another caveat: people's needs and desires usually exceed their ability or the capacity of the system to deliver on them. There never seems to be enough money, stuff, or emotional gratification to satisfy us. That is a formula for inevitable disappointment.

By 2016, a large cadre of pollsters and commentators had arisen to interpret the malaise that appeared to have fallen across the land. "Every political commentator has become an amateur sociologist," observed *Washington Post* columnist Michael Gerson, "trying to explain how rapid economic, social and cultural change has resulted in a populist backlash against elites."[3] The mood of discontent seemed to be deepening, even as employment levels and the stock market continued to move on up. "We're living in a world that's not the one we knew just a short time ago," observed Pulitzer Prize-winning historian Richard Rhodes. "It's leading somewhere and, right now, it's not a very comfortable place." Others echoed the sentiment. "The 2016 campaign made the quirks of our era more obvious," wrote Scott Canon and Dave Helling in the *Kansas City Star*. "A variety of forces—online and otherwise—upend our commerce, our culture, our politics. They make our lives less private and more fractious in large part because of how they put grievance on display. Rural America feels left behind and dismissed. Young black men feel themselves in danger. Police officers feel underappreciated. The poor and middle class feel shut off from schools, jobs and insider connections that pave the way to Easy Street. Women feel harassed. White men feel they get all the blame. These old grudges air in new ways. Sometimes it's healthy. Often, it makes for more anger."[4]

While many things were driving discontent, most complaints revolved around two poles: economic grievances and social issues. Most problematic were the economic woes many families were experiencing, still hurting from the effects of the Great Recession but now worried as much or more about the future than about current conditions. The long post–World War II expansion had ended around 1973, and for the next four decades real wages for a large segment of the population had stagnated or even slipped backwards. Good middle-class employment seemed to be disappearing, and globalization, the export of jobs, and a growing squeeze between incomes and rising housing, college, and medical costs were raising anxiety levels to new highs. Realizing that increasing gaps in income and wealth were a global phenomenon was small comfort to those caught in their grip. Between 1945 and the late 1970s, the richest 10 percent of the population had garnered 33 to 35 percent of total national income. By 2007, that figure was up to 50 percent. Meanwhile, the richest 1 percent's share had risen from around 10 percent in 1980 to 24 percent three decades later.[5]

Political consultant Scott Miller identified what he thought was the key political fact of our time: "Over 80 percent of the American people, across the board, believe an elite group of political incumbents, plus big business, big media, big banks, big unions and big special interests—the whole Washington political class—have rigged the system for the wealthy and connected." More than half of Americans believe "something has changed, our democracy is not like it used to be, people feel they no longer have a voice."[6] Voter alienation spread across the urban working classes as well as in rural areas, where residents saw population declining, jobs disappearing, and little on the horizon to promise better days ahead. Several regions of the country seemed especially affected by economic and political disillusionment. Appalachia, parts of the midwestern "Rust Belt," and areas in the South drew special attention from analysts. J.D. Vance's remarkably popular memoir of growing up in eastern Kentucky and southwestern Ohio, *Hillbilly Elegy: A Memoir of a Family and Culture in Crisis* (2016), remained on or near the top of the bestseller lists for over a year. Arlie Russell Hochschild's book focusing on southwestern Louisiana, *Strangers in Their Own Land: Anger and Mourning on the American Right* (2016), explained why so many people living in that region had lost faith in the American Dream. Nancy Fraser's *White Trash* (2016) about how poor people living in both urban and rural areas had been denigrated, made fun of, and treated badly throughout American history, reinforced the notion that there was something brewing in "left behind" parts of the nation. Beyond jobs, improved working conditions, and nicer lives, what many working class and middle-class Americans desired were simple respect and attention. They wanted their voices to be heard and someone to speak to them in a language they could relate to.

In that, many of them found their answer in Donald Trump. It seemed unlikely that a multi-billionaire, Manhattan-based, twice-divorced, real-estate mogul, reality-television, man-about-town would appeal to as many people as he did. Starting with the launch of his campaign for the presidency in mid–2015, most pundits and experts wrote him off as a viable candidate, perceiving his run as a personal vanity trip, a bid to widen his media appeal, or a pay-back journey of revenge against people who had crossed him in the past. There is reason to believe he saw little chance himself of winning the nomination. Right up to late in the primary season and then on up to election night in November, there were many who refused to believe that he could either win the nomination or capture the White House. His success, narrow as it turned out to be in the end, proved that 2016 was no ordinary election year; it was one of the most unanticipated and confounding moments in American political history. That lends no comfort to those who would downplay its possible implications. Many political commentators during and since the election have expressed deep concern about what Donald Trump's rise might mean for American democracy. On that, history is not reassuring. Democracies have been blind-sided in the past. In our current situation, people cannot escape wondering about the prospects for democracy in the United States.

While Donald Trump extended his own special appeal to a large segment of the electorate, Hillary Clinton possessed her own unique appeal, and, of course, she won the popular count by three million votes. She was intelligent, educated at elite schools, highly experienced, well-intentioned, a policy "wonk" supreme, and surrounded by aides and advisors who should have been able to answer every question to which a candidate needed to attend. On the other hand, she carried a fair amount of political baggage, not the least of which was being married to Bill Clinton. She had a penchant for getting paid hundreds of thousands of dollars for speeches to various interest groups, being involved in questionable business ventures, bending or avoiding the truth on various questions, and making statements that came back to haunt her. Her friends admired her for what she accomplished and for who she was, but she also had made many enemies along the way. For all her evident interest in people's problems and desire to make things better for them, she seemed to have had a tin ear and to lack the kind of ability to connect with many ordinary people that both her husband and Donald Trump exhibited in spades.

Her opponent, on the other had, was 180 degrees removed from her in many ways. He lacked political experience and basic knowledge of how government works, a desire to learn, real empathy for non-successful people (despite saying he "loved the poorly educated"), and an understanding of his own limitations. Also, he was, by his own claim, among the richest men in America. Of course, that meant he was a man, and manliness was something that was obviously important to him. Despite all the GOP charges that Clinton lied and engaged in illegal activity, Trump was several leagues ahead of her in his questionable business practices, his willingness to break taboos and accepted norms, and his habitual exaggerated rhetoric and tendency to distance himself from the truth. Psychologists could use him as a classic example of "projection," as he continually referred to his opponent as "Lyin' Hillary." He exposed his angry, vengeful, and cruel side most clearly when he encouraged audiences to engage in physical violence against protestors at his campaign rallies and joined in with them in crying, with regard to Clinton, "Lock her up!"

While turning off some voters, these qualities made him appealing to many others. What a lot of people liked—even loved—about Trump was that he "talked like they did." They liked the flippant attitude he adopted toward Establishment figures, politicians, educators, intellectuals, and journalists. His backers said they could understand him when he spoke, whereas a lot of Clinton's policy-wonkery lost them. Despite his wealth, he seemed to understand their economic problems. At least, he expressed sympathy for people who had lost their jobs or who were stuck in dead-end ones. More importantly, he was full of promises—promises to bring back jobs, to stop the business exodus, to make things better, to get back at vaguely described wealthy CEOs, big bankers, Wall Street manipulators, and elitists of all types. He was a fighter. He was bold. He took no guff.

Besides seeming to side with blue-collar workers, rural dwellers, and the middle class in their continuing efforts to achieve economic progress, Trump connected with conservatives on many social issues, despite the fact that his background as a New Yorker and his activities as a playboy sort of figure should have worked against him. He abandoned his former advocacy of choice for women in the matter of abortion and reached out to Evangelical religious leaders, even though he had never been notable as a church-goer himself. Despite his previous record as a Democrat, his friendliness to liberal causes, his casino operations, and other activities that should have disqualified him with the right, he won around four-fifths of the Evangelical Christian vote and by and large stood in good stead with conservatives on religious values and salient social issues. They, too, were highly upset at toxic trends in American culture, but by siding with the Republican candidate, they gave their backing to actions that could potentially undermine American democracy.

As David Brooks looked at what is happening to the electorate, he perceived the largest split as resulting from technological, educational, and information-age developments. "The crucial social divide today is between those who feel the core trends of the global, information-age economy as tailwinds at their backs and those who feel them as headwinds in their face," he wrote. Today, the most significant social division "is between a well-educated America that is marked by economic openness, traditional family structures, high social capital and high trust in institutions, and a less-educated America that is marked by economic insecurity, anarchic family structures, fraying community bonds and a pervasive sense of betrayal and distrust."[7] Looked at differently, the bifurcation could be drawn along lines of religion, culture, race, and immigration on the one side and economic malaise and hollowing out, deindustrialization, job loss, and foreign competition on the other.

There was a major geographic dimension to Trump's appeal, especially pronounced in the "Heartland"—the Middle West (along with Pennsylvania)—otherwise known as the "Rust Belt," "Flyover Country," or "Tall Corn Country." The abandoned factories of Cleveland, Detroit, Gary, and Akron were a large part of the story, but especially observable was a rural-urban split that pitted a strong Trump element in the countryside and a more liberal contingent, especially among women, in the suburbs of the larger cities of the Midwest, as was the case elsewhere in the United States. Several locations especially drew the attention of the press during the 2016 election, for example, Wilkes-Barre, in Luzerne County in northeastern Pennsylvania, and Macomb County, Michigan, north of Detroit. Luzerne County, which hadn't gone Republican since 1988 and which Barack Obama had carried by five percentage points in 2012, went for Trump four years later by 20 points. Its shoe and dress industries and other factories had largely migrated abroad and many of the remaining jobs in the area were low-wage service ones in local hospitals, chain stores, and restaurants. As in many other working-class places that had suffered job loss and wage stagnation in the wake of globalization and industrial readjustment, many Macomb County residents welcomed Trump's promises of renegotiated trade deals and industrial revival. Voters there, who had gone for Obama twice, gave Trump a 54 to 42 percent edge in 2016. The excess votes that Trump captured there were a big reason for his winning Michigan's electoral votes and the election.[8]

The drop-off in working-class support for the Democratic party had been going on for several decades, but the more noticeable trend in recent years has been the increasing appeal that Republicans have for rural voters. The resentments and concerns of farm families and residents of small towns were memorably captured in University of Wisconsin political scientist Katherine Cramer's 2016 book, *The Politics of Resentment: Rural Consciousness in Wisconsin and the Rise of Scott Walker.*[9] Five years and dozens of trips out into rural communities around Madison acquainted her intimately with the anxious and often angry thoughts and opinions of ordinary people who think that public employees complain too much, that minorities often get too much special treatment, that they are not getting their fair share of the economic pie, and that they are being ignored and disrespected. Their sense of loss—that things were no longer the way they once had been—was palpable. Bernie Sanders and Donald Trump held some fascination for them, because both promised to really shake things up and bring about significant change.

As Sanders and Trump vied for their political support, growing gaps in income and wealth in the United States were becoming ever more pronounced. Increasing numbers of people were caught in the Great American Stagnation that left them with less net worth than they had possessed decades earlier. Middle-aged whites weren't living as long as they used to. The middle class was being squeezed out. Without a strong and large middle class, democracy was in jeopardy. The kind of poverty that during the Great Depression most people shared in now was made all the more distressing and intolerable by the visible presence of outlandish wealth possessed by the upper 1 percent or wherever one wants to draw the line. For a segment of the population, resentment of excessive wealth was a motivation, and Donald Trump appealed to some of them, but just as many of them probably wished *they* could achieve such success. It was not wealth per se that they objected to—rather the sense of privilege, arrogance, and distance that separated them from their others.

When they donned their red MAGA hats, Trump voters had more than dollars on their mind. They wanted to return to a time when opportunity beckoned, when a person without an advanced college degree could get a well-paying job, and when they received respect for who they were and what they were thinking. Donald Trump, as much as anything else, was a nostalgist. When he promised to bring back good times—"the way things used to be"— the vision he conjured up included good jobs, respect, honor, and security. But whatever listeners wanted to imagine could be part of the picture, too; it was up to the individual. Traditional family life and gender roles, prayers in the schools, conventional morality (even if the rules were not always observed), predictability, patriotism, American dominance abroad—whatever one desired or valued could be added to the vision. That was the appeal of his campaign slogan, "Make America Great Again." It was simple, but pointed. Yet it wasn't new, nor was it particularly profound. There was no blueprint for action contained within it. What the phrase represented was a perfect exhibit of symbolic politics—the kind that may not always win elections, since everybody engages in the practice, but one that might put a weak candidate who gets a few lucky breaks over the top. Like sports teams that try to stay close to their opponent right up until the last few minutes of play and then hope that the breaks go in their direction, Trump endeavored first to place himself in a position to win and then pulled no punches in working to drive home to victory.

Much of this was straight out of a textbook—"Political Campaigning 101." A great deal of it, however, was unfamiliar and had never been witnessed before—the extreme rhetoric, the over-the-top vilification of opponents, the threats to use the judicial system to imprison them once he was in office, the unlimited promises to solve every problem, the self-congratulatory assessments that were always stated in hyperbolic language—the "best," the "greatest," "perfect" and "wonderful." The simplistic language often left wide gaps open for interpretation and for people to project their own hopes and ideas onto the statements he made. Building walls, defeating enemies, solving problems, making progress, cutting government regulations and taxes—these accomplishments would not take a week or a year but might actually happen in a single day. Trump's enthusiastic followers based many of their hopes in him on the assumption that he did not always really mean what he said, but they trusted that in other matters he actually would follow through on his promises. In everything, strange manipulations were being done with words—the kinds of things that George Orwell warned about during the 1940s in his book *1984* and in essays such as "Politics and the English Language."

During the Watergate episode, President Nixon's attorney general, John Mitchell, had famously stated, "Watch what we do, not what we say." That is good advice to follow at any time. The problem is that politics and administering government are activities that, to a very large extent, revolve around words—both spoken and written. The health and preservation of democracy are largely dependent upon words—words in places like the Declaration of Independence, the Constitution, the Bill of Rights, Lincoln's Second Inaugural Address, Franklin Roosevelt's First Inaugural, Dwight Eisenhower's Farewell Address, and Martin Luther King, Jr.'s "I Have a Dream" speech. Words divorced from action possess little meaning, so follow-through is essential. Words have to be connected to reality. They have to be embodied in action. They have to be true. They have to be factual. Promises need to be kept. The distance between words and practice needs to be minimized.

The 2016 election thus signals the following dangers to democracy:

1. We should be concerned that some of Donald Trump's pledges and suggestions might actually be implemented, such as "Lock her up!"; unleashing unlimited nuclear destruction on North Korea; or changing the libel laws in order to punish one's political enemies.

2. The animosity and hatred exacerbated by the campaign has further tribalized politics, dividing people into warring groups that are willing to accept almost anything negative that is alleged about their opponents and to excuse or easily forgive the most venomous things said by their allies. This tribalism creates an untoward willingness to accept lies and misstatements of fact by one's own candidates and leaders.

3. These sorts of divisions also provide excuses for the violation of basic liberties and the breaking of long-held norms, e.g., amending the libel laws, deporting immigrants without due process, politicizing the legal system by pardoning favorites and by threatening to prosecute opponents, limiting or abandoning formal news conferences, and denying access to news reporters. Two decades ago, the philosopher Richard Rorty made a remarkably prescient—or lucky—prediction in his book *Achieving Our Country*. At some point, he speculated, low-wage workers concerned about stagnant incomes, the export of jobs overseas, and dismal economic prospects for them and their children, would come to realize that the government was not really try-

ing to improve their situation. "At that point, something will crack," he wrote "The non-suburban electorate will decide that the system has failed and start looking around for a strongman to vote for—someone willing to assure them that, once he is elected, the smug bureaucrats, tricky lawyers, overpaid bond salesmen, and postmodernist professors will no longer be calling the shots." Philosophers probably aren't any better than historians at predicting the future, but after people heard about his prediction in a *New York Times* story shortly after the 2016 election, remaining copies of the book quickly sold out and it had to be reprinted by the publisher.[10]

4. In identifying with and making promises to people who were falling behind in the competition for jobs, better compensation, and living the good life, Trump was participating in, by trying to take advantage of, a huge socio-economic transition that possesses threatening implications for democracy. While a limited portion of Americans are doing quite well and a tiny fraction are making out like bandits under the current economy, the largest segment of the population struggles to make ends meet and to get by day to day. For the first time in our history, as many as half or more of the population think their children will be in a worse economic condition than they are as they go through life. As scholars such as David M. Potter, Seymour Martin Lipset, and Fareed Zakaria have pointed out, prosperity and economic growth are closely associated with and indeed operate as a major factor in promoting democratic political institutions. In 1954, Potter, a historian, published *People of Plenty: Economic Abundance and the American Character*, which argued that "there is a strong case for believing that democracy is clearly most appropriate for countries which enjoy an economic surplus and least appropriate for countries where there is economic insufficiency. In short, economic abundance is conducive to political democracy."[11] Potter was writing in the middle of a quarter-century following World War II when annual economic growth rates in the United States averaged upwards of 4 percent, based heavily upon productive growth rates of around 2.4 percent. For various reasons, growth slowed after 1973, and during the decade after the Great Recession began in 2008, productivity growth slowed down to under 1 percent and GDP growth to around 1.5 percent a year.[12] When abundance is placed in jeopardy in a nation or when segments of the public find themselves insufficiently provided for, they may become vulnerable to undemocratic political appeals.

Especially important to take account of are the differential effects of economic change. The impacts of technology, including information technology, globalization, shifts in manufacturing, education, and other factors fall differently in different places. This was notably true with regard to the extended fallout from the Great Recession of 2008. Every section of the country was deeply affected by job loss, mortgage foreclosures, and economic decline, but metro-area employment had largely recovered to pre-crisis levels within five years, while non-metro employment never did. It is necessary to look behind aggregate figures on the economy to observe how many places in the United States are doing quite well economically and how many others are not. "The unequal geographic distribution of opportunity helps explain the 2016 election in so many ways," writes book author and political commentator Timothy P. Carney in *Alienated America: Why Some Places Thrive While Others Collapse* (2019). Even more important than the unequal distribution of wealth and income, in his opinion, are unequal opportunity and hope. "And if you travel across the country and crunch the numbers, you see how unevenly these are scattered," he notes.[13] While voters will always differ in their voting patterns within particular places, at least as if not more important are the ways in which they sort themselves out differentially between places. Election returns and political polling in recent elections have shown that rural places and former manufacturing regions which have experienced especially large job losses and business failures—where factories and stores on Main Street stand vacant—have been especially vulnerable to voter discontent and susceptible to political fantasy and illusion.

Challenge 8—Polarized Politics

No political development in recent years has been more obvious or more disconcerting than the increasing polarization that characterizes politics at every level, especially in Washington, D.C. While Donald Trump's campaign description of the scene there as "a swamp" that needs to be drained may have sounded overblown to most listeners, frustration and indeed anger with Washington characterize more and more Americans. What many or most people often seem to forget is the large number of beneficial things the federal government provides and enables, such as national security, protection from terrorism, Interstate highways, safe food, factory safety, air traffic control, clean air and water, scientific research, support for education, Social Security, Medicare, Medicaid, and financial protections. When many of these programs were first proposed—e.g., Social Security, Medicare, and labor legislation—warnings were raised that they would destroy people's freedom, undermine the economy, and bankrupt the government. People tend to take for granted the advantages obtained from these types of programs and activities, while they often feel frustrated and are quick to complain about the costs and problems associated with them—taxes, regulation, and additional paperwork.

Partisan differences over governmental programs have ebbed and flowed over the decades, especially as government expanded its reach beginning in the late 1800s. Party identity revolved to a considerable degree around how far the country should go in extending regulation and increasing spending for various functions. As time went by, discussion tended to focus on "more-or-less" rather than on "either-or," but there was always a fair amount of cross-party coalition building as both "liberal" or "moderate" Republicans crossed the aisle to vote with Democrats on these proposals. Congressional affairs largely rotated around this kind of bipartisan maneuvering. President Franklin Roosevelt was highly successful in working with progressive Republicans and southern conservative Democrats, as well as with his own kind of New Deal Democrats, during the 1930s. Dwight Eisenhower cooperated with moderate Democrats during the 1950s; much of the time, he actually found it easier to work with them than with members of his own party. Ronald Reagan was unusually successful in passing legislation through Congresses that featured Democratic majorities in either one or both houses. This kind of mutual cooperation began to falter during the 1960s, declined further during the 1970s, and began to completely break down by the later 1980s and 1990s.

The historian Geoffrey Kabaservice notes that "movement conservatism finally succeeded in silencing, co-opting, repelling, or expelling nearly every competing strain of Republicanism from the party, to the extent that the terms 'liberal Republican' or 'moderate Republican' have practically become oxymorons."[14] Eisenhower, Nixon, Ford, and probably even Reagan would have a hard time getting nominated by today's Republican party. Congressional leaders from Everett Dirksen, Hugh Scott, and Howard Baker to Bob Dole, John Rhodes, and Bob Michel would find no home in the party today. Former Republican governors such as Nelson Rockefeller, George Romney, and William Scranton would hardly feel comfortable now in the Republican party. Reagan and George H.W. Bush, both of whom passed major tax increases during their terms of office, would have violated the current GOP's "Axiom One," installed by Grover Norquist, president of Americans for Tax Reform, in 1986—a no-tax-increase pledge that virtually every Republican in Congress would later sign.[15] Liberal columnist E.J. Dionne, Jr., suggests that "ever since Bush 41 agreed to that tax increase, conservatives and Republicans in large numbers have shied away from any deal-making with liberals. They have chosen instead to paint us as advocates of dangerous forms of statism. This has nothing to do with what we actually believe in or propose.

Every gun measure is decried as confiscation. Every tax increase is described as oppressive. This simply shuts down dialogue before it can even start."[16]

Polarization in Congress is asymmetrical, which is also reflected in the voting public. The Republicans have moved to the right in recent decades, while the Democrats have tended to push to the left, but not nearly as far.[17] The departure of segregationist southern Democrats from the party, predicted by Lyndon Johnson when he pushed through the 1964 Civil Rights Act, eliminated the most right-wing members of the party. But Democrats still maintain a place for some moderate and even conservative "blue-dog" adherents, while liberal and even moderate Republicans have become virtually extinct. A *Wall Street Journal*/NBC News poll revealed that while Democrats who were willing to identify themselves as "very liberal" doubled from 13 to 26 percent between 1990 and 2015, the percentage of Republicans identifying themselves as "very conservative" jumped from 12 to 28 percent during the same period of time. Commentator William Galston sums up the situation: "While Democrats have moved toward the left, Republicans have moved much further right." Political scientist Alan Abramowitz, in turn, observes that party loyalty is at the highest levels ever achieved in the history of survey research, and ticket-splitting is at the lowest.[18]

Evidence of the extreme level to which political polarization has arisen in the United States is abundant. Pollsters and political scientists used to analyze a wide variety of factors influencing people's votes at election time—race, ethnicity, gender, class, status, education, religion, geographic region, and so forth. Many of these characteristics still matter, but nothing matters as much these days as party identification. This would have seemed counterintuitive to researchers several decades ago. They were taking note of the declining influence of parties and were speculating about their possible demise. Today, public opinion polls predictably reveal the strength of partisan influence on people's thinking.[19]

A typical example is a Gallup poll taken in May 2018 asking people how they evaluated President Trump's moral leadership. Among Democrats, 2 percent rated it "very strong," 6 percent "somewhat strong," 13 percent "somewhat weak," and 78 percent "very weak." Among Republicans, on the other hand, 22 percent rated it very strong, 55 percent somewhat strong, 14 percent somewhat weak, and 8 percent very weak. Democrats were more critical in their negative opinions than Republicans were supportive in their positive assessments, but the results provided almost mirror images of each other.[20] Similar patterns occur time after time on issue after issue. Even more obvious were shifts that occurred after Donald Trump was elected president. Republican and Democratic expectations for the economy switched dramatically after the November balloting in 2016. Republican consumer expectations, which had been hovering around an index of 65, immediately jumped to 120. Democratic numbers, meanwhile, tumbled from around 85 to approximately 60. Both indicators leveled off in succeeding months.[21] Voters clearly are living in two separate realities.

As in Europe, the political middle in the United States has been shrinking, along with the middle class. In the U.S. House of Representatives, the percentage of moderates among Democrats has declined to around 10 percent and among Republicans to virtually nothing. The situation greatly reduces any incentive to discuss, deliberate, or negotiate on the floor or behind closed doors, while encouraging both sides to seek to win at all costs.[22] According to Greg Ip, chief economics commentator for the *Wall Street Journal*, "The demise of the political middle has made it far harder to assemble the coalitions or negotiate the compromises that governing requires."[23] Complex interactions among economic, social, cultural, and political factors escalate the stakes of conflict and reduce the possibilities for agreement. Weakness in one area hampers efforts in others, just as strength conditions progress. Political polarization has the effect of throwing a monkey wrench into the works.

Over centuries of development, the "American Experiment" has benefited from a constellation of supporting myths that have inspired, energized, and undergirded people's efforts to advance their interests and improve their situations. Whether we think of it as an "errand into the wilderness," a "city upon a hill," a "frontier adventure," the "melting pot," or the "American dream," the story of American progress is one of a people holding in uneasy tension the rights and liberties of individuals, on the one hand, and the common good, duties, and responsibilities of the community, on the other. *E pluribus unum* has been our motto, the American flag our emblem, the American dollar our bulwark, and the American eagle—a symbol of freedom— our inspiration. "One nation, under God, indivisible" is in our pledge, but lately a reversion to tribalism has been our scourge. The result of political polarization has been to break apart that tenuous construct of the melting pot and to lead us to revert back to groupishness. As *New York Times* reporter and columnist Timothy Egan puts it, "We are retreating to our tribal, ethnic and primitively prejudicial quarters. Everything is about race or identity. We choose politicians based on whether they help our tribe or hurt People Like Us."[24]

While a high degree of political polarization was a common feature of American politics from the very beginning, the period between the end of World War II and around 1980 witnessed unusually low levels of polarization, accompanied by a considerable amount of cross-party cooperation.[25] It is highly ironic that during the 1950s American political scientists concluded that national progress was being stymied by the presence of two unfocused, non-ideological political parties, both of which contained liberals, conservatives, and more moderately inclined members. A special committee of the American Political Science Association issued a famous report entitled "Toward a More Responsible Two-Party System." It argued that the Republicans and Democrats needed to be restructured into more ideologically coherent, internally unified, and adversarial entities which would operate more like parliamentary democracies do in countries such as Great Britain and Canada. The dream of more cohesive, coherent, and consistent parties actually went back to the New Deal years, when Franklin Roosevelt privately indicated his desire to establish a more progressive party in place of the ramshackle conglomerate of urban liberals, labor union members, progressive ruralites, ethnic groups, and southern conservative segregationists that made up his Democratic coalition. His effort to "purge" the Democrats of conservative elements during the 1938 off-year elections, however, went nowhere, and no comparable push for party coherence was attempted after that.

University of Wisconsin political scientist Austin Ranney dissented from his colleagues' recommendations on political realignment, warning that the American constitutional system, with its separation of powers and constraints on majority rule, demanded interparty cooperation and compromise for it to function effectively. His skepticism proved prophetic, since what the APSA wished for at mid-century largely became true by the early 2000s. The result was the most deadlocked, dysfunctional Congress in decades.[26] Fareed Zakaria observed that the political scientists who had hoped U.S. political parties would become more pure and coherent had finally gotten their wish and "the result is abysmal—and predictable … a political system whose chief characteristics are venom, dysfunction and paralysis." To get anything done, the parties have to cooperate, and doing that had now become more difficult than ever.[27]

This development was a warning that the best of intentions can often lead to unintended consequences. Not only do the practices of politicians and leaders foster obstruction and breakdown in Congress, the very language they use becomes something that is not conducive to clarity and accuracy. Neil Irwin observes that "in recent years members of the two parties don't merely emphasize different topics; they often use different language to refer to the same thing."[28] While Democrats are likely to talk about the "estate tax," "tax loopholes," and "tax cuts," Republicans will refer to the "death tax," "tax relief," and "tax reform." "Expert panels" become "death panels," "affirmative action" becomes "unfair advantage," "women's right to choose" becomes "the murder of the unborn," and "global warming" becomes "unproven climate change."

A few years ago, linguist George Lakoff and other language experts were tutoring politicians on how to better "frame" their arguments. Political pundits and observers had been referring to this practice as "spin" for years. Everybody does it, but the language game now gets played continuously and it appears there is no escaping from it. When language morphs into mere language games, the retention of claims to truth, factuality, and accuracy becomes increasingly difficult, if not impossible. The temptation to exaggerate, mischaracterize, fuzz up the truth, and deliberately lie ramps up greatly. "Gaslighting" has become a popular term for describing the misleading use of words to demonize one's opponents while one's own colleagues and supporters are characterized in the best possible light. (The word derives from a 1944 George Cukor film in which a manipulative husband drives his wife mad by employing a series of small, insidious falsehoods.) "The excessive use of 'gaslighting,'" observes writer James B. Meigs, "is a case study in how political speech is evolving from a discourse of persuasion to one of demonization."[29]

This helps explain why some politicians, from the president on down, have adopted a sort of gladiatorial rhetorical style in recent years, one that expresses outrage even while its own delivery is outrageous. Driven by talk-show hosts like Rush Limbaugh and Sean Hannity and reinforced by websites, Twitter feeds, and podcasts, this manner of speaking tickles the emotions, elevates anger, and undermines rational deliberation. Perfected by Fox Network and other political talk show platforms, the approach turns domestic politics into "a combination of war, sport, and entertainment all at once."[30]

In sum, according to Thomas E. Mann and Norman J. Ornstein in *It's Even Worse Than It Looks: How the American Constitutional System Collided with the New Politics of Extremism*, "Political polarization is undoubtedly the central and most problematic feature of contemporary American politics. Political parties today are more internally unified and ideologically distinctive than they have been in over a century. The pattern is most evident in Congress, state legislatures, and other bastions of elite politics, where the ideological divide is wide and where deep and abiding partisan conflict is the norm. But it also reaches the activist stratum of the parties and into the arena of mass politics, as voters increasingly sort themselves by ideology into either the Democratic or Republican Party and view politicians, public issues, and even facts and objective conditions through distinctly partisan lenses."[31]

Investigators disagree over whether elites are more polarized than the general public, or vice versa, and in which direction causality flows. Suffice it to say, divisions at both levels are substantial, mutually reinforcing, and arise from a multitude of influences. Peggy Noonan in the *Wall Street Journal* commented, "What we are living through in America is not only a division but a great estrangement." Among the many divisions she identifies are Trump supporters vs. those who despise him, left vs. right, divisions between the two parties and between their bases and their leaders in Washington, religious believers vs. nonbelievers, cultural progressives vs. cultural conservatives, the coasts vs. the heartland, and those who think bakeries should be required to bake cakes for same-sex weddings vs. those who don't. "We look down on each other, fear each other, increasingly hate each other," Noonan contends.[32]

While disagreement on a variety of issues is rife, the divisiveness goes much deeper than the above suggests. "Democratic and Republican voters don't just disagree about the right way to reform health care or the true intentions of President Trump," write reporters Emily Badger and Niraj Chokshi. "Many despise each other, and to a degree that political scientists and pollsters say has gotten significantly worse over the last 50 years." Shanto Iyengar, a political scientist at Stanford, reports that partisan animus is at an all-time high. People think the other side is not just misguided, but that it is dangerous. A 2016 Pew poll showed that 41 percent of Democrats and 45 percent of Republicans thought the other side's policies posed a threat to the nation. About 55 percent of Democrats and close to half of Republicans say the other party makes them "afraid." In 1960, 4 percent of Democrats and 5 percent of Republicans indicated they'd be unhappy if a child of theirs married someone from the other party. By 2010, the share that would be "somewhat" or "very upset" had jumped to one-third of Democrats and one-half of Republicans. These days, by some accounts, partisan prejudice exceeds racial hostility in its effect on people's thought patterns.[33]

Explanations for the divisions that exist range from genuine ideological differences, gridlock in Washington, economic decline, the rise of political tribalism and populism, the end of the Cold War, and the need to find a new enemy to hate to technologies that allow people to follow and listen only to messages they agree with, gerrymandering of political districts, residential sorting in which like-minded people are more likely to live near each other, more openly partisan media, an explosion of negative political messaging, and the impact of Donald Trump and other unorthodox politicians who have transformed the nature of political maneuvering. A commonly held view, especially among liberals, is that polarization has been asymmetrical, with Republicans being more responsible for divisiveness than they are themselves.[34]

Bill Bishop's 2008 book, *The Big Sort: Why the Clustering of Like-Minded*

America Is Tearing Us Apart, achieved wide attention for its description of how Americans are increasingly living near others not only of like status and income but also holding similar attitudes and views. Little of this was planned or conscious, but the results are the same is if it were. Neighborhoods become more homogeneous—either Democratic or Republican—and more polarized. Once people are surrounded by neighbors who generally lean toward similar views, they feel less need to explain themselves to each other or to try to persuade people one way or another. Their views also become more extreme. The middle ground begins to shrink. This, in turn, finds expression in voting patterns and political outputs.[35]

Political divisiveness is a form of tribalism, which has been a major element of human societies from the very beginning. In normal times, people display a tendency to associate and work with people of their own kind; this intensifies during times of stress, danger, and crisis. The psychologist Jonathan Haidt writes about people's dual nature, which begets a remarkable "groupishness" that in turn influences the moral impulses that determine our behavior. He isolates six broad moral foundations that enter into the considerations of everyone: care, fairness, liberty, loyalty, authority, and sanctity. Both liberals and conservatives agree, to one degree or other, on the first three, but conservatives are much more committed to the latter three than are liberals, who regard them ambivalently.[36] Recent years have witnessed the decentralization and fragmentation of society along many lines of division, much of it accentuated by the internet and social media. All of this feeds into the polarization that afflicts our politics.

Crucial for explaining this phenomenon is the concept of "negative partisanship" (or "negative polarization"), which refers to the kind of highly charged fear and animosity that can motivate intense dislike and demonization of one's political opponents. Large portions of the electorate today are united more by hatred for the other party or opposition candidates than by attachment to their own party and its leaders.[37] This is the politics of "backlash," a "zero-sum game of tribal loathing," fueled by grievance, antagonism, and pure hatred. "This is a time of the politics of the apocalypse," writes *Washington Post* reporter Dan Balz, "an all-or-nothing view of the difference between winning and losing an election and of holding power or not holding it. There is no middle ground on what winning or losing mean." Lance Morrow, a senior fellow at the Ethics and Public Policy Center, goes a step further, observing, "U. S. society has been fragmented by identity politics into warlord states and has become, here and there, almost psychotic." He continues, "The public narrative is filled with alternate fantasies of annihilation.... Conjectural nuclear or environmental apocalypse flickers just over the horizon."[38] David

French writes in the *National Review*, "The net 'cold' rating that members of each major party give the other one—do they feel 'very' or 'partly' cold about the opposition?—has roughly doubled since the Reagan years, and most partisanship is 'negative partisanship.' In other words, a person belongs to his party more because he dislikes the other side than because he likes his own. It's polarization based on antipathy."[39]

This phenomenon might help explain why many voters for whom Donald Trump was their last choice in the 2016 presidential primaries nevertheless gave him their votes in the general election. They were voting in perceived self-defense, and the New York real estate tycoon, whose personal traits differed from theirs in most respects, was fighting hard against their perceived enemies. It might also explain their willingness to buy into the notion of "fake news" and "alternative facts." Their opposition to the Democrats in general and to Hillary Clinton in particular was so intense that they were willing to listen to accusations from the presidential candidate, from his entourage, and from conservative media outlets regarding the nefarious activities of their opponents and to label anything that called those statements into question as "fake news."

Studying history can be instructive. In their 2018 book, *How Democracies Die*, Harvard professors of government Steven Levitsky and Daniel Ziblatt, whose research has focused on Latin America, Europe, and the developing world, warn that "extreme polarization can kill democracies."[40] In recent years, elected leaders have undermined democratic institutions in countries ranging from Venezuela, Nicaragua, and the Philippines to Poland, Turkey, and Russia. Beyond constitutions and institutions, governments need to be guided by practices and norms that preserve toleration, deliberation, debate, collaboration, and restraint. High degrees of political polarization can lead citizens and government leaders to accept the use of institutions as partisan political tools, packing and "weaponizing" courts and other government agencies, bullying reporters and undermining trust in journalism and other sources of information, and manipulating electoral processes to rig election outcomes.

A consideration of the divisions that have split the electorate of late helps us to understand the current challenges being posed to democracy in this country. Differences of opinion and opposing interests have been with us from the very beginning, as was notably pointed out in James Madison's *Federalist #10*. The question always is how to moderate the dangers posed by faction, allow majority opinion generally to hold sway, and still protect the rights and freedoms of minorities. Politics, in essence, relates to the resolution of conflict through debate and deliberation and the establishment out of it of some sort of consensus. Of late, this task has become more and more difficult to achieve and the dangers posed to democracy as a result are becoming more concerning.

Challenge 9—Congress Throws Out the Textbook

J. Ronald Pennock, in *Democratic Political Theory*, lists a set of criteria essential to the healthy functioning of democracy, including "attitudes favorable to compromise; habits of political moderation; [and] commitments to procedures designed to limit arbitrariness and to ensure that decisions are not made without hearing all sides and without adequate information and deliberation." If he were writing today, he might have added to this list the necessity to limit the influence of money in politics. Most objective observers would have to agree that Washington currently is failing on all counts. Pennock goes on, "Mass man has sometimes been defined as the man who does not think of the morrow but governs his life by considerations of immediate advantage. Insofar as this characterizes the average person, a successful democracy will clearly depend upon institutions that check impulsive action and upon deeply entrenched respect for these institutions."[41] Here, too, we can only conclude that we are failing. People demand many things from government, even when they are not willing to acknowledge the fact, but they are often reluctant to pay the price for them, whether it be serving in the military, running for office, participating in elections, informing themselves adequately in order to make intelligent decisions at the polls, or, perhaps most obviously, paying taxes. To a considerable degree, in Shakespearean terms, "the fault, dear Brutus, is not in our stars, but in ourselves." There is plenty of responsibility to go around. Suffice it to say, democracy's health and thriving will depend upon our leaders picking up their game and on our citizens picking up their own game.

When I was a student, I learned about government the same way everybody else did—from a textbook. The textbook version of governance—whether you're a K-12 or a college student, an immigrant studying for your naturalization test, a viewer watching a television program, or a foreigner trying to learn about how the American system of government works—is that Congress makes the laws, the president enforces and administers them, and the courts interpret them when disputes arise. To depict the process, textbooks often contain an illustration with lots of arrows pointing in different directions showing how a bill becomes law. This includes the holding of hearings, committee consideration and marking up of the bill, debate on the floors of both houses, voting the bill up or down, the reconciliation process if the bill passes muster, and sending the bill over to the White House to have the president sign or veto it, with the possibility of having Congress override a veto if it can do it by a two-thirds vote. It all looks so simple, clean, and transparent. It probably never worked exactly the way it was intended, but it certainly doesn't now.

Overriding everything is the seemingly irresistible force of money, as it impinges upon the conduct and outcome of elections, the passage of legislation, and the everyday conduct of governmental operations. To show how far we have come in the past half or three-quarters of a century, I just have to recall the subject of my Ph.D. dissertation—Governor Philip F. La Follette of Wisconsin—who won three elections (and lost two) during the 1930s while he was still in his thirties, earning enough respect and recognition for his leadership and creativity that he was considered, by some at least, to be a legitimate presidential possibility. His campaigns for office largely consisted of driving around the state in a car driven by his even younger law partner, while he sat in the back seat sipping on a bottle of orange juice. He would thumb through a little black book filled with names, addresses, and notes about party leaders in each little town they came to in order to remind himself, in preparation for visiting with them, what to talk about. Short speeches would have been scheduled for delivery in the half dozen or so towns they managed to get to in a day, and newspaper reporters would be handed press releases on the subject of the day, suggesting what La Follette wanted them to write about in their stories. At night, he and his driver would often stay in people's homes, cutting down on expenses. The total bill for his campaigns came to around $4,000 for each one.[42] Wisconsin U.S. Senator William Proxmire's campaigns from the late 1950s through the early 1980s reported spending only a few hundreds of dollars on each one. Those days are long gone.

Today, as author Robert G. Kaiser writes in *So Damn Much Money: The Triumph of Lobbying and the Corrosion of American Government*, our elections are awash in money. Members of Congress spend so much time dialing for dollars, they have little time left to do their jobs adequately. The deterioration of Washingtonian political culture mirrors that of the rest of the country. The role of money in American politics has been problematic for decades, but recently the stakes have risen and the numbers have soared. The money culture in Washington, Kaiser writes, is so pervasive that "raising money is a chronic condition, a constant subject of conversation, and the basis for a little-known industry of political action committees and professional fund-raisers." It led Senator Chris Dodd of Connecticut to comment that "it's now basically all money." Commenting on his own time in office in Washington, he observed, "It's changed dramatically, I mean *dramatically*. I don't want to sound melodramatic, but the republic's at risk. Truly at risk because of this."[43]

Since the mid–1980s, the amount of money spent on elections has grown faster than even college tuition and health care costs. Between 1984 and 2012, while median household income rose by 128 percent, private college tuition increased by 311 percent, health care costs by 425 percent, and spending on political campaigns by 555 percent.[44] A network of donors put together by the Wichita billionaire Koch brothers spent $400 million in 2012 on the candidates they favored.[45] Four years later, they were planning to double the ante to secure a conservative president. It is not only about politics per se, but about the entire American culture surrounding it. "Their network of super-wealthy conservatives is underwriting efforts to remake America's state legislatures, universities, law schools, think tanks, public-television stations, and even its museums," according to media critic Eric Alterman.[46]

Not that the Republicans are alone in their quest for big money to run their campaigns. Democrats play the same game. According to former GOP National Committee chairman Reince Priebus, "They've made a living off campaign talking points, when, in reality, they've been raking in more money from millionaire donors than Republicans for quite a while." The Democrats, it appears, have tended to out-produce the Republicans when it comes to moneys that need to be reported, while the latter have done better at tapping funds that are not required to be reported, the so called "dark money" that gives the title to Jane Mayer's detailed 2016 book focused on the Koch brothers.[47]

The fact that upwards of one-half of all election contributions during the 2016 presidential campaign were coming in from fewer than 400 wealthy families is problematical for a democratic political system.[48] The influence thus bought or implied is a serious issue. Beyond that, however, is the way that money dictates public servants' outlooks and expenditures of time. The first consideration for anyone running for a U.S. Senate or Congressional seat, a governorship, or the presidency now is how much money he or she commands at the outset or will be able to raise as the election proceeds. Once in office, there is the constant daily grind of dialing up dollars.[49] And then there are the improbable, or impossible, candidates who are able to get into a race simply because they have the necessary resources. Rick Santorum's and Newt Gingrich's bids for the GOP nomination in 2012 were personally sponsored by two men—business investor Foster Friess and casino magnate Sheldon Adelson respectively.[50] Columnist Frank Bruni pointedly inquires "about the ways in which politicians' frenzied competition for donations warps their views of the world. They now spend so much time among the country's plutocrats, sowing friendship wherever the funds are, that their bearings and their yardsticks surely change, as must their sense of their station."[51] Author Thomas Frank states things more bluntly: "Over the course of the past few decades, the power of concentrated money has subverted the professions, destroyed small investors, wrecked the regulatory state, corrupted legislators en masse, and repeatedly put the economy through the wringer. Now it has come for our democracy itself."[52]

Americans have always harbored highly ambivalent attitudes about their government in Washington. On the one hand, they wear their patriotism on their sleeves, praise their soldiers and veterans, honor the American flag and all the other iconic symbols of nationhood, insist that their country is exceptional, and bestow honor and adulation on their political heroes, from Washington, Jefferson, and Lincoln to the Roosevelts, John F. Kennedy, Ronald Reagan, and whomever else they happen to side with that today. On the other hand, they constantly complain about high taxes, government waste, failed services, political corruption, inefficiency, and malfeasance. Their loves and hates come in about equal proportions, unless they take a more measured view, as some do, or take no interest in politics at all, as far too many do.

For over two hundred years, citizens have aimed their venom and barbs at virtually every leader, regardless of accomplishment, and with great predictability. The object of their ire is almost always the leader of the opposition party. Whether it be spending programs, tax increases, unpopular wars, corrupt practices, presidential scandals, administrative breakdowns, dictatorial tendencies, intrusive regulations, shady cronies, failed initiatives—there are always an excess of targets for critics to aim their weapons at. In what is essentially a two-party system, support for either one tends not to rise much above 60 percent or drop much below 40 percent. There seems to be an inherent equilibrium in the party system that leads to a rough balance between the two major parties, even if one of them usually wins elections for a period of time. Constant pressure from the party out of power tends to keep the majority party on its toes.

Governing is a messy business. The problems begin with Congress and with its ongoing relationship with the president. The Constitution's Framers had Article I of their foundational document deal with Congress for a reason: they expected it to be the basic rule-making body for the country, the one that would set the course for government and be primarily responsible for the health and welfare of the citizenry. Article I, Section 8 defined the powers granted to Congress in 17 separate paragraphs, with a final one adding that it was empowered to "make all laws which shall be necessary and proper for carrying into execution the foregoing powers." In addition, the goal of promoting the "general welfare," as laid out in the preamble, has been interpreted to grant Congress other implied powers. Article I, Section 9 contains nine paragraphs specifying specific actions that Congress may not take. Both the House of Representatives and especially the Senate were intended to be places where the representatives elected by the people could engage in reasoned deliberation, bring the facts to bear, entertain argument, and arrive at consensual agreement on the best course of action to take, whatever the matter at hand.

Of late, the mess in Washington, referred to in various quarters as the "swamp," the "quagmire," and the "deep state," has aroused the ire and frustration of millions of Americans, high and low, something the polls continuously attest to. Accepting that most Americans take too many things for granted, that most of them would not prefer to live elsewhere, and that they are more apt to complain about things than to give credit where credit is due, it remains true that there are many elements that are confounding, worrisome, and, much too often, offensive to democracy. Increasingly, serious dangers arise to democracy itself. One thing is certain: the system doesn't operate the way school textbooks say it does, or should.

For several decades after World War II, Congress and its committees functioned relatively effectively to formulate legislation and worked cooperatively with the White House to address and come to grips with social and economic problems facing the country. But a variety of factors during the seventies and eighties coalesced to undermine the working relationships that had been established over time.[53] The kinds of dissatisfaction felt by observers and complaints that continually got expressed about Congress since then have grown recently to a crescendo level. "If the country was once seen as the world's most effective and enduring democracy, the latest events tell a far different story, that of a nation at war internally and with its institutions under assault," veteran *Washington Post* political reporter Dan Balz commented in September 2018. He perceived circuit overload occurring in government and politics at the time, as Brett Kavanaugh underwent Senate hearings on his nomination to the Supreme Court, people wondered how long Attorney General Jeff Sessions and Deputy Attorney General Rod Rosenstein would hold onto their jobs, special counsel Robert Mueller's investigation into Russian interference in the 2016 election seemed to be in jeopardy, and a number of other controversies swirled about. "There is too much happening at once," Balz observed. "Everyone is at battle stations awaiting the latest development, the latest accusation, the latest meeting, the latest tweet, the latest counteroffensive—ready to pounce, and often to reach premature conclusions."[54] The pyrotechnics and noxious behavior that routinely erupt on Capitol Hill these days resemble the epidemic of bad behavior that some parents exhibit at their children's athletic events.

Speaking of the Kavanaugh nomination, Democratic Senator Patrick Leahy referred to Republican claims that the process had been thorough and transparent as "downright Orwellian." Having gone through nineteen Supreme Court fights over more than four decades in the Senate, he called this one "the most incomplete, most partisan, least transparent vetting" he had ever seen. Republicans fired right back. Judiciary Committee chairman Charles Grassley offered that what had been truly novel was when Democrats had blocked Robert Bork's nomination in 1987, calling that "an unprecedented smear campaign." The willingness of senators to pick and choose their arguments solely on the basis of partisan advantage could be seen in the way in which Majority Leader Mitch McConnell, who had justified his choosing not to even holding hearings for President Obama's pick of Merrick Garland in 2016 by saying that the American people should be given a chance first to voice their opinion in the fall election that year, now explained why he would be willing to back a Trump nominee in 2020 if the occasion arose. He claimed that the precedent of not confirming a nomination during a presidential election year applied only when the Senate and the White House were controlled by different parties. These kinds of mental gymnastics are easily swallowed by voters who belong to the party of the person who utters them, but they fuel backlash and cynicism in members of the other party.[55]

Reporter Nicholas Fandos saw the Kavanaugh imbroglio as one that exposed "just how far the Senate has drifted from the rules of decorum that once elevated senatorial prerogative over party, leaving behind the kind of smash-mouth partisan politics that have long divided the unruly Senate."[56] Senators themselves were increasingly speaking out about how dysfunctional their body had become. "The Senate has literally forgotten how to function," observed Independent Senator Angus King of Maine. "We're like a high school football team that hasn't won a game in five years. We've forgotten how to win." Republican Ben Sasse of Nebraska remarked, "Congress is weaker than it has been in decades, the Senate isn't tackling our great national problems, and this has little to do with who sits in the Oval Office." Both parties, he believed, were obsessed with their political survival and the next election. Neither chamber, King and Sasse thought, was working the way it was supposed to.[57]

Beyond obvious concerns about incumbents' re-election chances, primary challenges from more extreme members of their own parties, the constant drive for dollars, burgeoning accumulations of problems to consider, and lack of time to work on them due to changing weekly schedules, members of Congress are burdened by their own lack of expertise on a wide range of issues. Life in America gets constantly more complicated. The difficulty of comprehending the nature of the challenges facing them often puts congressmen and senators at a disadvantage, but few in their position feel confident enough to admit their own lack of knowledge or imagine that they could benefit from such a confession. Robert Kaiser's book *Act of Congress*, centered on the Dodd-Frank financial regulation bill of 2010, describes how "many members of Congress are politics-obsessed mediocrities who know little about the policy they're purportedly crafting and voting on." As a result, much of the actual work getting done is performed by staff members, aides, lobbyists, influence peddlers, and think tank advisers. "Members' ignorance empowers lobbyists and staff," Kaiser writes.[58] The many reasons why Congress seems increasingly unable to get their job done are virtually endless, and no quick or easy solution is in sight.

While both parties obviously are implicated in the process, most objective observers consider Republicans more blameworthy for the problem.[59] Encouragingly, some members of Congress have been willing to step in and make more than innocuous statements about the seriousness of the situation. Unfortunately, many of them tend to be those who have just retired or are about to retire, such as Jeff Flake, John McCain, Trent Lott, and Tom Daschle. Especially notable have been former Senate majority and minority leaders Lott and Daschle, who often went head to head in opposition to each other while they were serving in that body. They wrote a book and took their act on the road in joint speaking appearances to talk about the seriousness of the situation. In an op-ed piece in the *Washington Post* they warned that the country and its political leaders have never been more sharply divided. They offered four criteria for candidates, governments, and the public to judge their own actions: (1) Compromise: "Representative democracy is not winner-take-all. The Constitution was designed as a harmonizing system, balancing the competing interests of all the people toward something that serves everyone." (2) Chemistry: "But our representatives in Washington no longer know one another as people.... We need to look for candidates who understand the necessity of getting to know the other side." (3) Leadership: "It's about governing—not necessarily winning—and finding common ground that leads to action." (4) Vision: "What we haven't seen is a vision of where we can all come together, inclusively, as a nation." In the end, they advise, "democracy requires active engagement, mindfulness, and tolerance."[60]

Strong majority and minority leaders in the Senate and House of Representatives and Speakers of the House, such as Joseph Martin, Sam Rayburn, Lyndon Johnson, Everett Dirksen, Mike Mansfield, Tip O'Neill, Newt Gingrich, Nancy Pelosi, and Mitch McConnell have used their power to move or block important legislation and thereby write themselves into the history books. The arrival of future Speaker Newt Gingrich in the House of Representatives in 1979 marked a particularly significant turning point in bringing about the changes that now define the role of Congress. His goals were to nationalize congressional elections and to paint Washington as being so awful and corrupt that anything would be an improvement over the status quo. "You're fighting a war," he intoned in seeking recruits for his cause. "It is a war for power.... Don't try to educate. That is not your job. What is the primary job of a political leader? To build a majority."[61] He achieved that majority in 1994 when the Republicans captured control of the House for the first time in forty years. Part of his agenda as Speaker was to launch an attack on the use of science and facts in the making of public policy, a seemingly strange thing to do for a former college professor. Or maybe not. By abolishing the Office of Technology Assessment, a congressional agency designed to have scientists offer objective analyses on questions relating to defense, climate, energy, and other such matters, he was able to claim that what he had done was a cost-cutting measure, while he simultaneously concentrated power in his own office. It was a defining moment. A message had been sent: in the future, ideology would trump evidence.[62]

Gingrich's successor as Speaker, Dennis Hastert of Illinois, raised the ante during the second Bush administration when he introduced a custom that became known as the "Hastert Rule" in the House of Representatives. Relying on Republican votes alone to pass bills, the GOP caucus would allow for consideration on the floor only bills that possessed "a majority of the majority," i.e., a majority of Republicans in favor of them. Few amendments would be permitted, and bills would be written by party leaders rather than in committee. The opposition party would be largely excluded from conferences to reconcile differences between the two houses in the passage of bills.[63]

Over in the Senate, Mitch McConnell operated in similar take-no-prisoners mode as majority leader during the Obama administration. Shortly after the inauguration in 2009, at a retreat of Republican leaders to discuss strategy, he is reported to have said, "We do not take him on frontally. We find issues where we can win, and we begin to take him down, one issue at a time. We create an inventory of losses, so it's Obama lost on this, Obama lost on that. And we wait for the time where the image has been damaged to the point where we can take him on." Besides defeating or attempting to defeat administration bills, he and his party colleagues blocked dozens of appointments to courts and federal agencies and refused even to conduct hearings on an appointment to the Supreme Court after Justice Antonin Scalia died. McConnell admitted to a *National Journal* reporter in October 2010, "The single most important thing we want to achieve is for President Obama to be a one-term president."[64] He failed in that, but he succeeded in contributing to an atmosphere of extreme partisanship and gridlock in Washington leading up to the 2016 election. Republican Senator George Voinovich said that McConnell's approach to Obama from the start was "If he was for it, we had to be against it."[65] However, "McConnell not only failed to destroy Obama," writes Robert G. Kaiser, "he helped create Donald Trump. Trump's success was surely a consequence, in part, of the stalemate in Washington to which McConnell contributed so much."[66]

The GOP narrative of the failure to achieve the kind of bipartisanship that Obama had talked about during his campaign for the presidency lays the fault for causing gridlock during his eight years in office squarely on the president. Rather than their own intransigence, they say, it was his initial approach to them that made things difficult. He made it clear, they contend, that the Democratic majority in Congress would push through an economic stimulus bill with or without Republican support. As it happened, the stimulus package passed with three Republican votes in the Senate and none in the House. Mutual recriminations escalated after that, peaking during the battle over health care reform. The Affordable Care Act passed in early 2010 without a single Republican vote. When Democrats incurred major losses in the mid-term elections later that year, giving the Republicans control of both houses of Congress, stalemate became entrenched.[67]

In all of this, Democrats were by no means completely innocent. A number of the kinds of actions and techniques that Republicans later applied more vigorously during the Obama years and into the Trump administration had been practiced to lesser effect earlier by the Democrats. For example, in 1987 they had several times violated a generally accepted custom of the House to allow fifteen minutes for members to get to the floor and vote on a bill by leaving the vote open for several extra minutes. Once, in unusual circumstances, they had extended the time allotted for voting on an important budget bill for a longer period of time. Republicans, however, made stretching the time allowed to vote a routine practice when they were soliciting or trying to arm-twist enough votes to squeak a bill through. In November 2003, while considering President George W. Bush's prescription drug bill under Medicare, with the decision teetering on the edge of a knife, voting was kept open for two hours and fifty-one minutes, as party leaders converged on wavering members, importuning them with sticks and carrots to get them to hold fast or change their votes. Afterwards, House minority leader Nancy Pelosi reproved the Republicans for their actions and for poisoning the well. "The Medicare vote will be remembered as one of the lowest moments in the history of the House," she admonished. Other Democrats joined in with "Shame, shame."[68]

Democrats also established a model for future judicial nominations in 1987 when their harsh attacks on law professor Robert Bork succeeded in blocking his path to the Supreme Court. The process introduced a new word into the political vocabulary—"borking." Twenty-nine years later, when Republicans refused to even consider President Obama's nomination of Merrick Garland during an election when the nastiness rose to an unprecedented degree. Nor had Republicans been alone in using their dominance in state legislatures to redraw congressional districts after decennial censuses. Gerrymandering is a practice going all the way back to the early years of the republic. Again, however, the GOP has taken the technique to new extremes, as it has with using the filibuster in the U.S. Senate, denying minority party participation in conference committee deliberations, and raising spending by political action committees in elections.

If the executive branch poses the largest potential threat to democracy, the shenanigans of Congress in recent years present more direct and concrete violations of the democratic spirit and tradition. Thomas E. Mann and Norman J. Ornstein provide a summary of many of the challenges thus posed in their book *The Broken Branch: How Congress Is Failing America and How to Get It Back on Track*. Among the problems they mention are Congress's decline of institutional identity, the collapse of ethical standards, their shrinking schedule, indifference to reform, disappearance of oversight, tolerance of executive secrecy, excessive use of the filibuster in the Senate, decline of deliberation, demise of regular order, dominance of "machine politics," susceptibility to lobbyists, gerrymandering, and the practice of voter suppression, including the disfranchisement of convicted felons and discriminatory requirements for voter identification.[69]

Some of these failings are more obvious or egregious than others. The increased resort to the filibuster in the Senate—with four cloture motions in 1961–62; 24 in 1971–72; 31 in 1981–82, 60 in 1991–92; 71 in 2001–02; and 110 in 2011–12[70]—means that, in effect, on major pieces of legislation these days majority rule in that body requires 60 percent of the vote, not 50 percent plus one. Both parties have resorted to the tactic, depending on which one happens to be in the minority.

One could go further into details in describing the various strategies, tricks, manipulations of the rules, and other practices both parties have used, to greater or lesser effect, in Congress and in the state legislatures to try to gain political advantage over the other side. Gerrymandering takes place within the context of unprecedented party polarization and has made for a toxic atmosphere that works against the cooperative spirit of debate and compromise that democratic governance requires. In the end, perhaps the most serious concerns we should have about Congress's workings are its decline of deliberation and the demise of regular order.

The Founding generation deliberated in reasoned and mature fashion for four months in 1787 in Philadelphia about the details of the document that still guides our democracy today. Deliberation by reasoned debate, argument, and eventually voting on questions lies at the heart of democratic procedure. Today, however, everything seems to hinge on the vote itself and the votes are, to a great extent, predetermined before debate begins. When the most conservative Democrat is more liberal than the most liberal Republican and there is little or no overlap in ideological positions in either house of Congress, there is much less chance that discussions on the floor will change anybody's mind and therefore that they will really matter. Compounding this is the effect of many changes in practice and habit in recent decades that make it almost impossible to do what the Constitution makers wanted senators and representatives to do: deliberate. Blame it on air travel if you will. In order to allow members to go home almost every weekend, many, if not most, of them fly in Tuesday morning and fly out Thursday night, leaving only parts of three days for actual work—Tuesday, Wednesday, and Thursday. How much time does this leave for committee and subcommittee meetings? Not enough. How much time does it allow for the kind of schmoozing and interactions that used to occur among members of both parties? Very little. How much do they even talk to each other? Certainly not as much as they used to.

According to Mann and Ornstein, the average number of days in session during the 1960s and 1970s was 323. By the 1980s and 1990s, that had declined to 278, and by the early 2000s it was down below 250. Their verdict: "The change from the past—and the lack of time spent in meaningful floor debate—has been striking." Beyond that, much committee work has been shunted aside. Major bills that used to require weeks of hearings and days of being marked up in committee now take only a fraction of the time and often get none of the detailed, line-by-line analysis they used to receive. Often, much of the real action occurs behind closed doors with small groups of staff people, industry reps, and a few majority party members rushing the bills through committees and subcommittees with little debate. Minority members may be shut out of the action altogether. The number of House committee and subcommittee meetings held in the 1960s and 1970s averaged 5,372 a year; in the 1980s and 1990s, 4,793; by 2003–4, they were down to 2,135. Without reasoned discussion and debate, we may still have democracy of a sort. But it certainly is not the kind the Founders intended.[71]

Other obstacles to traditional democracy fall under the heading of the demise of regular order. During the final decade or so of Democratic rule in the House, which lasted from 1955 until the big Republican off-year triumph in 1994 that elevated Newt Gingrich to the position of Speaker of the House, the majority party often used its leverage to deny effective Republican participation in the legislative process, according to Mann and Ornstein. In 1993, Republican members of the House Rules Committee issued a critical report condemning the practices of the Democrats in shutting down "deliberative democracy." They contended that they were being denied the opportunity for a "full and free airing of conflicting opinions through hearings, debates, and amendments" designed to improve bills under consideration. If anyone thought things would change when the Republicans took over the House in 1995, they were mistaken, for similar practices continued, just under different auspices. Under Republican leadership, committee deliberations on contested bills became "increasingly partisan and formalistic, with the serious work being done by the committee chair, party leadership, administration officials, and lobbyists." The pattern held true in conference committees. In addition, there was an increasing tendency to include many significant issues in large omnibus bills without allowing members time to even read or learn what was in them before being called upon to vote on them. Not only was this undemocratic, it was inefficient, because many bills that were passed under tight deadlines included embarrassing and damaging mistakes that could have been caught with a little more scrutiny.[72]

Republican Rules Committee chairman David Dreier of California acknowledged that he and his colleagues were now practicing tactics they had condemned when the Democrats were in the majority, rationalizing, "But now that I'm in the majority, I have this responsibility to govern. It's something I didn't completely understand when I was in the minority." He may have been right up to a point, but what the congressman failed to mention, according to Mann and Ornstein, was that his party had "manipulated the process to serve partisan interests far beyond what the Democrats did during their forty-year reign in the House." All of this came with a steep price "in the suspect content of the legislative product, the diminished institutional standing of the Congress, and the rancorous tone of public life in Washington and in the country."[73]

And the beat goes on. One can debate which party has been more at fault in setting the tone (or the lack of it) in Washington affairs. From the outside, there seems little hope of turning things around, as each side feels compelled to employ tactics it condemns in the other just to protect itself. It calls to mind an analogy used by historian Daniel Boorstin in describing the direction that American society was moving in 1973 at the time he was writing *The Americans: The Democratic Experience*. Much like physics researchers describe the force of momentum as the product of a body's mass and its velocity, a similar notion, he thought, could be applied to society. "Translated into social terms, this was the sense not of moving but of being moved, not of pushing but of being pushed. Momentum kept things going the way they were already going."[74] In congressional affairs, momentum meant that the legislative process became like a game of chicken: whatever outrage one party used to outmaneuver the other, the second party usually felt obliged to adopt the practice in order to protect itself.

If one were to apply this concept to democracy itself, the notion that momentum or inertia would keep things going toward a greater and greater perfection of the democratic ethos would be a welcome message. Applied instead to what appears to most people currently as dysfunction in the system, however, it is disconcerting and upsetting. Our task now is to understand, diagnose, and, we hope, shift direction in order to render our democratic ideals real again.

Challenge 10—The Rise of the New Imperial Presidency

The publication of historian Arthur M. Schlesinger, Jr.'s *The Imperial Presidency* in the midst of the Watergate controversy in 1973 struck a nerve with readers who had become increasingly concerned about the growing powers concentrated in the presidential office. Schlesinger, who as a liberal Democrat had written prize-winning books praising strong presidents like Andrew Jackson, Franklin D. Roosevelt, and John F. Kennedy, was writing in a new political environment in the early 1970s—one shaped by the Vietnam quagmire and the unfolding Watergate scandal. The excesses of concentrated power in the White House had come home to roost in a way that liberal Democrats like him had previously hesitated to consider. Though his complaint in the book was primarily directed at the war-making powers of the chief executive, his treatment of presidential excesses across the board directed readers' attention to the office as a whole.

His warnings about expanding presidential power and the threat it posed to democratic governance presaged the backlash that would occur during the next several years in the wake of Watergate. Laws limiting executive authority, while simultaneously increasing congressional prerogatives, helped restore balance to the traditional tug of war that went on between the legislative and executive branches. "Throughout the 1970s the efforts of Congress to regain the powers of the purse and the sword, along with its general institutional standing, were extensive and ambitious," wrote political scientist Andrew Rudalevige in his 2005 follow-up to Schlesinger, *The New Imperial Presidency: Renewing Presidential Power after Watergate.* "By the 1980s some argued that the truly imperial branch was not the presidency but Congress," he wrote.[75] But then came along Ronald Reagan, and after him the two Bushes, Clinton, and Obama, setting the stage for Donald Trump. By the turn of the twenty-first century, the long drift toward presidential dominance was very much back in evidence, and the post–Watergate decline in presidential power began to look more like a mere speed bump than a permanent shift in conditions. Of all the threats posing challenges to democracy today, the specter of a strong man or woman emerging in the White House is the one that poses the greatest worry. An unbridled presidency seems the most likely (but not the only) path to tyranny.

That prospect would not have surprised, and certainly would have disturbed, the American Founders, for it was primarily against tyrannical kingly rule that they revolted in 1776, and it was the executive office that stimulated their largest concern while formulating the Constitution a decade later. The Declaration of Independence, after its initial rhetoric about natural rights, was mostly a long list of complaints about the actions of George III. So fearful were patriot leaders of executive overreach that their first constitution—the Articles of Confederation—included no executive branch in it at all. Little at Philadelphia in 1787 during the writing of the Constitution occupied the delegates' attention more than questions surrounding the executive functions of the new government: whether to have a separate branch at all, whether it be singular or plural in form, length of tenure, number of terms of office, method of selection, powers exercised, and so forth. Article I dealt with the legislative branch, Article II with the executive—a clear signal about which branch the assembled delegates considered to be more important. An extensive list of powers was specified for the new Congress, while the statement of presidential powers was quite brief and vague. Only because everyone assumed that the first president would be George Washington were many of the assembly willing to allow the executive as much power and leeway as they did.

For more than a century, the office of the presidency, in fact, remained a largely ceremonial one. With only a few exceptions—the major ones being Jefferson, Jackson, and Lincoln—no one before Theodore Roosevelt resembled the kind of strong presidents the electorate would become accustomed to in the twentieth century. After what some historians have referred to as Lincoln's "wartime dictatorship," White House occupants during the Gilded Age were mostly a mediocre lot with the possible exception of Grover Cleveland. But with the arrival of the first Roosevelt, Taft, and Wilson, things began to change rapidly.

William McKinley had already moved in that direction before 1900. The Spanish-American War of 1898 was a key turning point. With the acquisition of a small landed empire, the United States became an imperial overseas power, intervened regularly in Latin American affairs, expanded economically into Asia, and intervened in World War I to bring victory to the Allies. The wartime bureaucracy and violation of civil liberties that came along with it were both quickly dismantled and discontinued afterwards, but a precedent had been established. Franklin Roosevelt's New Deal resurrected lessons that had been learned during the war in establishing some of the federal alphabetical agencies during the 1930s. The best example was the National Recovery Administration, which bore strong resemblance to the War Industries Board of 1917–1918 and whose administrator, Hugh Johnson, had played a prominent role in the wartime mobilization.

In his inaugural address on March 4, 1933, at the low point of the Great Depression, President Roosevelt indicated that if ordinary measures did not work to pull the country out of the economic difficulties that were dragging it down, he would resort to broad executive authority, an idea that enjoyed widespread support at the time among elite elements in the United States as well as among the general populace, both Democratic and Republican. Soon, however, as he signed legislation creating new governmental agencies of all kinds, accusations of "dictator" began to fill the air. Most voters were grateful and supported the changes going on in Washington, but a hard core of conservative opposition quickly arose, forming the nucleus of anti–New Dealism that persisted for many decades. The American Liberty League emerged in 1934 to unite critics who believed the Constitution was being trampled. Libertarians warned that innovations like Social Security, minimum wages and maximum hours legislation, and the National Labor Relations Board would destroy American freedom. They employed the same kinds of language and arguments that later would be directed against Medicare, the Affordable Care Act, environmental legislation, and various welfare provisions.

During the twentieth century, along with the growth of the welfare state, federal income taxation, corporate regulation, and an expanded role for the

United States abroad, there arose a greatly expanded Office of the Presidency and a much more visible presence of the person occupying the position. For many people, this was a welcome development. Presidential leadership was viewed as the most logical means of bringing about desirable social and economic change. For others, it was worrisome, contradicting what they viewed as traditional constitutionalism and threatening personal freedom. As time went by, however, a simple formula emerged that pretty accurately predicted what one's attitude toward presidential power would be at any particular time: when your party occupied the office, you favored strong presidential leadership; when the other party was in power, you were skeptical or opposed to it.

For most of the twentieth century, liberals touted strong presidents, ticking off ones they admired for getting things done: the first Roosevelt, Wilson, FDR, Truman, Kennedy, and Johnson (of the Great Society, not the Vietnam War), while conservatives tended to belittle them. Eisenhower, while he was in office, was unusually popular with the public but widely criticized in the media and academy for being passive and weak. It took awhile for observers to appreciate his virtues and what Princeton political scientist Fred Greenstein referred to as his "hidden-hand" method of leadership—getting things done by subtle means, without demanding much personal credit for them.[76] But it was the ascendancy of Ronald Reagan that made conservatives appreciate more fully the virtues of strong presidents. By the time George W. Bush was in office, legal counsel John Yoo and other lawyers in the White House were arguing for the expansion of presidential authority on the basis of a theory called "the unitary presidency."

Whichever party one belonged to and whatever historical tradition had been, by the 1980s and 1990s, presidents and their minions continually asserted expanded prerogatives for themselves and developed plausible legal justifications for them. Sometimes Congress pushed back; often it didn't. The Greeks, who invented political theory and along with it democracy, considered tyrannical rule by one man to be the worst form of government. They, for the most part, were not enamored of democracy, which most of them considered to be a way station on the way to tyranny. Ordinary citizens, they feared, were too susceptible to demagoguery. Their warnings were attended to by the American Founders, who rejected direct democracy and instead established a republican form of governance.

The paradox of Abraham Lincoln's presidency was that while he came closest to playing the role of a single-handed tyrant in American history, he did it during wartime in the name of preserving democracy and wound up becoming the nation's most honored hero. Franklin D. Roosevelt, who was much more careful of civil liberties during World War II than Lincoln had been during the Civil War (because he was able to), wound up second in the presidential pantheon for his service to democracy, but he, too, violated people's rights, most notoriously with the internment of Japanese Americans. The quick emergence of the Cold War with the Soviet Union during the late 1940s led many Americans to question the long-term viability of the democratic system. In fact, the secrecy enshrouding United States nuclear weapon development; the big buildup of a military-industrial complex; McCarthyism and the anti-communist crusade; and a series of real or potential military confrontations, ranging from the Korean War, the Suez Crisis, the Bay of Pigs, and the Cuban Missile Crisis to the Vietnam War, invasions of the Dominican Republic and Grenada, and interventions in Nicaragua and Lebanon, all worked to concentrate power in the hands of the president. Under Nixon and Trump, actual decision-making occurred more within the White House and the National Security Council than in the State Department. World War II was the United States' last declared war. The war-making power, originally assigned to Congress by the Constitution, has long been effectively in the hands of the President.

Along with visible developments came a wide range of less obvious shifts in the locus of power, resulting in the diminution of Congress and the enhancement of the president. The process generally was one of accretion by seemingly small actions rather than by dramatic or newsworthy power grabs. In fact, secrecy or anonymity was generally preferable to public acknowledgment. A good place to start is with the expansion of the staff employed in the White House Office. What was just a handful of aides, secretaries, and advisers under Franklin Roosevelt ballooned to 400 staffers under Lyndon Johnson and close to 600 in the Nixon White House. The numbers employed in the entire Executive Office of the President expanded from 1,400 in 1952 to 5,600 twenty years later.[77]

President Nixon was notorious for his frequent impoundment of funds and refusal to spend money on a variety of things authorized by congressional legislation. Justified as a means of saving money and balancing the budget, such manipulations more often reflected the president's policy preferences and were a way of negating congressional intent. Nixon was doing much more extensively what Lyndon Johnson and others before him had done, going all the way back to Franklin Roosevelt. They were, in effect, employing a line-item veto that Congress by no means had intended to give them. Nixon, also to a greater extent than his predecessors, engaged in selective enforcement of laws, for example, in 1969 failing to cut off federal funds to colleges that refused to desegregate, as mandated by the 1964 Civil Rights Act.[78]

Most recent presidents going back at least to Eisenhower have claimed executive privilege to avoid answering questions or requests for information from Congress. Bill Clinton, for example, officially resorted to the claim fourteen times in refusing to answer questions about the Whitewater investigation, his relations with Monica Lewinsky, and other matters—this in comparison to its use once by George H.W. Bush and three times by Ronald Reagan. The bigger problem for Congress, the press, and ordinary citizens in trying to obtain information from the executive branch was its excessive secrecy, slowness or refusal to respond to Freedom of Information requests, reduction in holding regular press conferences or even providing press briefings, and increased classification of documents. President Trump's attitude toward the press is that he doesn't need it. With the rise of social media and other forms of a proliferating array of media, presidents now have ways of communicating more directly with their audiences rather than relying upon traditional forms of communication.

Beyond the unilateral decision to use military force in a variety of situations all over the globe, presidents have increasingly engaged in bypassing formal treaties, which require two-thirds Senate ratification, in favor of executive agreements, presidential decision memoranda, and similar methods as a way of implementing decisions without having to obtain specific legislative authorization. As Rahm Emanuel, an adviser to Bill Clinton, described the situation in 1998, "sometimes we use [an executive order] in reaction to legislative delay or setbacks. Obviously, you'd rather pass legislation that can do X, but you're willing to make whatever progress you can on an agenda item."[79] One of the most common devices for ignoring congressional direction and oversight was the use of signing statements when legislation was presented for the president's signature. These could legitimately provide guidance for executive agencies in interpreting laws and drafting rules or making other decision about implementation. But increasingly they became stratagems for simply ignoring parts or all of the legislation that was being signed. They became, in effect, line item vetoes. Courts have sometimes rejected them, but more often they get implemented if Congress does not push back, which it seldom does. These and other methods of conducting end-runs around Congress, skirting the law, or actually doing illegal or legally questionable things became increasingly commonplace through successive administrations, regardless of the party in power. Some, obviously, were more egregious than others in their use, however.

The doctrine of the separation of powers, which lay at the heart of the philosophy guiding the authors of the Constitution in their attempt to prevent single individuals or small groups from dominating governmental decision-making and thereby undermining representative government, depends heavily on each branch of government fulfilling its assigned responsibilities. As James Madison put it in *Federalist #51*, "Ambition must be made to counteract ambition" in such a way as to prevent any single entity from taking over absolute control of the government. For a brief period during the 1970s, Congress stepped up to aggressively play out its constitutional role in the aftermath of the Vietnam debacle and the Watergate scandal. A number of laws were passed to dilute presidential power and enhance that of Congress, including the Case-Zablocki Act of 1972 (requiring submission to Congress of international agreements, other than treaties, within sixty days); the War Powers Resolution of 1973 (putting restrictions on the presidential sending of troops into foreign countries); the Independent Counsel Act of 1982 (creating a permanent, independent special prosecutor's office); the Congressional Budget Act of 1974 (which reshaped the legislative budget process); the Impoundment Control Act of 1974 (which required budget deferrals and recissions to be submitted to Congress); and the Foreign Intelligence Surveillance Act of 1978 (which sought to provide oversight on presidentially authorized wiretapping).

These combined to one degree or another to help reshape the behaviors of interactions between President and Congress during subsequent years, but it did not take long for old habits and practices to reappear. In a complicated world, full of danger and challenge, sometimes bordering on chaos and one in which large groups of individuals (such as the U.S. House of Representatives and the U.S. Senate) are at loggerheads on many issues and unable to achieve consensus or to act quickly even if they did, reliance upon a single person (like the president) or a small group of people (like those gathered around the president) often looks to be the counsel of wisdom. By 2001, when it came to the foreign policy realm, according to Andrew Rudalevige, "presidents found themselves in a comfortably familiar spot: if not the 'sole organ' of foreign policy, then certainly the maestro of a powerfully amplified orchestra." Then came 9/11, and with the collapse of the twin towers, pressures to concentrate power back in the Oval Office intensified. Shortly before the United States bombed Baghdad in the spring of 2003, Vice President Cheney expressed a common administration feeling: "For the 35 years that I've been in this town, there's been a constant, steady erosion of the prerogatives and the powers of the president of the United States, and I don't want to be a part of that." Among the impediments he listed were the War Powers Act and the Congressional Budget Act.[80]

George W. Bush's taking the United States into the "war on terror" and Barack Obama's subsequent response to the financial crisis of 2008, different as they were and opposed as the men were on most issues, reflected the common approach that both parties' leaderships took when they occupied the White House: to push their powers to the limits, and sometimes beyond. With a new sort of leader installed in power there after the election of 2016, the situation ramped up to a new, unprecedented level. Donald Trump possessed no background in electoral politics, expressed no evident interest in the history of White House practice and little curiosity about what contemporary elites understood and expected, and believed himself equipped to "drain the swamp" in Washington and replace it with his own brand of leadership, which derived from his own experience as a deal-maker and from his own self-confident, gut reaction to situations. With his arrival on the scene, two highly combustible elements came into proximity with each other: as previously described, a long history of centralization of power in the White House and an occupant of the place who acted a bit like an unguided missile—one who felt unconstrained by precedent, common expectations, or legalisms; one whose confidence in his own ability to transform reality seemed limitless; and one who was willing to bend or ignore rules, norms, and principles to get what he wanted. Furthermore, he possessed an uncanny ability to connect personally with a significant segment of the electorate, who found him to be honest, refreshing, outspoken, and understanding of their own problems. He had the makings of a classic demagogue, and his willingness to break precedents and his ability to upset predictions made him the kind of elusive actor who was difficult to pin down. Highly predictable in his unpredictability, transparent in many of his psychological traits, naked in his neediness and ambition, he also was enough of an eccentric and creative artist that he might be able to achieve some things that other more predictable, buttoned-down politicians could never hope to accomplish. There was just enough of a possibility that some good could come out of his time in office that one could not count him out as a political leader.

Other possibilities were much grimmer. Without perceivable boundaries on what actions he might take, with a willingness to make up stories and explanations that might justify a particular situation, and with a seeming willingness to sacrifice any individual, group, or cause for his own desired end, there seemed to be no limit to what he might be willing to do if people around him did not succeed in holding him back.

Almost all of the members of his own party—many, if not most, of whom had derided and denounced him during the primary election season—fell into line in support either after his nomination or after his election in November 2016. The person they had once referred to as a "con artist," a "delusional narcissist," or a "cancer on conservatism" now had their backing. Now and then, one was willing to speak out, either obliquely or sometimes forthrightly, in opposition to his rhetoric or his actions. Senators Jeff Flake, Bob Corker, Lisa Murkowski, John McCain, Mitt Romney, and Susan Collins come to mind. Several other Republicans, such as Senators Lindsay Graham and Ben Sasse, occasionally spoke up, but most remained silent. Several Cabinet members and top White House officials, such as Secretary of State Rex Tillerson and White House Chief of Staff John Kelley, openly contradicted the president in the press, and Secretary of Defense Jim Mattis summarily resigned his post when the president announced an immediate withdrawal of American troops from Syria (later rescinded). When Trump referred to a judge who had ruled against his immigrant asylum policy as "an Obama judge," Chief Justice John Roberts rebutted the notion, calling it a profound misunderstanding of the role that judges play in the American system. Conservative political columnists such as Charles Krauthammer, George Will, and Jonah Goldberg were outspoken in their criticism. None of this seemed to have much effect, however. Asked how he would grade himself after two years in office, the president replied, "Look, I hate to do this, but I will do it, I would give myself an A-plus. Is that enough? Can I go higher than that?"[81]

"There is no end to what Trump will ask of his party," David Brooks observed. "He is defined by shamelessness, and so there is no bottom. And apparently there is no end to what regular Republicans are willing to give him."[82] Emerging in recent years is the willingness of the party in power to grant greatly expanded powers to "their man" in office, while those on the outside remain intent on limiting that power. It is like almost everything else in national politics—party preference largely determines which side of the coin one ends up on. Paradoxically, after years of party decline—as they have lost many of their primary functions, including the ability to influence the nomination of candidates, their sway in determining party principles and platforms, and their setting of the political agenda—they have exerted almost unprecedented control over congressional voting on crucial issues.[83]

This kind of partisanship undermines the separation of powers established by the Constitution to guard against excessive power developing in any one of the separate branches or in any one individual's hands. In these circumstances, the system of checks and balances ceases to work. The most likely threat to democracy remains one-man rule, and preventing it depends upon individuals and groups working inside and outside of government to block such a takeover. As Arthur Schlesinger and others have pointed out, the most vulnerable target for a would-be dictator is in the realm of foreign policy. The war-making power provides limitless possibilities for mischief, and ever since Hiroshima and Nagasaki, the nuclear genie has been out of the bottle. We have managed to survive the atomic age thus far with no more nuclear weapons being dropped, but the possibility that such a thing might happen increases as time goes by, raising the specter of the ultimate nightmare of nuclear catastrophe.

The less dangerous but more likely development, however, lies in the more mundane accumulation of smaller actions and events that gradually concentrate power in a single person's hands. From the beginning, Donald Trump indicated a willingness to flout long-established rules, norms, and even legalities. His continued connection to his business interests, appointment of underqualified children and relatives to high position, demand for personal loyalty from all members of his administration, extreme condemnation of criticisms directed at him, reliance upon gut instinct rather than upon informed advice, and reluctance to accept constraints upon his personal whims all made for a volatile mix of unpredictability and dangerous gamble. "You've got someone who is defining the presidency very differently," observes presidential historian Michael Beschloss. "Trump is essentially saying, 'I'm not going to operate just within the boundaries that the founders might have expected for 200 years. I'm going to operate within the boundaries of what is strictly legal, and I'm going to push those boundaries if I can.'"[84]

Trump's contempt for legal niceties, and even for the law itself, manifested itself in a variety of ways. During the 2016 campaign, he took pleasure in threatening to put Hillary Clinton in jail if he won. He egged audiences on when they shouted, "Lock her up." He encouraged fans to physically assault people who voiced dissent in his crowds. He called the election rigged until he won it and threatened not to accept the verdict if he lost, suggesting that people resist it, only to tout his victory afterwards in extravagant terms. Once in office, he constantly belittled his attorney general, Jeff Sessions, whom he had appointed to the office. He unloosed Twitter barrages at any criticism directed against him. He called special counsel Robert Mueller's investigation of his administration a "witch hunt" and wrongly characterized the make-up of its staff. He embraced and extravagantly praised foreign dictators, such as Russia's Vladimir Putin, North Korea's Kim Jong Un, China's Xi Jinping, Egypt's Abdel Fatah al-Sissi, and the Philippines' Rodrigo Duterte. He denied and excused villainous behavior, such as the murder of *Washington Post*'s Jamal Khashoggi by Saudi operatives, the death of American student Otto Warmbier in North Korean prisons, and the participation of Russia's Vladimir Putin in the American election of 2016. He issued presidential pardons to friends and allies, such as Arizona sheriff Joe Arpaio and author Dinesh D'Souza. And the list continues.

President Trump's assault on the rule of law presents his most immediate and worrying threat to democracy. That, however, according to Charles Krauthammer, is "the very core of his appeal: his persona of the tough guy you can trust to protect you."[85] The appeal of the strong man has resurrected itself many times and in many places across the course of history, but not very often in the United States. To the degree that it reflects a large segment of public opinion in this country, it undermines the long-held notion of American exceptionalism. What Trump offers, according to author Robert Kagan, "is an attitude, an aura of crude strength and machismo, a boasting disrespect for the niceties of the democratic culture that he claims, and his followers believe, has produced national weakness and incompetence."[86]

American nationhood, incubated in the Revolution and instantiated in the Constitution, ultimately rests upon the rule of law—the notion that no person is above the law. Whatever name we give to the system by which we are governed—a democracy, a republic, self-rule, or something else—the greatest threat to its survival lies in its possible capture by some unprincipled tyrant. The most likely breeding ground for such a result is the presidency, and thus it is something we must keep a watchful eye on.

Challenge 11—Disappearing Norms and General Dysfunction in Politics

The United States is a paradoxical place. Large, powerful, and imposing, it can also appear at times to be small, intimate, and vulnerable. Idealistic, dreamy, and high-minded, it can also show itself as practical, clear-sighted, and tough-minded. Generous and hopeful as it often is, it also displays signs of self-centeredness and pessimism. Built on progress, it can also succumb to bouts of gloom and depression. These anomalies derive in part from the nation's vast size and diversity; the varieties of people who populate it; their many attitudes, beliefs, and assumptions; and the conflicting interests, groups, and organizations that seek recognition and preferment. It also derives from the contradictoriness, ambivalence, and indecision of the individuals who make up those groups. People can be up one minute, down the next; hopeful and optimistic today, down and dejected tomorrow. Time casts its pervasive shadow, and people are liable to change from moment to moment, only to revert to where they had been previously. Life is predictable only in its unpredictability.

The kinds of contradictions that characterize American society in general carry over into the political realm. The pride people take in the nation and the deference they pay its flag, the Constitution, its monuments, symbols, and all of the other accouterments of government live side by side with the contempt many of them display toward public officials, the criticism they voice toward governmental activities, the lack of confidence and trust they express to pollsters, and the dearth of knowledge and appreciation they display for what government does. People react strongly against any hint that Social Security benefits might be reduced, that potholes won't be filled, that snow won't be cleared, or that peace and order won't be maintained. At the same time, they resist higher taxes, avoid military service, pay little attention to news from the capital, and don't know much about history. Their low estimates of Congress as a body rest easily side by side with generally high opinions of their own representatives in Washington. In sum, Aristotelian logic, which tells us that A is A and cannot be B, is in short supply. In the current world of politics, A *is* B and B *is* A, depending upon the situation and upon people's mood of the moment.

Politicians in a democracy act the way one might expect them to act under the circumstances, being responsive to the many conflicting ideas, ideals, pressures, assumptions, hopes, and fears of the people they are elected to represent. If any motivating factor stands out above the rest, it is that most elected officials most of the time are highly concerned about the next election. That is one of democracy's strengths, but it can also have negative consequences. Too often, short-term thinking blinds people to long-term impacts. Money tends to talk louder than public need. Partisanship overwhelms commitment to the public good. Parochialism overshadows broad-mindedness. Ignorance stands in the way of knowledge. Fear overwhelms hope. Cycles of prosperity and recession, progress and regression, and high hopes and dark pessimism confuse the situation. Yet, above it all, few people express a desire to move elsewhere, and the United States has for generations been a magnet for those around the world who hope to enjoy freedom, better themselves, and pursue their dreams.

Disagreement and contentiousness are inevitable in any society, and the United States is no exception. American history is riddled with conflict, from disagreements over slavery, westward expansion, monetary policy, taxation, and immigration to battles over labor unions, jobs, corporate regulation, war and foreign affairs, environmental policy, and morality. Individual differences of opinion coagulate in organizational activity and pressure groups that form to push particular policy agendas. From the very beginning, governmental leaders have had to figure out how to balance the imperative for majority rule, which democracy demands, with minority rights, to which it is sworn to defend. They have had to pay deference to tradition and continuity even while they have sought to advance change and progress. Always, they face the necessity of adjudicating countless quarrels and disagreements among competing interests, belief groupings, geographical sections, and economic classes.

Quickly moving beyond the Founders' aversion to the establishment of political parties, early national leaders found themselves adjusting to the inherent tendency of the populace to divide into factions, as discussed by James Madison in *Federalist #10*, thus establishing the presence of a "loyal opposition" as a fundamental part of the system. Thomas Jefferson eloquently expressed the necessity for accommodation and forbearance after the bitter election of 1800, when he memorably stated in his inaugural address, "We are all republicans, we are all federalists." Ever since, the health and success of democracy have depended upon people's willingness to engage in deliberation and debate and to compromise on issues when no consensus is forthcoming. Political scientist Pendleton Herring wisely observed that "for a loyal opposition to function and for parties to be accepted as salutary influences, there must be common acceptance of the procedures and institutions by which men are to struggle for political power."[87]

Unfortunately, as has already been described, such acceptance has lagged of late in Congress and in the executive branch. Further evidence of dysfunction can be found in the bureaucracy, in governmental activity at other levels and in other places, and in the populace at large. We can start with the judicial branch. Part of the notion underlying the separation of powers, as it was built into the Constitution, is that judges at every level, culminating in the Supreme Court, will adjudicate cases fairly, honestly, and nonpolitically. No person is above the law, and when the law is applied, it will be done in an impartial and nonpartisan fashion. Most judges and juries, in fact, do operate this way. Our legal institutions and the judges who preside over them are bulwarks of the system and protectors of democracy. There are always some bad apples, some who bow to pressures and bribes, some who are incompetent or unknowledgeable, and some who have bad intentions.

The greatest threat to democracy in this area is the way in which partisanship, which manifests itself most obviously in legislative and executive channels and in the public mind, seeps more and more directly into judicial appointments and into legal deliberations. Throughout American history, partisan thinking has threatened to intrude in judicial issues, never more so than in recent years. Slavery before the Civil War, the regulation of corporate behavior during the Gilded Age, civil rights and civil liberties in the twentieth century, and now abortion, gender relations, government regulation, gun rights, and other hot-button issues have made and will continue to make judicial nominations controversial. The battles that take place regularly now over appointments to the Supreme Court have made it one of the most divisive pressure points in the system. Not since the 1930s, when the "Nine Old Men" on the Court ruled a number of New Deal laws to be unconstitutional, precipitating a constitutional crisis, has the situation been more rancorous. Judicial nominees' promises to act merely like referees in a sporting contest and not to intrude their own opinions in their decisions do not receive much credence any more. It is important, however, that judges do, in fact, endeavor to make the goal of impartiality a reality and that the public maintain trust that the system is working in fair and honest fashion.

Just as judges bear duties and responsibilities to the law, appointed governmental officials and civil service employees possess a mandate to carry out their assigned duties as effectively, impartially, and economically as possible. During the late 1800s, when the rise of corporate, institutional, and governmental bureaucracies emerged to prominence, the term "bureaucracy" was still a neutral one, describing a function necessary to be performed. Referred to variously as the "new class," the "technocracy," and the "white collar" work force, the executives, officials, and office workers who compose a bureaucracy are essential to making any business, organization, or government agency get the job done. Over time, however, the term "bureaucrat" has emerged as more of a pejorative label than a descriptive signifier. People using it tend to imply that they don't approve of what bureaucrats do. Yet, these same individuals then and now expect their Social Security checks to arrive on time, their streets to get cleaned, their food to be kept safe, their air to be kept breathable, and their water to be kept drinkable.

The challenges government bureaucracy presents to democracy are primarily two-fold: first, that it will grow to be too large, intrusive, oppressive, and costly. Too many rules, regulations, quotas, and petty annoyances: some of these are clearly necessary but many of them seem overboard and simply annoying. The second problem occurs when the regime in power has no stake in making the system work efficiently and instead is primarily interested in undermining the system and gumming up the works.

The first thing many people think of when the term "government bureaucrat" is mentioned is the huge size of the beast and the imperviousness to outside criticism of the bureaucratic work force. "The insidious power of the unelected administrative state is easy to understand," author Victor Davis Hanson suggests, since it governs so many important sectors of American life: national security, surveillance, taxes, regulation, criminal justice, and so forth. He observes that by 2017 there were nearly three million civilian federal workers along with 19 million state and local workers.[88] The growth rate of the federal work force, however, has been much more modest than those at other levels of government and in the private sector. Whereas the total number of private sector jobs grew from 28.2 million to 126.7 million between 1940 and 2018, corresponding numbers for state and local government workers were 3.2 million and 19.6 million and for federal government workers were 1.0 million and 2.8 million. After increasing steadily during the 1950s and early 1960s, the number of federal jobs has remained relatively level for the past half century.[89]

Beyond the question of the actual size of the federal bureaucracy, however, has been its impact in directly affecting people's everyday lives. Rules, regulations, paperwork, and red tape give big government a bad name. Author James Miller describes public reaction to all of this, saying that a widespread feeling is that "those who govern have become increasingly remote, often making democracy in practice seem like a puppet show, a spectacle in which hidden elites pull all the strings."[90] Back in the nineteenth century, European social theorist Robert Michels coined the phrase "iron law of oligarchy" to describe how institutions of all types tend to harden, undergo organizational drift, and become attached to the status quo. Author Jonathan Rauch invented the term "demosclerosis" to describe the immobility and inability of our current political setup to react effectively to the challenges confronting it.[91]

The most common criticisms of government throughout our nation's history have been its growing size, its increasing intrusiveness, its inefficiency, and its expanding reach into people's pocketbooks. Nineteenth century "laissez-faire" advocates seemed to resent government's mere presence, at least in principle. Where they would have stopped in stripping it of its functions is hard to say. Laura Ingalls Wilder's daughter, the writer Rose Wilder Lane, along with Ayn Rand and Isabel Paterson, was one of the three founding intellectual "godmothers" of the modern Libertarian movement in the United States. All three of them published books in 1943 that served as texts for true believers on the far right. Lane, in *The Discovery of Freedom*, appeared to be willing to decommission not only Social Security and almost every New Deal agency but also public high schools and even publically financed roads.[92]

By the 1960s and 70s, these kinds of extreme ideas were in retreat and "Social Darwinism," as it had been known since the late 1800s, appeared to have been put to rest. But then Ronald Reagan entered the White House announcing that "government isn't the solution to our problems; it *is* the problem." With Proposition 13 and other anti-tax initiatives arising in California and elsewhere around the same time, and with Grover Norquist getting almost every Republican member of Congress to sign his pledge never to raise taxes, a "New Social Darwinism" emerged to reintroduce laissez-faire type thinking into the realm of intellectual and political respectability. The key practical question remained, "Where exactly do you draw the line on governmental activity?"

Dwight Eisenhower had made his peace with the New Deal during the early 1950s, promising voters that he would administer federal programs more efficiently and frugally and slow down the growth of governmental bureaucracy. Reagan, despite his frequently extremist anti-government rhetoric, proved equally adept at appealing to his political base with well-received words and phrases while also not cutting back very much on actual programs. More extreme conservative academics, talk-show hosts, cable-TV heads, and political pundits, ranging from George Will, Jonah Goldberg, and Charles Krauthammer to Ann Coulter, Rush Limbaugh, Sean Hannity, and Jerome Corsi, constantly egged on presidents and congressional leaders to become more aggressive in slashing taxes and reducing spending, but they did not have to deal with actual people's problems or run for re-election the next time around.

Jonah Goldberg, one of the more historically informed and intellectually respectable conservative pundits and critics of government, traced the fatal turning point in American history to the early 1900s, with the expansion of state power during the progressive era. Intellectuals such as Herbert Croly, Richard T. Ely, Edward A. Ross, Walter Rauschenbusch, and John Dewey joined forces with political leaders such as (especially) Woodrow Wilson, Theodore Roosevelt, and, later on, Franklin D. Roosevelt to build an ever-expanding "administrative state" that subverted the Constitution and rolled over the kinds of practices and traditions that had made America great. Goldberg's assessment: "The regulatory state represents the elevation of a new class, an aristocracy, of men and women who are above the law. This was the original intent of the progressives who set up the administrative state."[93]

In recent decades, federal expenditures have remained in the range of one-fifth of the Gross Domestic Product, with a brief jump to around one-quarter after the financial debacle of 2008. Other indicators of federal activity and regulations show it becoming more intrusive. Federal income tax forms get more and more complicated. Rules and regulations in a variety of areas, ranging from employment practices, work place safety, and food processing to trade rules, automobile emissions, and gender equity, make their weight felt. The *Federal Register*, the official journal of the federal government, which contains agency rules, proposed rules, and public notices, grew from 2,620 pages at first issue in 1936 to 29,000 pages in 1972 and to 97,000 pages in 2016. After Roosevelt's "New Deal," Truman's "Fair Deal," Kennedy's "New Frontier," and Johnson's "Great Society," all of which promoted ambitious programs extending the reach of the federal government, Jimmy Carter proved to be something of an enigma as president, consciously seeking to achieve more of a balance between private activity and government assistance, thus leaving many observers and even members of his own party wondering just where he stood on the political spectrum. Bill Clinton, while generally perceived as being on the left side of the political spectrum, was a leader among a group of "New Democrats" serving as governors around the country during the 1980s, famously observing, "The era of big government is over." Nevertheless, the size and reach of government continued to expand on his watch.

During the 1940s and 50s and later, as the reforms introduced by the New Deal became institutionalized in American life, as Keynesian and other ideas about how to influence economic growth through the use of fiscal and monetary policy came to be accepted, and as various rights revolutions emerged and combined to work for making Bill of Rights guarantees more real, Americans engaged in a continuing debate over just how far the government could and should go in promoting the general welfare. While debates regarding specific programs could generate a fair amount of rancor and heated discussion, there was a lot of rational give and take, individuals in both parties were willing to "cross the aisle" to join with the other side, and often compromises were engineered to prevent stalemate. Arthur Schlesinger captured the tone of moderate left Democrats in his book *The Vital Center* in 1949, pointing toward a middle-of-the-road path to improvement. Harvard economist Alvin Hansen, the key figure in popularizing Keynesian ideas in the United States, was a whirlwind of activity at mid-century in promoting the idea of a "mixed economy," one that blended the best elements of government protection with free market initiative. Pluralist political scientists advanced models of cooperative interaction that relied upon bipartisan support to advance social and economic goals. Democracy seemed to be working effectively when authors such as Daniel Boorstin could write about *The Genius of American Politics* (1953), Henry Steele Commager gained plaudits for writing *The American Mind* (1950), and Daniel Bell captured attention for his book *The End of Ideology* (1960).

There is no advantage to be gained in wishing that we could resurrect a time when greater consensus existed among intellectuals and the general populace. Nostalgia will not bring those times back, and, in many ways, we would not want to go there. But there is this to say for them. Back then, there was much more intellectual interaction and reasoned debate in the corridors of Congress, party battles were not as weaponized, deliberation and compromise were real, money was less of an issue, and democratic norms were more respected. When people asked, *Can Democracy Survive the Cold War?* (1964), it was more of a theoretical issue than an insistent question like it would be today. In the current atmosphere, the possibility of the destruction of our democracy is not such a far-fetched notion. That is something worth pondering.

Also serious in its implications for effective democratic governance is that sometimes elected officials actually attempt to deliberately sabotage government by intentionally making it unworkable. One way to do this is to reduce an agency's effectiveness by "starving the beast," a term frequently heard during the Reagan years. The situation escalated during the Trump era due to his appointments record, attitude toward, and actions directed toward his own Cabinet and other agencies and officials. In *The Fifth Risk*, author Michael Lewis describes what happened in the Energy Department after the president appointed former Texas governor Rick Perry to be Secretary of Energy. In a 2011 presidential debate, Perry had been unable to remember the name of the department after ticking off the first two of three Cabinet departments he wanted to abolish once he became president. By 2017, when he was appointed Energy secretary, he still seemed to have gained little comprehension of what the department actually does. He and other lower ranking officials who were newly appointed to office took almost no interest in learning about the department they were about to run or in working to make it operate effectively. They avoided talking to outgoing Obama administration officials and appeared to disdain anyone they happened to meet there. "They mainly ran around the building insulting people," one outgoing Energy Department official recalled. "There was a mentality that everything that government does is stupid and bad," said another.[94] With regard to the other Cabinet departments, after two years in office, President Trump still had failed to nominate people to fill many positions at all levels, far beyond the record of his predecessors in this respect.

Over at State, Secretary Rex Tillerson was uncommonly slow is filling many high-ranking positions, lowering the morale of many career service employees. Scott Pruitt at the Environmental Protection Agency and Ryan Zinke at Interior, both of whom possessed strong industry ties, were notorious for their aggressive efforts to de-regulate and benefit the industries and interests they were supposed to be overseeing. Both were gone within a couple of years. For White House strategist Steve Bannon, who had played a major role in Trump's election campaign and during his short tenure in Washington in his swashbuckling style had sought to implement his vision of "deconstructing the administrative state," all of this was heartening. In a cover story published a year after the election, *Time* magazine described the entire operation as "The Wrecking Crew: How Trump's Cabinet Is Dismantling Government as We Know It."[95]

Government has always appealed to some schemers as a lucrative target for self-enrichment. Federal officials in many administrations of both major parties have been suspected of or convicted of shenanigans of all kinds. In this one, the President himself and his children were accused of using the office for their own financial benefit. In *America, Compromised*, Harvard law professor Lawrence Lessig writes of a more pervasive, insidious kind of corruption that afflicts government at all levels, contributing to the low regard and low level of trust the public has in its political institutions. Lessig aims his guns not so much at the people who occupy the offices as at the kinds of "institutional corruption" that render ineffective not only political but also social and economic institutions. Damage is done, he contends, "Not by evil souls, but by good souls. Not through crime, but through compromise." In finance, the ratings agencies give excessively high ratings. The media pander to public taste rather than making truth their highest goal. Academic research gets tainted by misplaced bias. The law fails to indict corrupt business leaders who deserve punishment for their wrongdoings. In like fashion, elected leaders spend too much time dialing for dollars and not enough legislating for the public good.[96]

Ultimately, the breakdown and bad behavior of governmental officials and institutions derives less from the actual breaking of the law and more from a lessening respect for and attention to well-established norms and practices that have been put in place over time. As has often been observed, institutional structures and rules alone are not sufficient to channel behavior along correct lines. Rather, it is the internal mechanisms and ethical guidelines that lead people to act in the way they do that matter most. Virtue, in other words, is a prime prerequisite. The Greeks understood this two and a half millennia ago. We understand it, too, today if we stop to think about it.

If our ethical and institutional norms were working more effectively today, our political leaders would not be as polarized as they are in their activities. They would not conduct the public business as if it were a war rather than with mature and reflective deliberation about what can contribute best to the public good. They would not be so beholden to wealthy and powerful interests. They would not resort to trickery and subterfuge to win elections and to pass legislation or prevent the other side from passing theirs. They would shame their colleagues who resort to extreme rhetoric, who travel in lies and distortion, who "spin" so much they've forgotten what the truth is, and whose many poses give hypocrisy a bad name. They would attempt to tamp down partisanship and try to make real all their fine talk about compromise and reaching across the aisle. They would call down members of their own party who violate the norms rather than bowing meekly to what they consider to be the imperatives of getting re-elected.

If our political leaders adhered more closely to the norms and ideals of democracy, they would replace gerrymandering with impartial redistricting after every census.[97] They would cease ill-considered efforts to suppress the votes of people they know would predominantly cast their votes for the other party. That means that they would not place unreasonable limits on voter registration, voter identification, and alternative places and times of voting. They would not eliminate released felons and other whole categories of people from voting because of mistakes they once made.[98] They would not come in, as legislators did in Wisconsin and Michigan, to pass laws restricting the actions of newly elected government officials simply because they were members of the other party.[99] In the current highly polarized climate, these kinds of actions may not be immediately understood for what they are. In the sort of environment envisioned by the Founding Fathers, party had no place, and reason, common sense, and deliberation were what mattered. Maybe someday we will be more inclined to lean in that direction than we do today.

Challenge 12—The Natural Fragility of Democracy

The health and survival of democracy are never guaranteed. They are subject to historical forces and the results of human action and inaction, like everything else. Democracy is a fragile thing. It requires constant vigilance and energetic creativity. Since democracy is such a large and diffuse subject, efforts to define and understand it are inconclusive and never-ending, reminds Bernard Crick, emeritus professor of politics at Birkbeck College in London, whose book *In Defense of Politics* (1962) is recognized as a modern classic. In the most general sense, he says, "what most people mean by democracy is what the Greeks meant by 'polity' or simply political rule, a system that allows for peaceable compromises to be made between ever-present conflicts of values and interests." To get more specific, "good government should be democratic, in both an institutional and a social sense, but also include individual liberties, human rights, economic progress, and social justice—which is something more than equality of political rights."[100]

There are at least three separate ways to approach the subject of democracy: (1) as a principle or doctrine of government; (2) as a set of institutional arrangements or constitutional devices; and (3) as a set of values or types of behavior characterizing the people who make it up, that is, a way of life. In the United States, as this book has emphasized, when we talk about democracy as a system of government, we are really talking about "representative democracy" or "republicanism." Within that context, the two fundamental principles or doctrines that must be operative in a republican form of government are, first of all, popular sovereignty, majoritarianism, or "power to the people," and secondly, legally guaranteed individual rights and liberties and protection in general of minority rights. A healthy tension always exists between facilitating the will of the majority and protecting the basic rights and interests of minorities. The ultimate task of democracies is to avoid falling into the trap of tyrannical or autocratic rule.

Essential to any real democratic practice is a set of legal requirements and institutions that enable the principles of popular sovereignty and individual rights to be effectively maintained. At the heart of this is the rule of law, which bars public officials from the president on down from arbitrarily violating legal rules and principles or acting on their own to violate citizens' guaranteed rights. Among these protections are the Bill of Rights, the Fourteenth Amendment, an independent judiciary, the checks and balances that operate among the three branches of government, and other extra-constitutional rules and norms.

No less essential to the healthy functioning of democracy are the values, habits, and responsibilities that the system instills in the citizenry and in their leaders to inspire and regulate their behavior. Again, these include voting, running for office, or participating in political decision-making in other ways; dispositions such as tolerance, volunteering, responsibility, self-regulation, and openness to new ideas; and values such as freedom, liberty, equality, community, individual opportunity, fairness, justice, honesty, truthfulness, and mercy. Some people will disagree with some of these points, preferring to rely upon a "hidden hand" to produce beneficial results if each person pursues his or her own self-interest. These will be matters of continuing debate among students of democracy.

Beyond the eleven challenges already discussed that beset democratic rule in the United States today, others that could be listed or discussed at greater length include

- the economic problems attending increasingly unequal wealth and income, deindustrialization, job instability, and regional stagnation;
- the domination of the culture by entertainment and distraction, leading to its infantilization, with similar consequences for the citizenry;
- the tendency of the media and the public to grade their politicians as actors on a stage, as if politics were a performance art rather than a system of governance;
- the huge impact of the Internet, surveillance, government secrecy, and social media on elections and government activity;
- the rise of "populist" forms of protest around the globe, the growth of authoritarian regimes, and foreign interference in elections; and
- a growing tendency on the part of partisan leaders not only to seek to defeat their rivals but to actually annihilate the opposition.

Americans have always tended to think of themselves as being different, exceptional, and superior to other peoples, and in some respects they have been right. Clothed in metaphors such as "a city upon a hill," "a beacon to all mankind," and "a lamp lighting the world," our revolutionary example has inspired other freedom-seeking crusades abroad, from the French Revolution of 1789 to liberation movements in Latin America during the early 1800s, widespread upheavals in Europe in 1848, the efforts of the Vietnamese to achieve independence from French colonial rule after World War II, and African anti-colonial statehood movements in the 1960s. Ironically, considering our later intervention in Southeast Asia, Communist leader Ho Chi Minh quoted Thomas Jefferson's words in the Declaration of Independence in announcing Vietnam's own Declaration of Independence in Hanoi in September 1945. But the United States is not immune from the tides of history.

Today, as the nation continues to stand as an example of and defender of freedom around the world, it is also beset by serious challenges to its own longstanding democratic traditions and system of government. In a number of ways, democracy stands besieged here, as it does elsewhere around the globe. In November 2016, Jeff Colgan, in surveying evidence of democratic decline around the world, listed warning signs for those attempting to understand our current situation in the United States, including "media intimidation, the identification and even manufacture of crises or political paralysis to justify emergency measures, attacks on minorities, the scapegoating of foreigners, closing off space for civil society, the rhetorical rejection of the current political system, the weakening of the legislature and the intimidation of its members, the silencing of political opposition, and significant increases in internal security forces."[101]

In the face of serious challenges to the health of democracy, too many people ignore the facts facing them, consider themselves to be too busy to bother, lack the energy to get engaged, or simply succumb to apathy. They rely on polarized positions to sort things out. Economics columnist Robert J. Samuelson states the situation in pungent terms: "We Americans are increasingly given to political escapism. Regardless of our place on the political spectrum—Republican or Democrat, liberal or conservative—we prefer self-serving fictions to messy realities. We avoid unpopular choices by hiding behind ideological platitudes." Today's zeitgeist is conducive to notions of "fake news," "alternative facts," and "post-truth" pontificating, Samuelson says. "Our political culture increasingly values symbolism over substance. That's what I mean by Americans favoring 'self-serving fictions.' Political behavior is shaped by beliefs that are false and goals so impractical as to be unobtainable. But the symbolism has consequences because it inspires feel-

good agendas that elected leaders are expected to achieve. When they predictably fail, popular disillusion deepens. The dynamic works on both left
and right. We cannot govern, it seems, because ideological fervor crowds out
pragmatic realism."[102]

Connected to political dysfunction in Washington, state capitals, cities,
and towns across the country, other changes bode ill for the health of democracy, as has already been discussed. Problems and challenges can be identified
in our educational systems, the press and other mass media, family structure,
class divisions, crime, drug use, community lethargy, leadership vacuums,
and institutional matrix. Columnist David Brooks observes, "We used to
build things." That process includes institutions and public and private organizations. When one looks back to the progressive era of the early 1900s, one
is "struck by how many civic institutions were founded to address the nation's
problems. Not only the Forest Service, but also the Food and Drug Administration, the municipal reform movement, the suffrage movement, the Boy
Scouts, the 4-H clubs, the settlement house movement, the compulsory
schooling movement, and on and on." This was true, too, of other periods in
American life. "We've got just as many problems as previous generations
faced—as many as in the progressive era, I'd say," Brooks mentions. "Why
has there been this decline in civic institution building?" Such organizational
efforts, otherwise referred to as civic capital, continue to exist and to do good
work, but Brooks wonders if now there is "a malaise, a loss of faith in the
future and a loss of expertise in institution building, a sense of general fragmentation and isolation."[103]

The power of popular culture to attract people's attention away from
more serious matters along with reversions to the type of anti-intellectualism
that prevailed so often in the American past points people away from serious
political discussion. "The news is there for people who want it," writes Kevin
D. Williamson in *National Review*. "The problem is: Most don't. Intelligent
commentary has become, practically overnight, a rarified and specialized
interest, like opera."[104] While the tendency has been general, reliance upon
sloganeering and symbolism and the retreat from reasoned argument and
debate has fallen more heavily upon the GOP than it has upon the Democrats.
Richard Nixon finished third in his Duke Law School class, Gerald Ford and
the two Bushes had connections to Yale, and Ronald Reagan was an enthusiastic consumer of conservative political philosophy, but with Donald
Trump, who revealed his aversion to reading and consumption of unbiased
information in a multitude of ways, Republicans found themselves rapidly
drifting away from intellectual concerns.

With many partisans reacting strongly against Barack Obama—not least with regard to his law school professorship, his enthusiastic reading of books, and his well-spoken rhetorical style—there was more motivation to denigrate idea-oriented leaders like him. "The Republican Party's divorce from the intelligentsia has been a while in the making," writes the *Economist*'s Lexington columnist, observing that George W. Bush preferred listening to his "heart" over his "head" when making decisions. (Somewhat similarly, Donald Trump would frequently indicate how much he trusted his gut instincts while making decisions.) After several decades when the GOP claimed to be the party of ideas, Republicanism's "anti-intellectual turn" was a troubling development in the *Economist*'s way of thinking.[105]

Now, deep into the third century of American Democratic experiment, we would be well-advised to recall that the Revolutionary leaders and the writers of the Constitution were well-educated individuals who relied upon the method of intelligence to make their way through a thicket of snares that might have diverted them from their goals of promoting liberty and equality. They were working in a tradition dependent upon and fostering the advancement of reason, deliberation, and debate. No political system has ever been perfect, but within the constraints of human nature and the imperfection of institutions democratic or republican governance has ultimately relied upon the uncovering of facts, the sifting and winnowing of truth, and the application of reason to the solving of society's problems. The Greeks were the first to try; their experiments lasted only a short time. The Roman republic lasted longer but succumbed to history's vagaries, too. Florentines during the Renaissance revived the civic tradition, but it faltered when ranged against the tyrannical tendencies of the time. It was with the outbreaks of the American and French revolutions during the late 1700s that the modern history of democracy came into its own.

The democratic tradition has had a two-fold motivational engine driving it ever since: a strong penchant for individual liberty, freedom of choice, pursuit of opportunity, and protection of rights, on the one hand, and a determination to achieve the public good, on the other. Throughout most of American history, there has been no lack of attention to the first set of goals; much of American history can be written in terms of the waxing and waning of the impulse to achieve the second.

The desire to promote the public good requires that people look sideways, away from themselves, and toward the welfare of their neighbors and fellow citizens. It demands that they loosen their grip on their own individual interest and look toward the interests of others. In 1776, the same year that Jefferson drafted his famous words in the Declaration of Independence, Adam Smith, in *The Wealth of Nations*, introduced the world to his notion of the "invisible hand." This was the idea that when people pursued their own self-interest, through a mysterious process focused around the workings of a free marketplace, the welfare of the general public would be enhanced. His vision was profound and illuminating, but it was only half-right. The same sort of positive results can obtain when people look away from themselves and strive to promote the benefit of those around them—their neighbors, co-workers, community residents, and fellow citizens. When the invisible hand operates in this fashion, it means that each person's individual interests are enhanced by the collective working together of society. The healthy and fruitful tension that exists in the gap between individual and society provides the greatest likelihood that everyone will benefit and prosper together.

Too often in the recent past, the public good has been lost sight of, as attention has shifted toward individual rights and freedoms. That is the message of economist Robert Reich, who in his book *The Common Good* argues that the quality of our civic life has gone downhill of late, as people have lost a sense of connectedness to each other and to the ideals that had once animated them. "The past five decades," he contends, "have also been marked by growing cynicism and distrust toward all of the basic institutions of American society—government, the media, corporations, big banks, police, universities, charities, religious institutions, the professions. There is a wide and pervasive sense that the system as a whole is no longer working as it should." Reich is not naïve enough to believe that everyone can simply get together and eliminate or transcend all of their differences. Democracy was never meant to do that. Rather than trying to get everyone to agree on the common good, Reich wants people to "get into the habit and practice of thinking and talking about it, and hearing one another's views about it. This alone would be an advance." He is especially interested in promoting civic education in schools and enlightening the general public. How did the Founding fathers originally assume and how can we best promote democracy today? Reich's simple answer: "More than anything else, education."[106]

Education does many things, and there is nothing to be gained by oversimplifying it and trying to sum up its excellences in what today we would call a few "sound bites." But to tick off a few of its virtues: It teaches us a vocabulary and instructs us in a language that allows us to perceive, comprehend, interpret, understand, and perhaps critically come to terms with the world around us. It provides perspectives—historical, geographical, sociological, psychological, philosophical, ethical, and religious—that get us outside of our own skin and into a position that, if all goes well, enables us to empathize with other people of different backgrounds and circumstances. It infuses us with a desire to learn, with a sense of wonder and joy in expanding our knowledge and understanding of many things and to appreciate the unending variability of people and the preciousness of each one of them. It helps us to sort things out, to note the differences as well as the similarities of different objects and subjects, to accept that variability is the rule of life and that we all must somehow come to grips with that idea. It assists us when it comes time to assign values to things, actions, relationships, attitudes, and beliefs, and it encourages us to establish an ethical foundation for our lives. It is central to our developing sense of self, to our understanding of who we are and who we want to be. It guides us in our daily lives by helping us sort out our priorities, formulating goals, imagining possibilities, understanding duties and obligations, and appreciating what we have been given. In the end, it confers wisdom, something beyond facts, information, and knowledge— a goal we should all strive to achieve even as we realize our own blind spots and remain aware of our own ignorance.

In a perfect world, everyone would be a philosopher-king of the kind Plato imagined in ancient Greece. But then again, we know how that turned out. Plato was no democrat, and his utopian political vision turned into more of a nightmare than a revelation, more totalitarian than democratic. We can conclude from this that education alone leads to no panacea and that a democratic society requires many things—participation, leadership, tolerance, humility, good will, and decency among them. But as a proximate thing, education will do. It is needed in our leaders and in our followers. The better the education, the better the result. Put everything on a sliding scale and expect that some minimum level of education is achieved at every point.

That, in turn, raises the issue of culture. For, like everything else, education is wrapped up in culture, and if the culture is suspect, its elements will be tainted by the connection. Unfortunately, there is much not to like about current American culture, although it needs to be said that there is much that is admirable, bracing, worthy of respect, and just plain fun to be found in it. Life is complicated. American culture has been called, with some justice, a culture of celebrity, a carnival culture, an infantilized culture, a spectator culture, and more. Foreign correspondent Georgie Ann Geyer, who is in a good position to make comparisons, talks about a vulgarized culture. Airline pilot Chesley B. "Sully" Sullenberger III advises, "This current absence of civic virtues is not normal, and we must not allow it to become normal." Urbanologist Alan Ehrenhalt contends that the notion of character has become an obsolete idea. Government professor Charles Kessler compares the United States to Weimar Germany, suggesting that we are approaching a time in which our civic culture has become so debased that we lack "the virtues necessary to sustain republican government." We are reminded by writer Adam Gopnik that "civilization is immeasurably fragile, and is easily turned to brutality and barbarism. The human capacity for hatred is terrifying in its volatility." Democratic regimes are not immune from the threat. "Democratic civilization has turned out to be even more fragile than we imagined," Gopnik writes, going on to observe that "the resources of civil society have turned out to be even deeper than we knew."[107] In the end, that is our hope. That the forces of light will win out over the forces of darkness. Nobody, least of all our nation's Founders, ever said that maintaining a free society would be easy. Life is full of tensions. It is up to each one of us to resolve those tensions with the best of our will and the best of our effort.

4

A Program for Renewal

Defining and diagnosing problems are always difficult tasks. Proposing solutions poses an even greater challenge. My purpose in this short chapter is not to provide a blueprint or detailed plan of action. Rather, I simply intend here to propose a few suggestions and make some brief comments following from my own perspective. The task is multidimensional, and any effort to approach it must necessarily be multipronged. Institutional change in Washington, statehouses, and localities will be difficult, because practices are so entrenched and each party will be hesitant to do anything that might give the other party an advantage. Personal change, while not easy, is at least something that individuals have some control over in their lives.

I'm a reader, so naturally I think everybody would and should want to read, too. As discussed in this book, however, there are pressures operating against long-form reading by students, young people, and adults. Time-pressures, heavy work schedules, many distractions in the form of entertainment, sports competitions, and especially social media prevent a large portion of us from reading as many books and magazines as we used to. Many people testify that after a steady diet of e-mail, Facebook, Twitter, and so forth, reading more than two or three pages of anything at one time becomes a real challenge. Schools tend to go along with the flow. If you have a habit of browsing college bookstore shelves as I do, you will observe that fewer books are being assigned in classes today than in the past. Professors and observant outside critics have discussed this problem at length. Reading not only provides people with the facts, ideas, concepts, and intellectual schemata they need to perceive, comprehend, and interpret the way the world works. It actually rewires the brain so as to make one better able to understand the complexity, the interconnections, and the meaning of the world around us. The discipline of reading helps us think more clearly, more comprehensively, and more intelligently.

The second thing I would emphasize is making connections with other people that undergird a strong sense of community. A major problem of spending too much time on social media and screens of all kinds is that it diverts us from the kinds of face-to-face interactions that make for friendship, empathy, mutual support, and deep understanding of other people. These are the building blocks of community. Many researchers have noted that body language, eye contact, tone of voice, and speech patterns are equally important with the actual words that are spoken in communicating with other people. Employers want employees who can connect on a personal basis with clients, customers, follow workers, and other people in general. Young people who spend too much time playing video games and watching television and screens of all kinds tend to be more deficient in face-to-face communication than others who spend less time in those activities. These comments are not to deny that the Internet, Google, social media, and other forms of technology are hugely useful and informative. The goal should be to ration screen time, arrive at a useful balance, and pay as much attention to building community as to promoting one's own personal agendas.

Finally, cultivating character as well as creativity will result in people who behave ethically, become good people, play their assigned roles in society, fulfill their social duties and political responsibilities, and fashion a better society in which all people and groups can prosper and flourish. In the words of Walter Lippmann and others, they can build a "good society"—one that will simultaneously strengthen democracy. In this spirit, I offer the following recommendation

Personal Change

Promote interest in reading, from school-age children to older adults. Read history, philosophy, literature, current events, fiction, and other genres that inform us about how society works, how government operates, what makes people tick, how organizations function, how change occurs, and what needs to be done.

Promote newspapers and magazines. Educate people to critically appraise internet information. Inform yourself about political issues and public policy.

Support and promote organizations and institutions that bring people together to learn, cooperate, and solve problems.

Support efforts to inform the electorate and go to the polls on election day.

Promote citizen involvement in political debate, deliberation, and work within the political system.

Reduce use of social media—Twitter, Facebook, and surfing the Internet. Use them responsibly. There is much to be learned from the Internet, but balance is required, as in all things.

Consciously seek out information from a variety of different sources. Do not simply read, watch, or listen to media sources that confirm your already established views or political biases. Engage in critical thinking.

Take someone of different political opinion to lunch. Research shows that more time spent in face-to-face contact with other people reduces antagonism and breeds cooperation.

Cultivate good character in your children and seek to promote it in others by example, word, and deed.

Promote neighborhood and community organizations and activities. Seek to enrich a sense of local community.

Support efforts to research political and social issues. Demand objective reporting and analysis.

Demand honesty, open-mindedness, and integrity from political, economic, and social leaders.

Do not tolerate false accusations, extreme rhetoric, and frivolous statements by people. Demand facts, evidence, and logical reasoning.

When one is personally attacked with false information, be quick to rebut the misbegotten assertions and defend the truth, not depending upon people's good sense and fair-mindedness to automatically rectify the situation.

Trust, but verify. Be skeptical but not cynical. Support politicians, reporters, researchers, and authorities who act responsibly, fairly, intelligently, and adult-like.

Institutional Change

Restore long held norms, practices, and traditions of openness and fairness in committee hearings, floor debates, conference committees, and voting in both houses of Congress. Continue the filibuster in the U.S. Senate but only in unusual cases, not as a normal device to require 60 votes rather than the usual majority to pass legislation.

Abolish gerrymandering by replacing partisan committees with nonpartisan, objective boards to redraw election districts after each decennial census.

Encourage respectful conversation, interaction, and give-and-take between the parties both formally and informally.

Reduce incentives for senators and representatives to travel home frequently, starting out by reducing their travel compensation.

Do something to reduce the flood of dollars in politics. Enact campaign finance reform. Promote governmental funding of campaigns. Put practical limits on campaign spending while also maintaining the principle of freedom of speech.

Expect that the president will hold at least bimonthly formal and open press conferences and will make Administration officials similarly open for questions from the press. Make government activities and statistics open and available for press and public scrutiny.

Expect open positions in government (starting with Supreme Court justices) to be filled in timely fashion. Depoliticize the nomination and confirmation processes as much as possible. End the warlike atmosphere in Washington.

Value facts, information, scientific investigation, and expertise. Maintain the free flow of information. Engage in rational discussion and debate.

Back efforts to support and maintain newspapers, magazines, other forms of journalism, and independent research institutions that engage in fair and objective methods of getting at the truth.

Epilogue

Americans have traditionally viewed themselves as being different and, in many ways, exceptional. Unlike other nations, who have defined themselves by their history, geography, and bloodlines, the United States has identified itself by its ideas, its ideals, and its visions of a better life ahead. While history is important to it, the nation remains primarily a future-oriented one. During the 1830s, Alexis de Tocqueville observed that since Americans possessed no feudal past, no king, and no aristocracy against which to revolt, their Revolution was in a real sense a conservative movement. The patriots who sought independence from the mother country were in a real sense simply demanding the protection of their well-established "rights as Englishmen." Most of them were little interested in bringing basic change to society and economic relations. In England, conservative thinker Edmund Burke gave his blessing to their venture.

Ironically, Washington, Adams, Jefferson, Madison, Paine, and their cohorts were launching one of the most radical transformations in world history. Theirs was a revolution not of oppressed classes, fire-breathing ideologues, or violent street fighters. Rather, it was one of ideas—the kinds of ideas that were so concisely but eloquently expressed in the Declaration of Independence and then embodied practically in the framework of the Constitution and the Bill of Rights. Those ideas included first and foremost freedom, or liberty, and also equality, along with community, fairness, justice, and progress.

The revolutionaries' greatest fear was tyranny—specifically of the type exercised by King George III (his many transgressions inspired the bulk of the words of the Declaration) but even more so the prospect of greater tyrannical oppression in the future, which the colonists perceived to be implicit in the new taxes and coercive acts imposed upon them after the Seven Years' War. That worry about tyranny was more potential than real, but it seemed real enough to many Americans at the time.

The Constitution the Founders fashioned after the war was geared to ward off such tyranny by establishing a more powerful and effective framework of government, along with multiple safeguards and protections. While not inspired by democratic notions as they were understood at the time (direct rule by the people), it did contain the seeds of an evolving concept of democracy that would encompass, as time went by, equality for women, blacks, and other races; more direct input in political decision-making by average citizens; and a whole panoply of rights and privileges not yet widely accepted during the 1780s. There was a strong communitarian strain in the writings of Alexis de Tocqueville. He was impressed by Americans' prolific tendency to form and participate in voluntary associations, which he considered to be highly advantageous to the advancement of the egalitarian society that he saw shaping up. American democracy has prospered most mightily when high degrees of civic participation and community spirit obtained.

The presence of free political institutions and the protections provided by the legal system, combined with the energetic work habits of the populace, the presence of seemingly unlimited natural resources, and the creative and entrepreneurial spirit of businessmen and ordinary citizens worked together to unleash economic growth and development that brought unprecedented prosperity to the nation as time went on. As historian David Potter and others have pointed out, democracy was nurtured in the cradle of prosperity. Things begin to get more difficult when economic growth falters.

Just as democracy can be cultivated and nurtured in a variety of ways and can operate in different fashions, it can erode and die in different ways. Past flourishing is no guarantee of current health or future continuity. Our recent history has been disconcerting in this regard, and people naturally are wondering what is going on. The nation, in many minds, is veering off course, and clear guidance and direction are lacking. Democracy seems to be dumbing down. Is there a bottom to all of this, we wonder, and what can we do about the situation?

Some Americans in recent years have become more responsive to antidemocratic, autocratic ideas. It is part of a worldwide phenomenon. "But elite disenchantment with democracy has been rising for many years," notes British author Edward Luce. "According to the World Values Survey, which offers the most detailed take on the state of global public opinion, support for democracy has plummeted across the Western world since the fall of the Berlin Wall. This is particularly true of the younger generations."[1] It appears that we have a major educational task confronting us. Rather than simply waving the flag and relying on tradition to make a convincing argument, the times call for soberer, more realistic thinking, relying upon facts, clear-minded reasoning, and history. "Democratic politics can be an unsightly spectacle," cautions Jan-Werner Muller, author of *What Is Populism?* "Even idealists will sometimes be tempted to agree that the best argument against it is a five-minute conversation with the average voter. But it isn't an accident that democracy is also the system that provides the most room for freedom, however imperfectly, and does the best job of protecting basic rights." Democracy's ultimate resource is the ability, when things get really bad, to "throw the bastards out," and "knowing whether the bastards are doing a bad job" doesn't require "a tremendous amount of social scientific knowledge."[2]

In a hugely complicated, contradictory, and opaque environment, it is always the counsel of wisdom to try to work assiduously to enlarge our purview, to try to get our facts straight, and to be open to argument and evidence, while always being aware of our own limited knowledge and intelligence. Essential to the task is information obtained from a free and freewheeling press, whose reporters delve into their subjects with every bit of intelligence, experience, and verve at their command. We should always remember, in the words of *Washington Post* media critic Margaret Sullivan, that "there is a clear difference between truth and propaganda, between fact and falsehood. And that journalists in the reality-based press are on the saving side—if there is one—of that increasingly dangerous divide."[3] In the short run, we need to do everything in our power to support healthy and vibrant newspapers and investigative journalism. In the longer run, we need to promote education in general and civic education in particular so as to bolster the deliberations of our politicians and elected leaders and the participation of the electorate.

Temptation abounds to succumb to cynicism, disgust, apathy, anger, and just plain lack of attention. There have been times in our nation's history when people's lack of attention, as they went about their daily rounds of work, play, family, and social life, was perceived to be a healthy indicator that government institutions were functioning efficiently and effectively. They presumably did not need much oversight. That time has past. As economist Paul Krugman reminds us, institutions are essential, but they are not able to do it alone. They need people to stay alert, to pay attention, and to do the right thing. "For while we may congratulate ourselves on the strength of our political institutions," he writes, "in the end institutions consist of people and fulfill their roles only as long as people in them respect their intended purpose. Rule of law depends not just on what is written down, but also on the behavior of those who interpret and enforce that rule."[4]

We have all seen the warning signs. Around the world, the rise of populism, anger and discontent, illiberal democracy, and outright authoritarianism indicates that things are out of synch. The United States is not immune. Growing polarization, we have been warned, could lead toward an ungovernable America. This book has identified twelve major challenges to democracy today. Like all lists, this one is somewhat subjective and arbitrary. Many of the items could have been categorized or combined in different ways, and all of them are intertwined with the each other. But they provide a good starting point for further deliberation and discussion. The lessons to be drawn from this foray into the subject include

- the supreme importance of education, intelligence, reason, and adherence to facts and truth in all of our thoughts and actions;
- the reality of political polarization and reversion to tribalism in our society, which are unhealthy extensions of the fundamental realization that people will always differ in their opinions and that politics is all about resolving such conflicts and divisions;
- the necessity for genuine discussion, debate, and deliberation in our political decision-making;
- the importance of norms, traditions, and what Tocqueville referred to as the "habits of the heart" that govern political decision-making over and above the words and structural elements of institutions that are in place;
- the stylized dance, healthy tension, fruitful relationship, or whatever one may call it that exists between leaders and the public that elects them into office will determine whether we succeed or fail. We expect voters to be informed, vigilant, tolerant, and devoted to the common good. We expect no less of our leaders, but we also demand more from them. Instead of partisan particularity, we need to have opposing groups wedded to fact, willing to compromise, and devoted to what is best for society as a whole and not just their own personal interests; and
- character, ethics, and community are all interrelated, and upon them depends the ultimate outcome.

Finally, the contradictions and tensions to be found throughout our democratic polity are ever present and never ending. We solve problems one day only to be confronted with new ones the next. Democracy is never a "done deal," to put it in colloquial terms, but rather a continuous quest. Elusive, unfinished, seemingly distant, and finally unrealizable, it provides us with a process and extends to us an idealistic goal: that a large group of citizens, diverse in backgrounds and goals, conflicted among themselves in how to proceed and act, can find practicable ways of achieving a good society in which the majority generally holds sway, while those in the minority are protected in their rights and liberties. Beyond that, we cannot ask. It is up to us to achieve the promise.

Suggestions
for Further Reading

Alan I. Abramowitz. *The Great Alignment: Race, Party Transformation, and the Rise of Donald Trump*. New Haven: Yale University Press, 2018.

Emory University political science professor Alan Abramowitz describes shifts in election patterns during the past forty years. Donald Trump did not create today's party divisions, but he effectively leveraged them, relying upon negative polarization to appeal to long-building resentments and divisions in the electorate along racial, ethnic, religious, ideological, and geographical lines. Presidential elections turn on the results of a handful of swing states, deadlock prevails in Congress, and vituperative rhetoric characterizes political debate.

Madeline Albright. *Fascism: A Warning*. New York: Harper, 2018.

A former United States secretary of state draws upon her own family's experience as refugees from fascism, her academic training, her diplomatic career, and her continued watchfulness to answer the question: Could fascism come to America? Her qualified "yes" is worrisome. She focuses upon recent manifestations of the phenomenon in Russia, Poland, Hungary, Venezuela, and elsewhere, but also notes warning signs in the United States.

Kurt Andersen. *Fantasyland: How America Went Haywire, A 500-Year History*. New York: Random House, 2017.

America's current condition of "post-truth," "fake news," and mass delusion is not new but has characterized our culture from the very beginning. Founded by wishful dreamers, magical thinkers, and true believers, the United States also generated P.T. Barnum-type hucksters, mesmerists, Hollywood dream purveyors, UFO trackers, conspiracy-theory nuts, and many other sorts of fantasists.

Carol Anderson. *One Person, No Vote: How Voter Suppression Is Destroying Our Democracy*. New York: Bloomsbury, 2018.

Anderson, a professor of African American studies at Emory University, catalogues the myriad ways in which African American voting rights have been suppressed since the Supreme Court's 2013 decision in *Shelby County vs. Holder*. These include photo ID requirements, gerrymandering, voter roll purges, poll closures, and reduced time allowed for regular and early voting.

James Ball. *Post-Truth: How Bullshit Conquered the World*. London: Biteback Publishing, 2017.

Arguing that truth is under siege in the United States, Ball sees Princeton philosopher Harry Frankfurt's notion of "bullshit" as a form of thinking that discards the distinction between truth and falsehood. Taking note of Donald Trump's rise in the United States and the Brexit controversy in Great Britain, Ball describes who is spreading BS and why it works and offers suggestions for combatting it.

Max Boot. *The Corrosion of Conservatism: Why I Left the Right*. New York: Liveright, 2018.

Long-time Republican journalist and book author Max Boot left his party the day after the November 2016 election. After emigrating with his family from the Soviet Union at the age of six, he became an enthusiastic celebrant of American freedoms and a staunch defender of democracy, press freedom, rule of law, and ethical and political norms. He sees Donald Trump as a threat to all of these things and lambastes Republicans for not standing up to him.

Jason Brennan. *Against Democracy*. Princeton: Princeton University Press, 2016.

Brennan, a professor of economics and public policy at Georgetown University, weighs the virtues of "epistocracy" (a system granting special weight to the votes of people who possess higher degrees of knowledge or expertise) over against those of democracy. Brennan warns that weaknesses in democratic systems—especially low levels of information, participation, and commitment of average voters—expose them to danger.

David Callahan. *The Cheating Culture: Why More Americans Are Doing Wrong to Get Ahead*. New York: Harcourt, 2004.

The co-founder of the Demos public policy center provides a tour of cheating in America, citing instances when old rules and standards have been broken or simply bypassed. Corporate scandals, doping athletes, cheating students, and fraudulent tax deductions reflect the impact of an unfettered market place, increasing economic inequality, a multitude of temptations, and ethical agnosticism.

Timothy P. Carney. *Alienated America: Why Some Places Thrive While Others Collapse*. New York: Harper, 2019.

Carney, a visiting fellow at the American Enterprise Institute, attributes the alienation of the electorate to the differential effects of place. People living in areas doing well economically tended to vote for Hillary Clinton in 2016, and places suffering from job loss and lack of hope and opportunity were more likely to be attracted to Donald Trump. For many, the American Dream has become far less real than it used to be.

Nicholas Carr. *The Shallows: What the Internet Is Doing to Us*. New York: W.W. Norton, 2010.

The author's *Atlantic* magazine cover story "Is Google Making Us Stupid?" hit a cultural nerve at a time when the Internet and social media were rapidly transforming our lives. Carr, one of our most influential computer skeptics, warns that too much screen time can literally rewire people's brains, making it more difficult for them to read and think deeply, thus leaving them less able to concentrate, contemplate, and reflect.

William Davies. *Nervous States: Democracy and the Decline of Reason*. New York: W.W. Norton, 2018.

After tracing the rise of factual and scientific thinking over the last four centuries, Davies, a political economist at the University of London, examines developments in recent years that have caused people to retreat from facts and objective reasoning and to rely more heavily upon emotions and irrational thought processes. Words have become weapons and knowledge is less valued for its accuracy than for its impact on people.

Larry Diamond. *The Spirit of Democracy: The Struggle to Build Free Societies Throughout the World*. New York: Times Books, 2008.

Diamond, a senior fellow at the Hoover Institution and a professor at Stanford University, discusses the recent history of democratic institutions in countries around the world. After tracing the historical origins of democracy and describing its essential elements, he chronicles the worldwide democratic boom that occurred after 1974, followed by a recession in the phenomenon after 1999. His discussion of the internal and external factors driving democracy applies to the Unites States, as it does to every other country.

E. J. Dionne, Jr., Norman J. Ornstein, and Thomas E. Mann. *One Nation after Trump: A Guide for the Perplexed, the Disillusioned, the Desperate, and the Not-Yet Deported*. New York: St. Martin's, 2017.

Three eminent political observers ask how the U.S. got into the political mess it is in. Part I diagnoses the problem, with chapters on the meaning of the 2016 election, the crisis of the media and the rise of "alternative facts," the disappearing norms of American politics, our penchant for authoritarianism, "populism" and the new politics of the far right, and the impacts of immigration, culture, and economics on voters. Part II offers proposals for change.

Francis Fukuyama. *Trust: The Social Virtues and the Creation of Prosperity*. New York: Free Press, 1995.

Social scientist Fukuyama assesses a wide range of national cultures to locate practices and principles that create prosperous and successful societies. He concludes that moral bonds and social trust are crucial for well-functioning economies and societies. He argues that high degrees of social trust, vital civil associations, and cohesive communities are conducive to democratic development.

William A. Galston. *Anti-Pluralism: The Populist Threat to Liberal Democracy.* New Haven: Yale University Press, 2018.

A senior fellow at the Brookings Institution catalogs the challenges, dilemmas, and ultimate advantages of liberal democracy amidst growing populism in the United States and around the world. Like other Western democracies, the United States experiences increasing social divisions, economic insecurity, governmental failure, and public rancor. Despite difficulties and divergent interests, liberal democracy remains the best remedy available.

Jason Grumet. *City of Rivals: Restoring the Glorious Mess of American Democracy.* Guilford, CT: Lyons Press, 2014.

Grumet, the president of the Bipartisan Policy Center, says a divided public and a dysfunctional Congress are leading many people to wonder about the long-term viability of democracy. Although many forces have weakened Congress in recent years, he expresses optimism that the ship can be turned around and democratic decision-making can be made to work again.

Jonathan Haidt. *The Righteous Mind: Why Good People Are Divided by Politics and Religion.* New York: Pantheon, 2012.

Haidt, a professor of psychology at the University of Virginia, applies the lessons of moral psychology, anthropology, and history to understand why people divide into opposing groups and why they are so certain of their own righteousness. Their "groupishness" brings them joy but also divides them from others unwilling to join them.

Richard Hofstadter. *Anti-Intellectualism in American Life.* New York: Alfred A. Knopf, 1963.

Hofstadter's classic analysis helps place the current situation of "fake news," "alternative facts," and dumbed-down political discussion in historical context. Too many citizens fail to inform themselves on issues, respect facts, and seek the truth, instead settling for a comfortable, self-reassuring, but false, version of it. Writing in the wake of Senator Joseph McCarthy and rising right- and left-wing extremism, Hofstadter analyzed the "dark side" of mass politics and especially the hostility many people show toward elites and intellectuals.

James Davison Hunter. *The Death of Character: Moral Education in an Age without Good and Evil.* New York: Basic Books, 2000.

Hunter, a sociologist at the University of Virginia, bluntly asserts that "character is dead. Attempts to revive it will yield little. Its time is past." With all the current talk about the need to restore values and revive character, he suggests that most Americans don't want to pay the price, which would include the reassertion of moral authority, a commitment to bring our behavior into conformity with our stated values, and a renewal of creedal order that constrains, limits, obligates, and compels.

Michiko Kakutani. *The Death of Truth: Notes on Falsehood in the Age of Trump*. New York: Tim Duggan Books, 2018.

The former chief book critic for the *New York Times* explains how truth has become an endangered species in America and considers the implications this has for politics and governance. She catalogues a broad array of causal factors, including weaponized news organizations, the Internet, theories of postmodernism and deconstruction, historical relativism, a war on science and expertise, narcissism, and the embrace of subjectivity.

James T. Kloppenberg. *Toward Democracy: The Struggle for Self-Rule in European and American Thought*. New York: Oxford University Press, 2016.

Kloppenberg, a professor of intellectual history at Harvard, ranges back and forth across the Atlantic to trace how democracy was imagined, understood, and practiced from ancient Greek times to its modern emergence during the 1700s and 1800s. Primarily focused on the United States, the author observes that beyond being a set of political practices, democracy also constitutes an ethical ideal.

Lawrence Lessig. *America, Compromised*. Chicago: University of Chicago Press, 2018.

In five chapters on Congress, finance, the media, the academy, and the law, Harvard law professor Lawrence Lessig contends that Americans are uncomfortable with the way things are heading and concludes that "institutional corruption" is rampant. That includes compromise, corner-cutting, backsliding, and failing to pay attention, all of which undermine democracy.

Steven Levitsky and Daniel Ziblatt. *How Democracies Die*. New York: Crown, 2018.

Focusing on politics in Latin America, Europe, and developing countries, the authors show how democracies can die in ways other than by direct force and subversion. More common has been the slow process of democratic norms and freedoms being strangled and eliminated by elected leaders who systematically attack procedural safeguards, politicize legal institutions and the courts, punish or even jail political opponents, undermine independent governmental agencies, rig elections, and disable investigative journalists.

Michael Lewis. *The Fifth Risk*. New York: W.W. Norton, 2018.

Honing in on the first year and a half of the Trump administration, popular author Michael Lewis illustrates how political leaders guided by financial ambition, anti-government ideology, and incompetence can render democratic government ineffective. Focusing on the Energy, Agriculture, and Commerce Departments, he describes bureaucratic failure on many levels.

Edward Luce. *The Retreat of Western Liberalism*. New York: Atlantic Monthly Press, 2017.

Growing frustration with slow economic growth, increasing class divisions, declining trust and confidence in political and economic institutions, and political polarization are not confined to the United States. Retreat from liberalism is a worldwide phenomenon. Since 2000, some twenty-five democracies have failed, as democratic values, institutions, and practices come under assault.

Alasdair MacIntyre. *After Virtue: A Study in Moral Theory*, 2d ed. Notre Dame: University of Notre Dame Press, 1984.

A professor of philosophy at Vanderbilt argues that the language of morality is in a grave state of disorder. People have largely lost their comprehension, both theoretical and practical, of morality. Especially problematic is the doctrine of emotivism, holding that moral judgments are simply expressions of personal preferences, attitudes, and feelings and thus are not binding on others. Consequently, they have little ability to guide our actions.

Robert W. McChesney and John Nichols. *The Death and Life of American Journalism: The Media Revolution That Will Begin the World Again*. Philadelphia: Nation Books, 2010.

Statistics on declining readership, ad revenues, profits, staff levels, and the physical artifact making up daily papers are stark and troubling. Predictions of the actual demise of print journalism are rife. The authors explain the causes driving newspapers' decline, sketch possible solutions, and examine alternate business models that might provide a viable basis for ongoing reporting.

Lee C. McIntyre. *Post-Truth*. Cambridge: MIT Press, 2018.

This brief, but incisive, primer argues that challenges and even assaults on truth have occurred before but that never before have they been "so openly embraced as a strategy for the political subordination of reality." Separate chapters focus on science denial, cognitive bias, the decline of traditional media, the rise of social media and "fake news," and the intellectual influence of postmodernism.

John McWhorter. *Doing Our Own Thing: The Degradation of Language and Music and Why We Should, Like, Care*. New York: Gotham Books, 2003.

McWhorter, a professor of linguistics and cultural critic located at the University of California, traces a precipitous decline in the language used by ordinary Americans. Everyday speech, along with poetry, political oratory, and journalism, has abandoned formal usage in favor of casual expression. Arising out of the 1960s counter-culture, these changes make it difficult to convey ideas and arguments effectively.

Farhad Manjoo. *True Enough: Learning to Live in a Post-Fact Society*. Hoboken: Wiley, 2008.

Published more than a decade ago, *True Enough* was startlingly insightful in predicting the rise of media fragmentation, the decline of objectivity, information bias, and assaults on the notion of truth itself. Manjoo analyzed how constant technological change facilitated an increasingly skeptical, polarized, and partisan public willing to accept information that conformed to its preconceptions, while dismissing information that challenged or refuted them.

Thomas E. Mann and Norman J. Ornstein. *It's Even Worse Than It Looks: How the American Constitutional System Collided with the New Politics of Extremism.* New York: Basic Books, 2012.

Mann and Ornstein describe a political system heading toward institutional collapse and one characterized by polarization and partisan deadlock, refusal to compromise and collaborate, ideological extremism, and inability or unwillingness to persuade the public and their fellow legislators through factual analysis and reasoned argument. All of this is facilitated by an increasingly partisan media.

Pankaj Mishra. *Age of Anger: A History of the Present.* New York: Farrar, Straus and Giroux, 2017.

This erudite intellectual history of the last several centuries serves as a backdrop for the current world situation, in which people in many countries are expressing their disdain and, indeed, hatred for other groups, parties, and governments. Individuals and groups exhibiting paranoia, belligerence, racism, and misogyny trace their origins to thinkers and demagogues who attempt to make political capital out of the fears and concerns of ordinary people.

Ian I. Mitroff and Warren Bennis. *The Unreality Industry: The Deliberate Manufacturing of Falsehood and What It Is Doing to Our Lives.* New York: Oxford University Press, 1989.

Three decades ago, *The Unreality Industry* foretold the situation we are in today in an age of postmodernism, "fake news," and "alternative facts." The authors' prescience is evident in their discussion of many of the themes being sounded today, including artificial reality, pseudo reality, the trivialization of political rhetoric, the rise of "infotainment," and the childlike behavior of some of our leaders.

Tom Nichols. *The Death of Expertise: The Campaign against Established Knowledge and Why It Matters.* New York: Oxford University Press, 2017.

Why in a time when people have access to more information than ever before do they fall victim to fake news and fraudulent thinking while turning their backs on the experts who could provide them with valid knowledge? The rise of the Internet, where answers to questions are only a click away, leads people to overestimate their ability to sort things out and to think they are on an equal footing with doctors, diplomats, teachers, and politicians.

Cailin O'Connor and James Owen Weatherall. *The Misinformation Age: How False Beliefs Spread.* New Haven: Yale University Press, 2019.

Two professors of logic and the philosophy of science examine how people can succumb to mistaken reasoning and how false beliefs arise, persist, and spread. They train their sights on political polarization, confirmation bias, pressures to conform, information cascades, propaganda, misuse of reputation, and other factors undermining effective democratic deliberation.

George Packer. *The Unwinding: An Inner History of the New America*. New York: Farrar, Straus and Giroux, 2013.

Packer, a staff writer for the *New Yorker* magazine, suggests that seismic shifts over a single generation have led to a deeply divided society. Possessing unprecedented freedom in the realm of culture, Americans find themselves increasingly powerless to affect their lives economically and socially in a positive way. Packer alternates broad, sweeping sociological and historical analysis with focused narratives about a handful of typical Americans.

Thomas E. Patterson. *Informing the News: The Need for Knowledge-Based Journalism*. New York: Vintage Books, 2013.

Patterson, a professor of government and the press at Harvard University, calls for transforming journalistic education in the United States by expanding knowledge-based journalism to help practitioners become more deeply informed about the subjects they cover. Journalists must get their facts right, but they also need to help readers understand their significance by placing those facts in proper context.

Neil Postman. *Amusing Ourselves to Death: Public Discourse in the Age of Show Business*. New York: Penguin Books, 1985.

Translated into a dozen languages, *Amusing Ourselves to Death* is a classic analysis of how the electronic media have reshaped our culture. The book suggests that public discourse increasingly takes the form of entertainment, and it asks important questions: What happens when the public becomes infatuated with and seduced by media? Are the media conducive to freedom or do they imprison us? Do they enhance or degrade democracy?

Matthew Pressman. *On Press: The Liberal Values That Shaped the News*. Cambridge: Harvard University Press, 2018.

Pressman, a professor of journalism at Seton Hall, identifies the 1960s and 70s as decades when newsgathering transformed itself, adopting the basic practices and principles that guide it today. The ruling ideal of objectivity, which had arisen during the 1910s and later, gave way to increased analysis, interpretation, skepticism, and adversarialism. In catering to what consumers desired, newspapers became more reader-friendly at the same time that public trust in them waned.

Robert B. Reich. *The Common Good*. New York: Alfred A. Knopf, 2016.

An economist, former U.S. secretary of the Treasury, and best-selling author argues for elevating the notion of the "common good" in an environment dominated by division, self-interest, cynicism, and crass materialism. People's lost sense of connectedness with each other, he argues, has dire implications for democracy. Reich calls for revitalizing leadership, resurrecting truth, and recommitting to civic education for all.

Sophia Rosenfeld. *Democracy and Truth: A Short History*. Philadelphia: University of Pennsylvania Press, 2019.

    With truth in apparent crisis under current conditions facing modern democracy, University of Pennsylvania professor Sophia Rosenfeld investigates the causes of that crisis. She hones in on shifts in the mass media and entertainment and on the rise of the Internet as disruptive forces that undermine trust in authority and sources of factual information. She calls on journalists to remain committed to objective reporting along with increased efforts at fact-checking and urges support for institutions designed to promote fact-gathering and truth.

Zachary Roth. *The Great Suppression: Voting Rights, Corporate Cash, and the Conservative Assault on Democracy*. New York: Crown, 2016.

    Roth, a national reporter for MSNBC, describes a variety of schemes whereby Republicans seek to reduce the numbers of people who go to the polls in order to improve their chances for winning elections. Methods used include eliminating limits on money in politics, gerrymandering electoral districts, reducing early voting, installing voter ID laws, and disenfranchising felons.

Alan Rusbridger. *Breaking News: The Remaking of Journalism and Why It Matters Now*. New York: Farrar, Straus, and Giroux, 2018.

    Pulitzer Prize-winning author and former editor-in-chief of *The Guardian*, Rusbridger says the newspaper industry is a sickly thing in many parts of the world. He analyzes the radical transformation that news is going through, as technology reconfigures the process, the Internet rules everything, and wealthy individuals and profit-seeking corporations gobble up independent newspapers without being committed to traditional journalistic values.

Greg Sargeant. *An Uncivil War: Taking Back Our Democracy in an Age of Trumpian Disinformation and Thunderdome Politics*. New York: Custom House, 2018.

    Chapters on voter suppression, "democratic backsliding," the proliferation of lying and disinformation, political polarization, the withering of congressional norms, and executive aggrandizement convincingly lay out the problems challenging democracy. Sargeant offers a variety of proposals aimed at curing these problems but admits that no easy solutions are in sight.

Hedrick Smith. *Who Stole the American Dream?* New York: Random House, 2012.

    Citing the work of historian Arnold Toynbee, a former *New York Times* reporter warns readers that the United States could follow in the footsteps of twenty-one other great civilizations in a precipitate fall, after rising to the heights in previous decades. We have become two different countries, sharply divided by money, power, and ideology.

Timothy Snyder. *On Tyranny: Twenty Lessons from the Twentieth Century*. New York: Tim Duggan Books, 2017.

Yale history professor Snyder utilizes his expertise in Eastern European history to comment upon the current malaise characterizing American democratic institutions. His twenty warnings for the American people include: defend institutions, beware of the one-party state, believe in truth, investigate, contribute to good causes, and be kind to the language.

Cass R. Sunstein. *#republic: Divided Democracy in the Age of Social Media*. Princeton: Princeton University Press, 2018.

Sunstein, a Harvard law professor and former Obama administration official, addresses concerns about digital media, the new information environment, and the Internet. He describes echo chambers that merely repeat what people want to hear, warns against terrorist groups that exploit social media for their own ends, decries online fragmentation that stands in the way of conversation and deliberation, and urges planned encounters that expose people to other people, views, and ideas.

Michael Tomasky. *If We Can Keep It: How the Republic Collapsed and How It Might Be Saved*. New York: Liveright, 2019.

Tomasky, a columnist, author, and editor of *Democracy: A Journal of Ideas*, says political polarization is nothing new but has prevailed throughout most of the nation's history. Following thirty-five post–World War II years of unusual national consensus, the breakdown of comity in the 1980s resulted from many factors, including the ideological bent of the modern conservative movement, growing racial tensions, increased immigration, divisions on social issues like abortion, widening gaps in income and wealth, and a dramatically transformed media environment.

Peter Wehner. *The Death of Politics: How to Heal Our Frayed Republic after Trump*. New York: HarperOne, 2019.

To this long-time Republican political advisor, President Trump is the culmination of a long-developing trend in the United States—public contempt for politics. Many Americans have lost hope that we can collectively solve our problems. Our task must now be to recover practices of morality, religion, civility, deliberation, moderation, and compromise.

Diana West. *The Death of the Grown-Up: How America's Arrested Development Is Bringing Down Western Civilization*. New York: St. Martin's, 2007.

Syndicated columnist Diana West asks why it is so difficult to find grownups in the United States today. The culture has become infantilized, she contends, a place where it is difficult to differentiate adults from kids, where parents find it hard to set limits for their children and often act like them, where standards and values have given way to a bland relativism, and where people have forgotten how to tell right from wrong.

Alan Wolfe. *The Politics of Petulance: America in an Age of Immaturity.* Chicago: University of Chicago Press, 2018.

Boston College emeritus professor of political science Alan Wolfe locates the central problem currently facing American democracy not so much in the man sitting in the White House as in the electorate that put him there. Allowing that Donald Trump sometimes acts like a petulant child and that his ascendancy to power has been a disaster, Wolfe aims his primary critique at the immature culture of the United States and the people who compose it.

Kevin Young. *Bunk: The Rise of Hoaxes, Humbug, Plagiarists, Phonies, Post-Facts, and Fake News.* Minneapolis: Graywolf Press, 2017.

Kevin Young, a poet and the director of the Schomburg Center for Research in Black Culture at the New York Public Library, turns his attention to the long history of hoaxes, fantastic stories, humbugs, and what lately has been called fake news as they have developed over the course of several centuries in the United States. Americans have been peculiarly vulnerable to being taken in by fakers and frauds.

Fareed Zakaria. *The Future of Freedom: Illiberal Democracy at Home and Abroad.* New York: W.W. Norton, 2003.

After initial chapters defining democracy, describing its historical development, and placing it in its international setting, Zakaria addresses many current problems besetting democracy in the Unites States, including declining of trust in institutions, weakening political parties, distortions caused by money in politics, the death of authority, and the decline of elites.

Chapter Notes

Preface

1. Thomas Jefferson, letter to Charles Yancy, January 6, 1816.

Introduction

1. Robert Pogue Harrison, "The True American," *New York Review of Books*, August 17, 2017, p. 14.

2. Michael Kammen, *People of Paradox* (New York: Alfred A. Knopf, 1972); Kammen, ed., *The Contrapuntal Civilization: Essays Toward a New Understanding of the American Experience* (New York: Thomas Y. Crowell Co., 1971).

3. Franklin quoted in Walter Isaacson, *Benjamin Franklin: An American Life* (New York: Simon & Schuster, 2003), 459.

4. James Miller, *Can Democracy Work? A Short History of a Radical Idea, from Ancient Athens to Our World* (New York: Farrar, Straus and Giroux, 2018), 91, 99.

5. On the foundational principles of democratic, or republican, government, see, for example, Ralph Henry Gabriel, *The Course of American Democratic Thought*, 2d ed (New York: Ronald Press, 1956), chap. 2; J. Roland Pennock, *Democratic Political Theory* (Princeton: Princeton University Press, 1979), chap. 1; James T. Kloppenberg, *Toward Democracy, The Struggle for Self-Rule in European and American Thought* (New York: Oxford University Press. 2016), chaps. 6–9; and Fareed Zakaria, *The Future of Freedom: Illiberal Democracy at Home and Abroad* (New York: W.W. Norton, 2003), 18–20.

6. The "Moynihan Rule" was stated many different times in slightly different forms.

Chapter 1

1. Ralph Henry Gabriel, *The Course of American Democratic Thought*, 2d ed (New York: Ronald Press, 1956), 12; Harold J. Laski, *The American Democracy: A Commentary and an Interpretation* (New York: Viking, 1948), 17; John Keane, *The Life and Death of Democracy* (New York: W. W. Norton, 2009), 276–79.

2. Quoted in Richard Hofstadter, *The American Political Tradition* (New York: Alfred A. Knopf, 1948), 4.

3. Ibid., 5.

4. Quoted ibid., 6.

5. Seymour Martin Lipset, *The First New Nation: The United States in Historical and Comparative Perspective* (New York: Basic Books, 1963).

6. "Liberal democracy as we understand it today in fact only properly took root across the Western world in the early years of the new century," writes Simon Reid-Henry in *Empire of Democracy: The Remaking of the West Since the Cold War, 1971–2017* (New York: Simon & Schuster, 2019), 3.

7. Diane Ravitch, *The Revisionists Revised: A Critique of the Radical Attack on the Schools* (New York: Basic Books, 1978), 167–68.

8. Richard Hofstadter, *Anti-Intellectualism in American Life* (New York: Alfred A. Knopf, 1963).

9. Washington quotation from his Farewell Address; Madison quoted in Ross L. Finney, *The American Public School* (New York: Macmillan, 1921), 38.

10. The standard multivolume history of American education is Lawrence A. Cremin, *American Education*, 3 vols. (New York: Harper and Row, 1970, 1980, 1988). Other useful studies include Carl L. Bankstrom, III, *Public Education, America's Civil Religion: A Social History* (New York: Teachers College Press, 2009); Rush Welter, *Popular Education and Democratic Thought in America* (New York: Columbia University Press, 1962); and R. Freeman Butts, *Public Education in the United States: From Revolution to*

Reform (New York: Holt, Rinehart and Winston, 1978).

11. James T. Kloppenberg, *Toward Democracy, The Struggle for Self-Rule in European and American Thought* (New York: Oxford University Press, 2016), 257.

12. Quoted in Finney, *The American Public School*, 13.

13. James Davison Hunter, *The Death of Character: Moral Education in an Age Without Good and Evil* (New York: Basic Books, 2000), 37.

14. Bernard Bailyn, *Education in the Forming of American Society: Needs and Opportunities for Study* (Chapel Hill: University of North Carolina Press, 1960), 14.

15. Bankston and Caldas, *Public Education—America's Civil Religion*, 24–25.

16. Ibid., 28–29.

17. Butts, *Public Education in the United States*, 94.

18. Hunter, *The Death of Character*, 47–48.

19. Merle Curti, *The Social Ideas of American Educators* (Totowa, NJ: Littlefield, Adams and Co., 1966), chaps. 9, 11, 12, and 14.

20. Butts, *Public Education in the United States*, 188–89.

21. Ibid., 193.

22. Benjamin R. Barber, "America Skips School: Why We Talk So Much about Education and Do So Little," *Harper's*, November 1993, p. 43.

23. There is a vast literature on the history of American journalism. See, for example, Michael Emery and Edwin Emery, *The Press and America: An Interpretive History of the Mass Media* (Englewood Cliffs, NJ: Prentice Hall, 1988); Robert A. Rutland, *The Newsmongers: Journalism in the Life of the Nation, 1690–1972* (New York: Dial Press, 1973); Michael Schudson, *Discovering the News: A Social History of American Newspapers* (New York: Basic Books, 1978); and Christopher B. Daly, *Covering America: A Narrative History of America's Journalism*, 2d ed (Amherst: University of Massachusetts Press, 2018).

24. Matthew Pressman, *On Press: The Liberal Values That Shaped the News* (Cambridge: Harvard University Press, 2018), 23–31. Pressman's book about changes in press practices and in public reaction to them after the mid-twentieth century is hugely insightful, and my analysis here relies heavily upon it.

25. Kristol quoted ibid., 211.

Chapter 2

CHALLENGE 1

1. Richard Hofstadter, *Anti-Intellectualism in American Life* (New York: Alfred A. Knopf, 1963), 301.

2. David Leonhardt, "The Myth of Education Skepticism," *New York Times*, March 19, 2018.

3. Paul Begala, "Let's Ban Thinking!" *Newsweek*, July 16, 2012, p. 18.

4. Catherine Rampell, "Who Hates College? A Lot of Conservatives," *Washington Post*, December 29, 2017.

5. Reuven Brenner, "Accelerate Education," *American Affairs* 1 (Winter 2017): 20; Motoko Rich, "As Graduation Rates Rise, Experts Fear Diplomas Come Up Short," *New York Times*, December 26, 2015.

6. David Robinson, "Can U Read Kant?" *Wall Street Journal*, May 13, 2008.

7. Richard Arum and Josipa Roksa, *Academically Adrift: Limited Learning on College Campuses* (Chicago: University of Chicago Press, 2011), 36, 55, 59, 121.

8. Josh Mitchell and Douglas Belkin, "Fewer Americans Value a College Degree, Poll Finds," *Wall Street Journal*, September 8, 2017.

9. Jan-Werner Muller, "Blaming the People," *Nation*, October 9, 2017, p. 31; Jason Brennan, *Against Democracy* (Princeton: Princeton University Press, 2016), ix, 14, 23–53.

10. Lloyd Omdahl, "Republic if We Can Keep It," *Fargo Forum*, July 30, 2011.

11. Cal Thomas, "Ignorant Nation," *Aberdeen* (SD) *News*, September 19, 2017.

12. Sreve Chapman, "The Fiscal Fantasy," *Chicago Tribune*, August 21, 2011.

13. George Will, "The Price of Political Ignorance," *Washington Post*, January 2, 2014.

14. Thomas E. Patterson, *Informing the News: The Need for Knowledge-Based Journalism* (New York: Vintage Books, 2013), 5.

15. During the 1920s, Walter Lippmann stood out among those raising serious questions about democratic government. Georgetown University professor Jason Brennan's *Against Democracy* is a compelling recent book raising doubts about continued reliance upon democracy in the United States.

16. Diane Ravitch, *The Revisionists Revised: A Critique of the Radical Attack on the Schools* (New York: Basic Books, 1978), 4.

17. Jean M. Twenge, *iGen: Why Today's Super-Connected Kids Are Growing Up Less Rebellious, More Tolerant, Less Happy—and Com-*

pletely Unprepared for Adulthood (New York: Atria Books, 2017), 169, 284–86, 307–8.

18. Rod Dreher, "Intellectual Void Robs U.S. Society of Reason," *Sioux Falls Argus Leader*, December 2, 2009.

19. Mark Bauerlein, *The Dumbest Generation: How the Digital Age Stupefies Young Americans and Jeopardizes Our Future* (New York: Jeremy P. Tarcher/Penguin, 2008), 16.

20. Robinson, "Can U Read Kant?"

21. Jay Mathews, "Better Civics Classes Won't Save American Politics; Ignorance Is Part of Our Culture," *Washington Post*, March 5, 2018.

22. Edward Luce, *The Retreat of Western Liberalism* (New York: Atlantic Monthly Press, 2017), 121–22.

23. Christopher Dale, "What We Don't Know About Civics Can (and Will) Hurt Us," *Minneapolis Star Tribune*, December 23, 2017.

24. Gary Rosen, "Advanced Civics," *New York Times Book Review*, November 18, 2001, 64.

25. "Civic Education," *CQ Researcher*, February 3, 2017.

CHALLENGE 2

26. Robert A. Dahl, *On Democracy* (New Haven: Yale University Press, 1998), 85–86.

27. Philip Meyer, *The Vanishing Newspaper: Saving Journalism in the Information Age* (Columbia: University of Missouri Press, 2009), 19, 23, 43. Other books on the crisis in journalism include Jack Fuller, *What Is Happening to News: The Information Explosion and the Crisis in Journalism* (Chicago: University of Chicago Press, 2010); Robert W. McChesney and John Nichols, *The Death and Life of American Journalism: The Media Revolution That Will Begin the World Again* (Philadelphia: Nation Books, 2010); and David M. Ryfe, *Can Journalism Survive? An Inside Look at American Newsrooms* (Malden, MA: Polity, 2012).

28. David T. Z. Mindich, *Tuned Out: Why Americans Under 40 Don't Follow the News* (New York: Oxford University Press, 2004), 2–5.

29. McChesney and Nichols, *The Death and Life of American Journalism*, x; Obama quoted on p. ix. See also Meyer, *The Vanishing Newspaper* and Ryfe, *Can Journalism Survive?*

30. "Trust in Media," *CQ Researcher*, June 9, 2017.

31. Penelope Muse Abernathy, *The Expanding News Desert* (Chapel Hill: University of North Carolina School of Media and Journalism, 2018), 12, 14, 27.

32. Ibid., 16–17; Abernathy and Steve Cavendish, interviewed by Judy Woodruff on *PBS News Hour*, January 31, 2019.

33. Abernathy, *The Expanding News Desert*, 28–29.

34. Robert Kuttner and Hildy Zenger, "Saving the Free Press from Private Equity," *American Prospect*, Winter 2018, pp. 22–24.

35. Margaret Sullivan, "Your Paper's Being Wrecked: Stand By It," *Washington Post*, January 29, 2019.

36. Abernathy, *The Expanding News Desert*, 30–31.

37. John Nichols and Robert W. McChesney, "The Death and Life of Great American Newspapers," *Journalists and Journalism*, April 6, 2009.

38. "The President-Elect," *Time*, December 6, 1968, p. 30.

39. Douglass Cater, *Power in Washington: A Critical Look at Today's Struggle to Govern in the Nation's Capital* (New York: Random House, 1964), 223–24.

40. Broder quoted in Richard W. Lee, ed., *Politics and the Press* (Washington: Acropolis Books, 1970), 62–64.

41. E. J. Dionne, Jr., Norman J. Ornstein, and Thomas E. Mann, *One Nation After Trump: A Guide for the Perplexed, the Disillusioned, the Desperate, and the Not-Yet Departed* (New York: St. Martin's Press, 2017), 37; Alex Shephard, "Paper Tiger," *New Republic*, January/February 2018, p. 10.

42. Farhhad Manjoo, *True Enough: Learning to Live in a Post-Fact Society* (Hoboken: Wiley, 2008), 4.

43. Mitch Landrieu, *In the Shadow of Statues: A White Southerner Confronts History* (New York: Viking, 2018), 88.

44. Max Boot, *The Corrosion of Conservatism: Why I Left the Right* (New York: Liveright, 2018), 19.

45. Report quoted in Eric Alterman, "Asymmetric Warfare," *Nation*, December 31, 2018, p. 6. See also Kathleen Hall Jamieson and Joseph N. Cappella, *Echo Chamber: Rush Limbaugh and the Conservative Media Establishment* (New York: Oxford University Press, 2008).

46. Nick Anderson, "As Trump Rips Media, More Flock to the Field," *Washington Post*, September 17, 2018.

47. Jaclyn Peiser, "Website Revs Up, With Magazine's Help, to Cover More New York News," *New York Times*, September 27, 2018.

CHALLENGE 3

48. John Maynard Keynes, *The General Theory of Employment, Interest and Money* (1936, reprint New York: Harcourt, Brace and World, 1964), 383.

49. Two spirited accounts of Americans' continuing penchant for fantasy and unreality are Kurt Andersen, *Fantasyland: How America Went Haywire, a 500-Year History* (New York: Random House, 2017) and Kevin Young, *Bunk: The Rise of Hoaxes, Humbug, Plagiarists, Phonies, Post-Facts, and Fake News* (Minneapolis: Graywolf Press), 2017.

50. Frederick Jackson Turner, "The Significance of the Frontier in American History," in his *The Frontier in American History* (New York: Henry Holt, 1920), 209–14.

51. Andersen, *Fantasyland: How America Went Haywire*, 84.

52. Michiko Kakutani, *The Death of Truth: Notes on Falsehood in the Age of Trump* (New York: Tim Duggan Books, 2018), 13, 17.

53. On the development of democratic ideas from the 1600s through the early 1800s, see James T. Kloppenberg, *Toward Democracy: The Struggle for Self-Rule in European and American Thought* (New York: Oxford University Press, 2016).

54. Morton White, *Social Thought in America: The Revolt Against Formalism* (New York: Viking Press, 1949). See also Paul K. Conkin, *Puritans and Pragmatists: Eight Eminent American Thinkers* (New York: Dodd, Mead and Co., 1968) and John Patrick Diggins, *The Promise of Pragmatism: Modernism and the Crisis of Knowledge and Authority* (Chicago: University of Chicago Press, 1994).

55. On the intellectual contributions of progressive thinkers, see, for example, Eric F. Goldman, *Rendezvous with Destiny: A History of Modern American Reform* (New York: Vintage Books, 1956); Michael McGerr, *A Fierce Discontent: The Rise and Fall of the Progressive Movement in America, 1870–1920* (New York: Free Press, 2003); Robert M. Crunden, *Ministers of Reform: The Progressives' Achievement in American Civilization, 1889–1920* (New York: Basic Books, 1982); and Charles Forcey, *The Crossroads of Liberalism: Croly, Weyl, Lippmann, and the Progressive Era, 1900–1925* (New York: Oxford University Press, 1961).

56. Kallen quoted in Goldman, *Rendezvous with Destiny*, 154.

57. Jon H. Roberts, *Darwinism and the Divine in America: Protestant Intellectuals and Organic Evolution, 1859–1900* (Madison: University of Wisconsin Press, 1988), 13, 31, 67, 87, 117.

58. Henry F. May, *The End of American Innocence: A Study of the First Years of Our Own Time, 1912–1917* (New York: Alfred A. Knopf, 1959), 6, 19, 393.

59. Peter Novick, *That Noble Dream: The 'Objectivity Question' and the American Historical Profession* (Cambridge: Cambridge University Press, 1988), 134–35.

60. Walter Lippmann, *A Preface to Morals* (1929, reprint Boston: Beacon Press, 1960), 3, 9.

61. Joseph Wood Krutch, *The Modern Temper: A Study and a Confession* (New York: Harcourt, Brace and World, 1929), 71.

62. Novick, *That Noble Dream* 145.

63. Ibid., 253–58.

64. Thurman W. Arnold, *The Symbols of Government* (New Haven: Yale University Press, 1935), 9, 17, 229; Arnold, *The Folklore of Capitalism* (New Haven: Yale University Press, 1937), 115.

65. Nietzsche quoted in Arthur C. Danto, *Nietzsche as Philosopher* (New York: 1965, reprint New York: Columbia University Press, 1980), 79; Bernd Magnus and Kathleen M. Higgins, eds., *The Cambridge Companion to Nietzsche* (New York: Cambridge University Press, 1996), 29–30.

66. Richard Rorty, *Philosophy and the Mirror of Nature* (Princeton: Princeton University Press, 1979), 315–18, 389–94; Putnam quoted in Paul Thagard, *The Brain and the Meaning of Life* (Princeton: Princeton University Press, 2010), 37.

67. Simon Blackburn, *Truth: A Guide* (New York: Oxford University Press, 2005), xiii.

68. See, for example, Charles Newman, *The Post-Modern Aura: The Act of Fiction in an Age of Inflation* (Evanston: Northwestern University Press, 1985); David Lehman, *Signs of the Times: Deconstruction and the Fall of Paul de Man* (New York: Poseidon Press, 1991); James Ball, *Post-Truth: How Bullshit Conquered the World* (London: Biteback Publishing, 2017).

CHALLENGE 4

69. Jill Lepore, *These Truths: A History of the United States* (New York: W.W. Norton, 2018), xiv–xv.

70. "Season of Statistics," *Time*, December 1, 1967, p. 38.

71. Trump quoted in Ruth Marcus, "A Nauseating Betrayal of American Values," *Washington Post*, June 16, 2018.

72. David Patrikarakos, *War in 140 Characters: How Social Media Is Reshaping Conflict in the Twenty-First Century* (New York: Basic Books, 2017), 264.

73. Margaret Sullivan, "It's Time to Take Mic Away from Conway," *Washington Post*, December 18, 2018.

74. Lee C. McIntyre, *Post-Truth* (Cambridge.: MIT Press 2018), 1, 5.

75. Margaret Sullivan, "We've Managed to Cheapen the Concept of 'Fake News,'" *Washington Post*, January 9, 2017; Ben Guarino, "Fake News Spreads 'Farther, Faster' Than Truth on Twitter, Study Finds," *Washington Post*, March 10, 2018.

76. David M. J. Lazer, et al., "The Science of Fake News," *Science* 359 (March 9, 2018): 1094–96; Seth Bernstein, "On Twitter, Tweets Spreading Fake Info" (AP story), *Sioux Falls Argus Leader*, January 26, 1919.

77. Jan-Werner Muller, "Blaming the People," *Nation,* October 9, 2017, p. 33.

78. Marvin Kalb, *Enemy of the People: Trump's War on the Press, the New McCarthyism, and the Threat to American Democracy* (Washington, D.C.: Brookings Institution Press, 2018), 128.

79. E. J. Dionne, Jr., Norman Ornstein, and Thomas E. Mann, *One Nation After Trump: A Guide for the Perplexed, the Disillusioned, the Desperate, and the Not-Yet Deported* (New York: St. Martin's Press, 2017), 37–38.

80. Michiko Kakutani, "Why *1984* Is a 2017 Must-Read," *New York Times*, January 27, 2017.

81. Wehner quoted in Karen Tumulty, "No Longer on the Campaign Trail, but Still Untethered by Facts," *Washington Post*, January 25, 2017.

82. Glenn Kessler, "Trump Averaged 15 False Statements a Day in 2018," *Washington Post*, December 31, 2018.

83. Schwartz and Sullivan quoted in Sullivan's column, "Vicious, Vile and Soulless," *Washington Post*, October 5, 2018.

84. Cailin O'Connor and James Owen Weatherall, *The Misinformation Age: How False Beliefs Spread* (New Haven: Yale University Press, 2019), 167.

85. Michael M. Grynbaum, "Challenge to President and His View of News," *New York Times*, February 2, 2019.

86. Jim Rutenberg, "Chipping Away at the Enemy," *New York Times*, October 29, 2018.

87. Frank Rich, *The Greatest Story Ever Sold: The Decline and Fall of Truth from 9/11 to Katrina* (New York: Penguin, 2016), 3–4.

88. Dionne, Jr., Ornstein, and Mann, *One Nation After Trump*, 60–61.

89. Nicholas Kristof, "Lies in Guise of News in the Trump Era," *New York Times*, November 13, 2016.

90. Kathryn Olmstead, "A Conspiracy So Dense," *The Baffler*, November/December 2018, p. 42.

91. Eric Zorn, "One Nation, Under Delusions," *Chicago Tribune*, January 6, 2017.

92. Charlotte Alter and Michael Scherer, "The Truth Is Out There," *Time*, October 17, 2016, p. 31.

93. Orwell quoted in Charles Lewis, *935 Lies: The Future of Truth and the Decline of America's Moral Integrity* (New York: Public Affairs, 2014), xii.

94. On people's receptiveness to deceitful and misleading statements, see Amanda Carpenter, *Gaslighting America: Why We Love It When Trump Lies to Us* (New York: Broadside Books, 2018).

95. Thompson quoted in Rick Hampson, "Next Commander in Chief Might Have to Play Entertainer in Chief," *USA Today*, February 21, 2016.

96. Harry G. Frankfurt, *On Bullshit* (Princeton: Princeton University Press, 2005), 60–61.

97. Ted Anthony and Ron Fournier, "The Mythic Presidency," *Mitchell* (SD) *Daily Republic*, February 1, 2008.

98. Timothy Egan, "Good News: Democracy Has a Pulse," *New York Times*, November 10, 2018.

99. David Brooks, "When Politics Becomes Your Idol," *New York Times*, October 31, 2017.

100. Max Boot, *The Corrosion of Conservatism: Why I Left the Right* (New York: Liveright, 2018), 129.

101. Richard Cohen, "The Bobblehead Brigade," *Washington Post*, May 16, 2017.

102. Tali Sharot and Cass R. Sunstein, "Why Facts Don't Unify Us," *New York Times*, September 4, 2016.

103. Steven Sloman and Philip Fernbach, *The Knowledge Illusion: Why We Never Think Alone* (New York: Riverhead, 2017).

104. See also, for example, Sophia Rosenfeld, *Democracy and Truth: A Short History* (Philadelphia: University of Pennsylvania Press, 2019); Ralph Keyes, *The Post-Truth Era: Dishonesty and Deception in Contemporary Life* (New York: St. Martin's Press, 2004); Simon Blackburn, *Truth: A Guide* (Oxford: Oxford University Press, 2005): and Lee McIntyre, *Post-Truth* (Cambridge: MIT Press, 2018).

105. Cass Sunstein, *#republic: Divided Democracy in the Age of Social Media* (Princeton: Princeton University Press, 2017), ix, 5–7.

106. Drew Harwell, "Scramble Is on to Detect, Stop 'Deepfake' Videos," *Washington Post,* June 13, 2019.

107. Franklin Foer, "Reality's End," *Atlantic,* May 2018, pp. 16, 18. See also Foer's provocative book *World Without Mind: The Existential Threat of Big Tech* (New York: Penguin, 2017), which discusses in greater detail the wide-ranging impact and threat of technology, computers, and new media in general. See also Kevin Roose, "Here Come the Fake Videos, Too," *New York Times,* March 4, 2018, and Thomas Kent, "The Next Threat to Truth: 'Deep Fake' Videos," *Washington Post,* September 7, 2018.

108. "Truth and Lies in the Age of Trump," *New York Times,* December 11, 2016.

CHALLENGE 5

109. Robert Samuelson, "The Center Sags, America Groans," *Washington Post,* July 3, 2016.

110. Francis Fukuyama, *Trust: The Social Virtues and the Creation of Prosperity* (New York: Free Press, 1995), 5.

111. E. J. Dionne, Jr., Norman Ornstein, and Thomas E. Mann, *One Nation After Trump: A Guide for the Perplexed, the Disillusioned, the Desperate, and the Not-Yet Deported* (New York: St. Martin's Press, 2017), 224–26.

112. David Brooks, "The Leaderless Doctrine," *New York Times,* March 11, 2014.

113. Graham Allison, "The Myth of the Liberal Order," *Foreign Affairs* 97 (July/August 2018): 133.

114. George F. Will, "Another Casualty of Vietnam: Trust," *Washington Post,* August 3, 2017.

115. Robert D. Putnam, *Bowling Alone: The Collapse and Revival of American Community* (New York: Simon & Schuster, 2000), 46.

116. Tom Nichols, *The Death of Expertise: The Campaign against Established Knowledge and Why It Matters* (New York: Oxford University Press, 2017), ix. 21, 158.

117. Charles P. Pierce, *Idiot America: How Stupidity Became a Virtue in the Land of the Free* (New York: Doubleday, 2009), 8.

118. William Davies, *Nervous States: Democracy and the Decline of Reason* (New York: W. W. Norton, 2019), 26–27, 60–61.

119. Edward Luce, *The Retreat of Western Liberalism* (New York: Atlantic Monthly Press, 2017), 120.

120. Christopher Lasch, *The Revolt of the Elites and the Betrayal of Democracy* (New York: W. W. Norton, 1995), 3–4.

121. Daniel Yankelovich, "Crowding Out the Public," *Phi Kappa Phi Journal,* Winter 1991, p. 11.

122. James M. Kouzes and Barry Z. Posner, *The Leadership Challenge,* 3d ed (San Francisco: Jossey-Bass, 2002); Fred I. Greenstein, *The Presidential Difference: Leadership Style from FDR to Clinton* (New York: Free Press, 2001); Lee Iacocca with Catherine Whitney, *Where Have All the Leaders Gone?* (New York: Scribner, 2007); Rob Jenkins, "What Makes a Good Leader?" *Chronicle of Higher Education,* March 8, 2013, p. A43.

123. Robert D. Kaplan, *Warrior Politics: Why Leadership Demands a Pagan Ethos* (New York: Random House, 2001); Archie Brown, *The Myth of the Strong Leader: Political Leadership in the Modern Age* (New York: Basic Books, 2014); Benedict Carey, "The Boss Unbound," *New York Times,* July 18, 2010.

124. Christopher Caldwell, "The Management Genius of Bill Belichick," *Wall Street Journal,* January 31, 2015; Michael Lewis, *The Fifth Risk* (New York: W. W. Norton, 2018); Douglas A. Ready, "How to Grow Great Leaders," *Harvard Business Review,* December, 2004, p. 93.

CHALLENGE 6

125. Colin Woodard, *American Character: A History of the Epic Struggle between Individual Liberty and the Common Good* (New York: Viking, 2016), 21–22; Peter Wehner, *The Death of Politics: How to Heal Our Frayed Republic After Trump* (New York: HarperOne, 2019), 39.

126. David Selbourne, *The Free Society in Crisis: A History of Our Times* (Amherst, NY: Prometheus Books, 2019), 238.

127. Robert N. Bellah and associates, *The Good Society* (New York: Alfred A. Knopf, 1991), 3–4.

128. Jeffrey Stout, *Democracy and Tradition* (Princeton: Princeton University Press, 2004), 28.

129. Hans Gerth and C. Wright Mills, *Character and Social Structure: The Psychology of Social Institutions* (New York: Harcourt, Brace and World, 1953), 10–11.

130. David Brooks, "Kennedy and Privatizing Meaning," *New York Times,* June 29, 2018.

131. See, for instance, Robert D. Putnam, *Bowling Alone: The Collapse and Revival of American Community* (New York: Simon & Schuster, 2000); Robert Wuthnow, *American Mythos: Why Our Best Efforts to Be a Better Nation Fall Short* (Princeton: Princeton University

Press, 2006); and Robert B. Reich, *The Common Good* (New York: Alfred A. Knopf, 2018).

132. Wuthnow, *American Mythos*, 25, 39; Michael J. Sandel, *Democracy's Discontent: America in Search of a Public Philosophy* (Cambridge: Harvard University Press, 1996), 4.

133. David Brooks, "The Moral Peril of Meritocracy," *New York Times*, April 7, 2019.

134. Putnam, *Bowling Alone*, 288–90.

135. Alasdair MacIntyre, *After Virtue: A Study of Moral Theory*, 2d ed (Notre Dame: University of Notre Dame Press, 1984), 2.

136. Ernest Hemingway, *A Farewell to Arms* (New York: Scribner's, 1929), 191.

137. Jonathan Haidt, *The Happiness Hypothesis: Finding Modern Truth in Ancient Wisdom* (New York: Basic Books, 2006), 164.

138. James Davison Hunter, *The Death of Character: Moral Education in an Age without Good and Evil* (New York: Basic Books, 2000), 4–5.

139. James B. Twitchell, *Carnival Culture: The Trashing of Taste in America* (New York: Columbia University Press, 1992), 2.

140. David Brooks, "Why Our Elites Stink," *New York Times*, July 13, 2002.

141. Adam Gopnik, "The Talk of the Town," *New Yorker*, February 13, 2017, p. 29.

142. Bryan Garsten, "Talk Show," *Wall Street Journal*, September 24, 2016.

143. Kelly Lawler, "Violence on TV May Have Finally Gone Too Far," *USA Today*, December 23, 2016.

144. Adam Haslett, "Vandal in Chief," *Nation*, October 26, 2016, p. 16.

145. Jennifer Peltz, "Politicians Talking Dirty," *Aberdeen* (SD) *American News* (AP story), July 7, 2012.

146. Paul Krugman, "How Republics End," *New York Times*, December 19, 2016.

147. Cantor quoted in Roxanne Roberts, "Also His Parachute?" *New York Times*, June 16, 2016.

148. Mitt Romney, "How a President Shapes the Public Character," *Washington Post*, January 2, 2019.

149. Andrew Root, "Young Adult Realities," *Christian Century*, October 4, 2011, p. 36.

150. Earl Shorris, "American Vespers: The Ebbing of the Body Politic," *Harper's*, December 2011, 67.

151. John Winthrop, "A Model of Christian Charity," in Daniel J. Boorstin, *An American Primer* (New York: New American Library, 1968), 40.

Chapter 3

CHALLENGE 7

1. David Schribman, "Nation to Take a Turn to the Right After Revealing Election," *Brookings* (SD) *Register*, December 28, 2016.

2. E. J. Dionne, Jr., Norman Ornstein, and Thomas E. Mann, *One Nation After Trump: A Guide for the Perplexed, the Disillusioned, the Desperate, and the Not-Yet Deported* (New York: St. Martin's Press, 2017), 22.

3. Michael Gerson, "The True Danger to Democracy Is Cynicism, Not Anger," *Washington Post*, July 7, 2016.

4. Scott Canon and Dave Helling, "Rising Mood of Discontent," *Kansas City Star*, November 6, 2016.

5. Robert Samuelson, "Should We Be Angry at the Rich?" *Chicago Tribune*, October 11, 2011.

6. Peggy Noonan, "America Is So in Play," *Wall Street Journal*, August 29, 2015.

7. David Brooks, "Time for a Realignment," *New York Times*, September 9, 2016.

8. Bob Davis and John W. Miller, "The Places That Made Trump," *Wall Street Journal*, November 12, 2016; Mark Binelli, "Trump County, USA," *Rolling Stone*, February 9, 2017, pp. 26–31.

9. Katherine J. Cramer, *The Politics of Resentment: Rural Consciousness and the Rise of Scott Walker* (Chicago: University of Chicago Press, 2016); Cramer, "Understanding Rural Resentment," *Christian Century*, August 2, 2017, pp. 10–11; see also Robert Wuthnow, *The Left Behind: Decline and Rage in Rural America* (Princeton: Princeton University Press, 2018).

10. Richard Rorty, *Achieving Our Country: Leftist Thought in Twentieth Century America* (Cambridge: Harvard University Press, 1998), 89; Jennifer Senior, "A Book from 1998 Envisioned 2016 Election," *New York Times*, October 21, 2016.

11. David M. Potter, *People of Plenty: Economic Abundance and the American Character* (Chicago: University of Chicago Press, 1954), 112; Fareed Zakaria, *The Future of Freedom: Illiberal Democracy at Home and Abroad* (New York: W. W. Norton, 2004), 69–70.

12. Robert J. Samuelson, "The Political Consequences of Slower Growth," *Washington Post*, February 26, 2018.

13. Timothy P. Carney in *Alienated America: Why Some Places Thrive While Others Collapse* (New York: Harper, 2019), 59–60.

CHALLENGE 8

14. Geoffrey Kabaservice, *Rule and Ruin: The Downfall of Moderation and the Destruction of the Republican Party from Eisenhower to the Tea Party* (New York: Oxford University Press, 2012), xvi.

15. Thomas E. Mann and Norman J. Ornstein, *It's Even Worse Than It Looks: How the American Constitutional System Collided with the New Politics of Extremism* (New York: Basic Books, 2012), 53.

16. E. J. Dionne, Jr., "A Start on Closing the Divide," *Washington Post*, June 19, 2017.

17. Alan I. Abramowitz, *The Great Alignment: Race, Party Transformation, and the Rise of Donald Trump* (New Haven: Yale University Press, 2018), 102–04, 107, 119; Thomas E. Mann and Norman J. Ornstein, "Let's Just Say It: The Republicans Are the Problem," *Washington Post*, April 27, 2012.

18. Gerald F. Seib, "Party Tumult Reflects Changed Face of Politics," *Wall Street Journal*, October 13, 2015; William Galston, "Americans Are as Polarized as Washington," *Wall Street Journal*, June 4, 2014; Abramowitz, *The Great Alignment*, 60–62, 71, 100–01, 112–13.

19. While most observers agree that political polarization in the United States is at a historically very high level and is unlikely to diminish any time soon, the Hoover Institution's Morris Fiorina and some other academics, pollsters, and pundits downplay the amount of divisiveness that actually exists within the electorate. See, for example, Morris P. Fiorina, Samuel J. Abrams, and Jeremy C. Pope, *Culture War? The Myth of a Polarized America*, 3d ed (New York: Pearson Longman, 2011); Stanley B. Greenberg, *The Two Americas: Our Current Political Deadlock and How to Break It* (New York: St. Martin's Press, 2005); Steve Chapman, "Deteriorating Relationships? The United States Only Seems to Be Polarized," *Chicago Tribune*, November 5, 2009; E. J. Dionne, Jr., "Less Divided Than We Think," *Washington Post*, August 21, 2014.

20. Charles M. Blow, "Where Trump Succeeded," *New York Times*, June 4, 2018.

21. "Survey: Election Shifted Party Views of Economy," *Washington Post*, June 23, 2017.

22. Darrell M. West, *Divided Politics, Divided Nation: Hyperconflict in the Trump Era* (Washington, D.C.: Brookings Institution Press, 2019), 168–69.

23. Greg Ip, "The Shrinking of the Political Middle," *Wall Street Journal*, January 22, 2019.

24. Timothy Egan, "A Narrative Shattered by Our National Crackup," *New York Times*, October 28, 2017.

25. Michael Tomasky, *If We Can Keep It: How the Republic Collapsed and How It Might Be Saved* (New York: Liveright, 2019), xx, 62–63, 85–89.

26. Mann and Ornstein, *It's Even Worse Than It Looks*, xiii–xiv.

27. Fareed Zakaria, "The Gridlock We Can Fix," *Washington Post*, July 21, 2011.

28. Neil Irwin, "Two Political Parties, Two Different Languages," *New York Times* July 26, 2016.

29. James B. Meigs, "A Gaslight unto the Nations," *Commentary*, January 2019, p. 43.

30. Michael Tomasky, "Trump," *New York Review of Books*, September 24, 2015, p. 12.

31. Mann and Ornstein, *It's Even Worse Than It Looks*, 44.

32. Peggy Noonan, "Rage Is All the Rage, and It's Dangerous," *Wall Street Journal*, June 17, 2017.

33. Emily Badger and Niraj Chokshi, "Partisan Relations Sink from Cold to Deep Freeze," *New York Times*, June 16, 2017; "15 Years After 9/11, America Lost Unity," *USA Today* (editorial), September 12, 2016.

34. Alan Murray, "The Divided States of America," *Wall Street Journal*, June 12, 2014; Thomas L. Friedman, *The American Civil War, Part II*," *New York Times*, October 3, 2018.

35. Bill Bishop, *The Big Sort: Why the Clustering of Like-Minded America Is Tearing Us Apart* (Boston: Houghton Mifflin Harcourt, 2008), 5–8.

36. Gary Rosen, "Conflicting Moralities," *Wall Street Journal*, March 19, 2012; Jonathan Haidt, *The Righteous Mind: Why Good People Are Divided by Politics and Religion* (New York: Pantheon Books, 2012), chaps. 7–8.

37. Abramowitz, *The Great Alignment*, 143–44, 164–68.

38. Cameron Tung, "Chain Reaction," *New York Times Magazine*, April 29, 2018, pp. 9–11; Lexington, "The Trump Cult," *Economist*, November 3, 2018, p. 33; Dan Balz, "Bomb Scares and the Politics of the Apocalypse," *Washington Post*," October 25, 2018; Lance Morrow, "Shall We Have Civil War or Second Thoughts?" *Wall Street Journal*, August 18, 2018; Henry G. Brinton, "Why U.S. Politics Devolves into Good vs. Evil," *USA Today*, January 23, 2012.

39. David French, "Mourning in America," *National Review*, September 12, 2016, pp. 16–17.

40. Steven Levitsky and Daniel Ziblatt, *How Democracies Die* (New York: Crown, 2018), 9.

CHALLENGE 9

41. J. Ronald Pennock, *Democratic Political Theory* (Princeton: Princeton University Press, 1979), 216–17.

42. John E. Miller, *Governor Philip F. La Follette, the Wisconsin Progressives, and the New Deal* (Columbia: University of Missouri Press, 1982), 96.

43. Robert G. Kaiser, *So Damn Much Money: The Triumph of Lobbying and the Corrosion of American Government* (New York: Alfred A. Knopf, 2009), 350.

44. Michael Scherer and Pratheek Rebala,"Campaign Inflation: The Cost of Campaigns Has Been Growing at a Staggering Clip," *Time*, November 3, 2014, p. 11.

45. Jim Newell, "Cash and Carry," *Bookforum*, Summer 2014, p. 8.

46. Eric Alterman, "Dissecting the Kochtopas," *Nation*, February 15, 2016, p. 10.

47. Philip Elliott, "Democrats Better at Tapping Rich" (AP story), *Minneapolis Star Tribune*, December 24, 2014.

48. Nicholas Confessore, Sarah Cohen, and Karen Yourish, "Small Pool of Rich Donors Dominates Election Giving," *New York Times*, August 2, 2015.

49. Jason. Grumet, *City of Rivals: Restoring the Glorious Mess of American Democracy* (Guilford, CT: Lyons Press, 2014), 197–99.

50. Elizabeth Drew, "Money Runs Our Politics," *New York Review of Books*, June 4, 2015, p. 22.

51. Frank Bruni, "Greed and the Presidency," *New York Times*, May 17, 2015.

52. Thomas Frank, "It's a Rich Man's World," *Harper's*, April 2012, p. 25.

53. Grumet, *City of Rivals*, 114–16.

54. Dan Balz, "From Rosenstein to Kavanaugh, World Leaders Get a Look at System Overload." *Washington Post*, September 25, 2018.

55. James Hohmann, "What's Unprecedented? The Senate's Breakdown," *Washington Post*, September 6, 2018; Elise Viebeck, "McConnell Would Back a Trump Court Nominee in 2020," *Washington Post*, October 2, 2018.

56. Nicholas Fandos, "Kavanaugh Hearings Show Drift from Decorum,:" *New York Times*, October 3, 2018.

57. King and Sasse quoted in Sheryl Gay Stolberg and Nicholas Fandos, "In Congress, Only Gloom Over the Dysfunction Is Bipartisan," *New York Times*, January 28, 2018.

58. Jonathan Martin, "How a Bill Becomes a Mess" [book review of *Act of Congress*], *Wall Street Journal*, May 11, 2013.

59. For example, see Catherine Rampell, "The Guilty Party," *Washington Post*, February 20, 2018; Greg Sargent, *An Uncivil War: Taking Back Our Democracy in an Age of Trumpian Disinformation and Thunderdome Politics* (New York: Custom House, 2018), 146–47; Thomas E. Mann and Norman J. Ornstein, *It's Even Worse Than It Looks: How the American Constitutional System Collided with the New Politics of Extremism* (New York: Basic Books, 2012), 51–58.

60. Trent Lott and Tom Daschle, "The Way Out of Partisan Gridlock," *Washington Post*, January 1, 2016.

61. Gingrich quoted in E. J. Dionne, Jr., Norman J. Ornstein, and Thomas E. Mann, *One Nation After Trump: A Guide for the Perplexed, the Disillusioned, the Desperate, and the Not-Yet Depressed* (New York: St. Martin's Press, 2017), 75.

62. Ibid., 76.

63. Ibid., 76–77.

64. Robert G. Kaiser, "The Closed Mind of Mitch," *New York Review of Books*, November 10, 2016, p. 40. McConnell claimed that his words had been taken out of context.

65. Voinovich quoted in Dionne, Jr., Ornstein, and Mann, *One Nation After Trump*, 77.

66. Kaiser, "The Closed Mind of Mitch," 40.

67. Christi Parsons and Lisa Mascaro, "Obama Leaves Behind an Unwanted Partisan Divide," *Chicago Tribune*, January 15, 2017.

68. Thomas E. Mann and Norman J. Ornstein, *The Broken Branch: How Congress Is Failing and How to Get It Back on Track* (New York: Oxford University Press, 2006), 4.

69. Mann and Ornstein, *The Broken Branch*, chap. 5.

70. Tom Udall, "Fibuster Abuse Has Broken Senate," *USA Today*, December 4, 2012.

71. Mann and Ornstein, *The Broken Branch*, 169–70.

72. Ibid., 171–73.

73. Ibid., 175.

74. Daniel Boorstin, *The Americans: The Democratic Experience* (New York: Random House, 1973), 558.

CHALLENGE 10

75. Andrew Rudalevige, *The New Imperial Presidency: Renewing Presidential Power After Watergate* (Ann Arbor: University of Michigan Press, 2005), 138.

76. Fred Greenstein, *The Hidden Hand Presidency: Eisenhower as Leader* (New York: Basic Books, 1982).

77. Specific figures and references for the growth of presidential power and authority here

and in the following pages, unless otherwise specified, derive from Rudalevige, *The New Imperial Presidency.*

78. Ibid., 63.

79. Emanuel quoted in Rudalevige, *The New Imperial Presidency*, 171.

80. Cheney quoted ibid., 211.

81. Trump quoted in Eugene Robinson, "When Will the Rats Flee the Sinking Ship?" *Washington Post*, November 20, 2018.

82. David Brooks, "The G.O.P. Is Rotting," *New York Times*, December 8, 2017.

83. On party decline, see, for example, David S. Broder, *The Party's Over: The Failure of Politics in America* (New York: Harper & Row, 1972) and Martin P. Wattenberg, *The Decline of American Political Parties, 1952–1996* (Cambridge: Harvard University Press, 1990).

84. Beschloss quoted in Peter Baker, "Under Trump, a Once Unimaginable Presidency Becomes Reality," *New York Times*, December 31, 2017.

85. Charles Krauthammer, "Evangelicals Buy Trump's Tough-Guy Routine," *Rapid City* (SD) *Journal*, March 7, 2016.

86. Robert Kagan, "How Fascism Comes to America," *Washington Post*, May 20, 2016.

CHALLENGE 11

87. Pendleton Herring, *The Politics of Democracy: American Parties in Action* (New York: W.W. Norton, 1965), 78.

88. Victor Davis Hanson, "Surviving at the White House," *National Review*, March 11, 2019, p. 31.

89. "Federal Government Jobs Are Few, Compared with the Private Sector," *New York Times*, January 17, 2019.

90. James Miller, *Can Democracy Work? A Short History of a Radical Idea, from Ancient Athens to Our World* (New York: Farrar, Straus and Giroux, 2018), 4.

91. Jonathan Rauch, *Demosclerosis* (New York: Random House, 1994), later published under the title *Government's End: Why Washington Stopped Working* (New York: Public Affairs, 1999).

92. Brian Doherty, *Radicals for Capitalism: A Freewheeling History of the Modern American Libertarian Movement* (New York: Public Affairs, 2007), chap. 3; Rose Wilder Lane, *The Discovery of Freedom: Man's Struggle Against Authority* (1943, reprint San Francisco: Fox and Wilkes, 1993), 213, 258–59.

93. Jonah Goldberg, *Suicide of the West: How the Rebirth of Tribalism, Populism, Nationalism,*

and Identity Politics Is Destroying American Democracy (New York: Crown Forum, 2018), 194.

94. Michael Lewis, *The Fifth Risk* (New York: W. W. Norton, 2018), 41–42.

95. Massimo Calabresi et al., "Demolition Crew," *Time*, November 6, 2017, pp. 22–31.

96. Lawrence Lessig, *America, Compromised* (Chicago: University of Chicago Press, 2018), ix and passim.

97. A 5–4 Supreme Court decision written by Chief Justice John G. Roberts in June 2019, capping decades of debate over the reach of federal authority into state elections, ruled that federal judges possess no power to intrude into the drawing of electoral districts with regard to partisan preference.

98. Zachary Roth, *The Great Suppression: Voting Rights, Corporate Cash, and the Conservative Assault on Democracy* (New York: Crown, 2016) and Carol Anderson, *One Person, No Vote: How Voter Suppression Is Destroying Our Democracy* (New York: Bloomsbury, 2018) catalogue a wide variety of methods being employed today in attempts to suppress voting by one's opponents and distort democratic decision-making.

99. Mitch Smith and Monica Davey, "In Wisconsin, a Power Play for the Road," *New York Times*, December 6, 2018; Astead W. Herndon and Jonathan Martin, "Midwest Power Grab May Fuel G.O.P. Backlash," *New York Times*, December 11, 2018.

CHALLENGE 12

100. Bernard Crick, *Democracy: A Very Short Introduction* (Oxford: Oxford University Press, 2002), 92–93.

101. Jeff Colgan, "Risk of Democratic Erosion—Reading List," quoted in Dionne, Jr., Ornstein, and Mann, *One Nation After Trump*, 97.

102. Robert Samuelson, "Paralyzed by Principle," *Washington Post*, November 17, 2014.

103. David Brooks, "We Used to Build Things," *New York Times*, October 13, 2017.

104. Kevin D. Williamson, "The Future Is Fake," *National Review*, February 11, 2019, p. 16.

105. Lexington, "Ship of Fools," *Economist*, November 15, 2008, p. 44.

106. Robert B. Reich, *The Common Good* (New York: Alfred A. Knopf, 2018), 4, 6, 176.

107. Georgie Ann Geyer, "Our Vulgarized Culture Corrupts Us All," *Brookings* (SD) *Register*, November 5, 2018; Chesley B. "Sully" Sullenberger, "This Is Not the America I Know," *Washington Post*, October 30, 2018; Alan Ehren-

halt, *The Lost City: Discovering the Forgotten Virtues of Community in the Chicago of the 1950s* (New York: Basic Books, 1995), 38–39; Kessler quoted in George Will, "Republicans: Save Your Party, Don't Give to Trump," *Aberdeen* (SD) *American News*, June 23, 2016; Adam Gopnik, "Americanisms," *New Yorker*, February 13, 2017, pp. 29–30.

Epilogue

1. Edward Luce, *The Retreat of Western Liberalism* (New York: Atlantic Monthly Press, 2017),

121. See also James Hohmann, "Poll Commissioned by Bush, Biden Shows Americans Losing Faith in Democracy," *Washington Post*, June 27, 2018; Catherine Rampell, "Getting Fed Up with Democracy," *Pierre* (SD) *Capital Journal*, August 19, 2016.

2. Jan-Werner Muller, "Blaming the People," *Nation*, October 9, 2017, p. 33.

3. Margaret Sullivan, "A Reality-Based Review of 2017," *Washington Post*, December 25, 2017.

4. Paul Krugman, "Conservatism's Monstrous End Game," *New York Times*, December 18, 2018.

Bibliography

Abernathy, Penelope Muse. *The Expanding News Desert.* Chapel Hill: University of North Carolina School of Media and Journalism, 2018.

Abramowitz, Alan L. *The Great Alignment: Race, Party Transformation, and the Rise of Donald Trump.* New Haven: Yale University Press, 2018.

Andersen, Kurt. *Fantasyland: How America Went Haywire, a 500-Year History.* New York: Random House, 2017.

Arnold, Thurman W. *The Folklore of Capitalism.* New Haven: Yale University Press, 1937.

_____. *The Symbols of Government.* New Haven: Yale University Press, 1935.

Arum, Richard, and Josipa Roksa. *Academically Adrift: Limited Learning on College Campuses.* Chicago: University of Chicago Press, 2011.

Bailyn, Bernard. *Education in the Forming of American Society: Needs and Opportunities for Study.* Chapel Hill: University of North Carolina Press, 1960.

Ball, James. *Post-Truth: How Bullshit Conquered the World.* London: Biteback Publishing, 2017.

Bankston, Carl L., III, and Stephen J. Caldas. *Public Education, America's Civil Religion: A Social History.* New York: Teachers College Press, 2009.

Bauerlein, Mark. *The Dumbest Generation: How the Digital Age Stupefies Young Americans and Jeopardizes Our Future.* New York: Jeremy P. Tarcher/Penguin, 2008.

Bellah, Robert N., and associates. *The Good Society.* New York: Alfred A. Knopf, 1991.

Bishop, Bill. *The Big Sort: Why the Clustering of Like-Minded America Is Tearing Us Apart.* Boston: Houghton Mifflin Harcourt, 2008.

Blackburn, Simon. *Truth: A Guide.* New York: Oxford University Press, 2005.

Boorstin, Daniel. *The Americans: The Democratic Experience.* New York: Random House, 1973.

Boot, Max. *The Corrosion of Conservatism: Why I Left the Right.* New York: Liveright, 2018.

Broder, David S. *The Party's Over: The Failure of Politics in America.* New York: Harper & Row, 1972.

Brown, Archie. *The Myth of the Strong Leader: Political Leadership in the Modern Age.* New York: Basic Books, 2014.

Butts, R. Freeman. *Public Education in the United States: From Revolution to Reform.* New York: Holt, Rinehart and Winston, 1978.

Carney, Timothy P. *Alienated America: Why Some Places Thrive While Others Collapse.* New York: Harper, 2019.

Carpenter, Amanda. *Gaslighting America: Why We Love It When Trump Lies to Us.* New York: Broadside Books, 2018.

Cater, Douglass. *Power in Washington: A Critical Look at Today's Struggle to Govern in the Nation's Capital.* New York: Random House, 1964.

Conkin, Paul K. *Puritans and Pragmatists: Eight Eminent American Thinkers.* New York: Dodd, Mead and Co., 1968.

Cramer, Katherine J. *The Politics of Resentment: Rural Consciousness and the Rise of Scott Walker.* Chicago: University of Chicago Press, 2016.

Cremin, Lawrence A. *American Education,* 3 vols. New York: Harper & Row, 1970, 1980, 1988.

Crick, Bernard. *Democracy: A Very Short Introduction.* Oxford: Oxford University Press, 2002.

Crunden, Robert M. *Ministers of Reform: The Progressives' Achievement in American Civilization, 1889–1920.* New York: Basic Books, 1982.

Curti, Merle. *The Social Ideas of American Educators.* Totowa, NJ: Littlefield, Adams and Co., 1966.

Dahl, Robert A. *On Democracy.* New Haven: Yale University Press, 1998.

Daly, Christopher B. *Covering America: A Narrative History of America's Journalism*, 2d ed. Amherst: University of Massachusetts Press, 2018.

Danto, Arthur C. *Nietzsche as Philosopher*. 1965, reprint New York: Columbia University Press, 1980.

Davies, William. *Nervous States: Democracy and the Decline of Reason*. New York: W.W. Norton, 2019.

Diggins, John Patrick. *The Promise of Pragmatism: Modernism and the Crisis of Knowledge and Authority*. Chicago: University of Chicago Press, 1994.

Dionne, E. J., Jr., Norman J. Ornstein, and Thomas E. Mann. *One Nation After Trump: A Guide for the Perplexed, the Disillusioned, the Desperate, and the Not-Yet Deported*. New York: St. Martin's Press, 2017.

Doherty, Brian. *Radicals for Capitalism: A Freewheeling History of the Modern American Libertarian Movement*. New York: Public Affairs, 2007.

Ehrenhalt, Alan. *The Lost City: Discovering the Forgotten Virtues of Community in the Chicago of the 1950s*. New York: Basic Books, 1995.

Emery, Michael, and Edwin Emery. *The Press and America: An Interpretive History of the Mass Media*. Englewood Cliffs, NJ: Prentice Hall, 1988.

Finney, Ross L. *The American Public School*. New York: Macmillan, 1921.

Fiorina, Morris P., Samuel J. Abrams, and Jeremy C. Pope. *Culture War? The Myth of a Polarized America*, 3d ed. New York: Pearson Longman, 2011.

Foer, Franklin. *World Without Mind: The Existential Threat of Big Tech*. New York: Penguin, 2017.

Forcey, Charles. *The Crossroads of Liberalism: Croly, Weyl, Lippmann, and the Progressive Era, 1900–1925*. New York: Oxford University Press, 1961.

Frankfurt, Harry G. *On Bullshit*. Princeton: Princeton University Press, 2005.

Fukuyama, Francis. *Trust: The Social Virtues and the Creation of Prosperity*. New York: Free Press, 1995.

Fuller, Jack. *What Is Happening to News: The Information Explosion and the Crisis in Journalism*. Chicago: University of Chicago Press, 2010.

Gabriel, Ralph Henry. *The Course of American Democratic Thought*, 2d ed. New York: Ronald Press, 1956.

Gerth, Hans, and C. Wright Mills. *Character and Social Structure: The Psychology of Social Institutions*. New York: Harcourt, Brace and World, 1953.

Goldberg, Jonah. *Suicide of the West: How the Rebirth of Tribalism, Populism, Nationalism, and Identity Politics Is Destroying American Democracy*. New York: Crown Forum, 2018.

Goldman, Eric F. *Rendezvous with Destiny: A History of Modern American Reform*. New York: Vintage Books, 1956.

Greenberg, Stanley B. *The Two Americas: Our Current Political Deadlock and How to Break It*. New York: St. Martin's Press, 2005.

Greenstein, Fred I. *The Hidden Hand Presidency: Eisenhower as Leader*. New York: Basic Books, 1982.

_____. *The Presidential Difference: Leadership Style from FDR to Clinton*. New York: Free Press, 2001.

Grumet, Jason. *City of Rivals: Restoring the Glorious Mess of American Democracy*. Guilford, CT: Lyons Press, 2014.

Haidt, Jonathan. *The Happiness Hypothesis: Finding Modern Truth in Ancient Wisdom*. New York: Basic Books, 2006.

_____. *The Righteous Mind: Why Good People Are Divided by Politics and Religion*. New York: Pantheon Books, 2012.

Hemingway, Ernest. *A Farewell to Arms*. New York: Scribner's, 1929.

Herring, Pendleton. *The Politics of Democracy: American Parties in Action*. New York: W.W. Norton, 1965.

Hochschild, Arlie Russell. *Strangers in Their Own Land: Anger and Mourning on the American Right*. New York: New Press, 2016.

Hofstadter, Richard. *The American Political Tradition*. New York: Alfred A. Knopf, 1948.

_____. *Anti-Intellectualism in American Life*. New York: Alfred A. Knopf, 1963.

Hunter, James Davison. *The Death of Character: Moral Education in an Age without Good and Evil*. New York: Basic Books, 2000.

Iacocca, Lee, with Catherine Whitney. *Where Have All the Leaders Gone?* New York: Scribner's, 2007.

Isenberg, Nancy. *White Trash: The 400-Year Untold History of Class in America*. New York: Viking, 2016.

Jamieson, Kathleen Hall, and Joseph N. Cappella. *Echo Chamber: Rush Limbaugh and the Conservative Media Establishment*. New York: Oxford University Press, 2008.

Kabaservice, Geoffrey. *Rule and Ruin: The Downfall of Moderation and the Destruction of the Republican Party from Eisenhower to the Tea Party*. New York: Oxford University Press, 2012.

Kaiser, Robert G. *So Damn Much Money: The Triumph of Lobbying and the Corrosion of American Government.* New York: Alfred A. Knopf, 2009.

Kakutani, Michiko. *The Death of Truth: Notes on Falsehood in the Age of Trump.* New York: Tim Duggan Books, 2018.

Kalb, Marvin. *Enemy of the People: Trump's War on the Press, the New McCarthyism, and the Threat to American Democracy.* Washington, D.C.: Brookings Institution Press, 2018.

Kammen, Michael. *People of Paradox.* New York: Alfred A. Knopf, 1972.

_____, ed. *The Contrapuntal Civilization: Essays Toward a New Understanding of the American Experience.* New York: Thomas Y. Crowell Co., 1971.

Kaplan, Robert D. *Warrior Politics: Why Leadership Demands a Pagan Ethos.* New York: Random House, 2001.

Keane, John. *The Life and Death of Democracy.* New York: W.W. Norton, 2009.

Keyes, Ralph. *The Post-Truth Era: Dishonesty and Deception in Contemporary Life.* New York: St. Martin's Press, 2004.

Kloppenberg, James T. *Toward Democracy: The Struggle for Self-Rule in European and American Thought.* New York: Oxford University Press. 2016.

Kouzes, James M., and Barry Z. Posner. *The Leadership Challenge,* 3d ed. San Francisco: Jossey-Bass, 2017.

Krutch, Joseph Wood. *The Modern Temper: A Study and a Confession.* New York: Harcourt, Brace and World, 1929.

Landrieu, Mitch. *In the Shadow of Statues: A White Southerner Confronts History.* New York: Viking, 2018.

Lane, Rose Wilder. *The Discovery of Freedom: Man's Struggle Against Authority.* 1943, reprint San Francisco: Fox and Wilkes, 1993.

Lasch, Christopher. *The Revolt of the Elites and the Betrayal of Democracy.* New York: W.W. Norton, 1995.

Laski, Harold J. *The American Democracy: A Commentary and an Interpretation.* New York: Viking, 1948.

Lee, Richard W., ed. *Politics and the Press.* Washington: Acropolis Books, 1970.

Lehman, David. *Signs of the Times: Deconstruction and the Fall of Paul de Man.* New York: Poseidon Press, 1991.

Lepore, Jill. *These Truths: A History of the United States.* New York: W.W. Norton, 2018.

Lessig, Lawrence. *America, Compromised.* Chicago: University of Chicago Press, 2018.

Levin, Yuval. *Fractured Republic: Renewing America's Social Contract in the Age of Individualism.* New York: Basic Books, 2016.

Levitsky, Steven, and Daniel Ziblatt. *How Democracies Die.* New York: Crown, 2018.

Lewis, Charles. *935 Lies: The Future of Truth and the Decline of America's Moral Integrity.* New York: Public Affairs, 2014.

Lewis, Michael. *The Fifth Risk.* New York: W.W. Norton, 2018.

Lippmann, Walter. *A Preface to Morals.* 1929, reprint Boston: Beacon Press, 1960.

Lipset, Seymour Martin. *The First New Nation: The United States in Historical and Comparative Perspective.* New York: Basic Books, 1963.

Luce, Edward. *The Retreat of Western Liberalism.* New York: Atlantic Monthly Press, 2017.

MacIntyre, Alasdair. *After Virtue: A Study of Moral Theory,* 2d ed. Notre Dame: University of Notre Dame Press, 1984.

Magnus, Bernd, and Kathleen M. Higgins, eds. *The Cambridge Companion to Nietzsche.* New York: Cambridge University Press, 1996.

Manjoo, Farhad. *True Enough: Learning to Live in a Post-Fact Society.* Hoboken: Wiley, 2008.

Mann, Thomas E., and Norman J. Ornstein. *The Broken Branch: How Congress Is Failing and How to Get It Back on Track.* New York: Oxford University Press, 2006.

_____. *It's Even Worse Than It Looks: How the American Constitutional System Collided with the New Politics of Extremism.* New York: Basic Books, 2012.

May, Henry F. *The End of American Innocence: A Study of the First Years of Our Own Time, 1912-1917.* New York: Alfred A. Knopf, 1959.

McChesney, Robert W., and John Nichols. *The Death and Life of American Journalism: The Media Revolution That Will Begin the World Again.* Philadelphia: Nation Books, 2010.

McGerr, Michael. *A Fierce Discontent: The Rise and Fall of the Progressive Movement in America, 1870-1920.* New York: Free Press, 2003.

McIntyre, Lee C. *Post-Truth.* Cambridge: MIT Press, 2018.

Meyer, Philip. *The Vanishing Newspaper: Saving Journalism in the Information Age,* 2d ed. Columbia: University of Missouri Press, 2009.

Miller, James. *Can Democracy Work? A Short History of a Radical Idea, from Ancient Athens to Our World.* New York: Farrar, Straus and Giroux, 2018.

Miller, John E. *Governor Philip F. La Follette, the Wisconsin Progressives, and the New Deal.* Columbia: University of Missouri Press, 1982.

Mindich, David T. Z. *Tuned Out: Why Americans Under 40 Don't Follow the News.* New York: Oxford University Press, 2004.

Newman, Charles. *The Post-Modern Aura: The Act of Fiction in an Age of Inflation.* Evanston: Northwestern University Press, 1985.

Nichols, Tom. *The Death of Expertise: The Campaign against Established Knowledge and Why It Matters.* New York: Oxford University Press, 2017.

Novick, Peter. *That Noble Dream: The 'Objectivity Question' and the American Historical Profession.* Cambridge: Cambridge University Press, 1988.

O'Connor, Cailin, and James Owen Weatherall. *The Misinformation Age: How False Beliefs Spread.* New Haven: Yale University Press, 2019.

Patrikarakos, David. *War in 140 Characters: How Social Media Is Reshaping Conflict in the Twenty-First Century.* New York: Basic Books, 2017.

Patterson, Thomas E. *Informing the News: The Need for Knowledge-Based Journalism.* New York: Vintage Books, 2013.

Pennock, J. Roland. *Democratic Political Theory.* Princeton: Princeton University Press, 1979.

Pierce, Charles P. *Idiot America: How Stupidity Became a Virtue in the Land of the Free.* New York: Doubleday, 2009.

Potter, David M. *People of Plenty: Economic Abundance and the American Character.* Chicago: University of Chicago Press, 1954.

Pressman, Matthew. *On Press: The Liberal Values That Shaped the News.* Cambridge: Harvard University Press, 2018.

Putnam, Robert D. *Bowling Alone: The Collapse and Revival of American Community.* New York: Simon & Schuster, 2000.

Rauch, Jonathan. *Demosclerosis.* New York: Random House, 1994.

Ravitch, Diane. *The Revisionists Revised: A Critique of the Radical Attack on the Schools.* New York: Basic Books, 1978.

Reich, Robert B. *The Common Good.* New York: Alfred A. Knopf, 2018.

Reid-Henry, Simon. *Empire of Democracy: The Remaking of the West Since the Cold War, 1971–2017.* New York: Simon & Schuster, 2019.

Rich, Frank. *The Greatest Story Ever Sold: The Decline and Fall of Truth from 9/11 to Katrina.* New York: Penguin, 2016.

Roberts, Jon H. *Darwinism and the Divine in America: Protestant Intellectuals and Organic Evolution, 1859–1900.* Madison: University of Wisconsin Press, 1988.

Rorty, Richard. *Achieving Our Country: Leftist Thought in Twentieth Century America.* Cambridge: Harvard University Press, 1998.

_____. *Philosophy and the Mirror of Nature.* Princeton: Princeton University Press, 1979.

Rosenfeld, Sophia. *Democracy and Truth: A Short History.* Philadelphia: University of Pennsylvania Press, 2019.

Rudalevige, Andrew. *The New Imperial Presidency: Renewing Presidential Power After Watergate.* Ann Arbor: University of Michigan Press, 2005.

Rutland, Robert A. *The Newsmongers: Journalism in the Life of the Nation, 1690–1972.* New York: Dial Press, 1973.

Ryfe, David M. *Can Journalism Survive? An Inside Look at American Newsrooms.* Malden, MA: Polity, 2012.

Sandel, Michael J. *Democracy's Discontent: America in Search of a Public Philosophy.* Cambridge: Harvard University Press, 1996.

Sargent, Greg. *An Uncivil War: Taking Back Our Democracy in an Age of Trumpian Disinformation and Thunderdome Politics.* New York: Custom House, 2018.

Schudson, Michael. *Discovering the News: A Social History of American Newspapers.* New York: Basic Books, 1978.

Selbourne, David. *The Free Society in Crisis: A History of Our Times.* Amherst, NY: Prometheus Books, 2019.

Sloman, Steven, and Philip Fernbach. *The Knowledge Illusion: Why We Never Think Alone.* New York: Riverhead, 2017.

Stout, Jeffrey. *Democracy and Tradition.* Princeton: Princeton University Press, 2004.

Sunstein, Cass. *#republic: Divided Democracy in the Age of Social Media.* Princeton: Princeton University Press, 2017.

Tomasky, Michael. *If We Can Keep It: How the Republic Collapsed and How It Might Be Saved.* New York: Liveright, 2019.

Turner, Frederick Jackson. *The Frontier in American History.* New York: Henry Holt, 1920.

Twenge, Jean M. *iGen: Why Today's Super-Connected Kids Are Growing Up Less Rebellious, More Tolerant, Less Happy—and Completely Unprepared for Adulthood.* New York: Atria Books, 2017.

Twitchell, James B. *Carnival Culture: The Trashing of Taste in America.* New York: Columbia University Press, 1992.

Vance, J. D. *Hillbilly Elegy: A Memoir of a Family and Culture in Crisis.* New York: Harper, 2016.

Wattenberg, Martin P. *The Decline of American Political Parties, 1952–1996.* Cambridge: Harvard University Press, 1990.

Wehner, Peter. *The Death of Politics: How to Heal Our Frayed Republic After Trump.* New York: HarperOne, 2019.

Welter, Rush. *Popular Education and Democratic*

Thought in America. New York: Columbia University Press, 1962.

West, Darrell M. *Divided Politics, Divided Nation: Hyperconflict in the Trump Era.* Washington, D.C.: Brookings Institution Press, 2019.

White, Morton. *Social Thought in America: The Revolt against Formalism.* New York: Viking Press, 1949.

Woodard, Colin. *American Character: A History of the Epic Struggle between Individual Liberty and the Common Good.* New York: Viking, 2016.

Wuthnow, Robert. *American Mythos: Why Our Best Efforts to Be a Better Nation Fall Short* Princeton: Princeton University Press, 2006.

_____. *The Left Behind: Decline and Rage in Rural America.* Princeton: Princeton University Press, 2018.

Young, Kevin. *Bunk: The Rise of Hoaxes, Humbug, Plagiarists, Phonies, Post-Facts, and Fake News.* Minneapolis: Graywolf Press, 2017.

Zakaria, Fareed. *The Future of Freedom: Illiberal Democracy at Home and Abroad.* New York: W.W. Norton, 2003.

Index